14 July 1961
The one millionth
passenger travels

September 1961
Lombard Bank invests
in Derby Airways

7 October 1961
DC-3 G-AMSW crashes
in the Pyrenees

1 April 1965
The move to East Midlan

18 May 1957
First inclusive tours
(IT) service

4 June 1967
Argonaut G-ALHG crashes
at Stockport

December 1968
Minster Assets invests
£150,000

12 March 1959
Derby Airways
registered
as an airline
company

1 October 1964
Change of name to
British Midland Airways

12 December 1964
BMA acquires
Mercury Airlines Ltd

18 March 1969
British Midland Airways
merges with Invicta Airways

3 November 1969
First scheduled service by
British Midland from Heathrow
to Teesside begins

1960

Miles Marathon

Canadair Argonaut

Handley Page Herald

Vickers Viscount

1970

BAC One-Eleven

1957
First non-stop passenger flight
from London to Vancouver

1969
British Airways and Air France
launch their supersonic Anglo-
French Concorde aircraft

1968
Terminal 1 opens at Heathrow

1962
First US/UK satellite
launched from Cape
Canaveral

1966
Freddie Laker launches
Laker Airways

bmi the story

and the history of Donington Hall

Celebrating 70 years in the business of aviation

Penny Olsen

Contents

Foreword

Eighteen years ago a history of Donington Hall was published after much interest had been expressed about the successful restoration of this classic 18th-century building and its subsequent use by bmi as the airline's headquarters.

The year 2008 has marked the 70th anniversary of the airline and more than 25 years has passed since they moved into Donington Hall thus providing the most appropriate opportunity for the original publication to be updated and expanded.

The original author, Penny Olsen, has returned not only to revise her work on the history of the Hall itself but to include a comprehensive history of bmi to mark its 70th anniversary.

I thank all members of our staff who have contributed their recollections, enabling the airline's history to be written, and especially Penny Olsen for her enthusiasm and patience in compiling this book.

Sir Michael Bishop, November 2008

Introduction

This is the story of a handful of remarkable men and their passion to start an airline. They were followed by three loyal and steadfast partners who stepped in and built that airline into a major carrier. During the past 70 years the company they formed have fought adversity when world events intervened and social habits changed, and have continued to survive in a precarious industry where so many others have failed.

bmi began in 1938 as Air Schools Ltd, a pilot training school, primarily for military personnel. When that eventually became redundant the operation became Derby Aviation in the exciting years of post-war civil aviation. The new carrier offered charter and cargo flights until in 1953 the first scheduled service took off from their base at Burnaston Airport to Jersey. Business grew slowly yet steadily but the grass airfield at Burnaston precluded further growth. In 1965, having already changed their name to British Midland Airways, the airline moved to East Midlands Airport.

In 1968, the merchant bank Minster Assets invested in the business and installed a more professional management team who developed the network of scheduled services with a fleet of Vickers Viscounts. There followed an adventure with Boeing 707 jets and long-haul charters, but this faltered so the company turned to wet-leasing to airlines in developing countries, running a successful aircraft leasing business. In 1978, the airline's ownership underwent a major change when (Sir) Michael Bishop and two co-directors acquired the shareholding of the business in a management buy-out.

For many years Michael Bishop fought a political battle with the national flag carrier, British Airways, for the right to compete on the UK's major trunk routes. The struggle was finally won in 1982 with the launch of BMA's scheduled service from Heathrow to Glasgow. The fight for European liberalization continued until that too became reality when the company began its DC-9 operation from Heathrow to Amsterdam in 1986. By the end of the decade the airline had a fleet of new Boeing 737s and were carrying more than two million passengers a year to 45 destinations across the UK and Europe.

As the new millennium approached the company was rebranded as bmi, and plans were resurrected to embrace the long-haul market with the acquisition of a fleet of Airbus jets. When tragedy struck on 11 September 2001, the aviation industry collapsed worldwide. bmi brutally cut their operating costs and soon began a steady climb back, despite hungry competition from the national carrier and the new low-cost airlines. By embracing new business opportunities and rethinking the product, customer numbers soared and prosperity returned. Since 2005, there has been a gradual increase in long- and mid-haul scheduled services out of Heathrow with an enormous injection of 17 new routes following the acquisition of BMed, a franchise operation. The challenge to win transatlantic open skies was finally achieved in 2007.

On 10 May 2008 bmi celebrated its 70th anniversary in the business of aviation, having grown to become a major player with 11.3 per cent of the take-off and landing slots at Heathrow and a fleet of 33 Airbuses and 17 Embraers flying 12 million passengers a year to and from four continents.

On 10 October 2008 Sir Michael Bishop exercised an option requiring Lufthansa to acquire his 50 per cent plus one share controlling interest in bmi marking the beginning of a new chapter in the history of the airline.

Early years

Air Schools Limited

The journey began on 20 May 1938 when a newly registered business, Air Schools Ltd, held their first meeting in readiness to begin an operation focusing on flying training. The company had already secured the lease on Derby Corporation's new all-grass municipal airport at Burnaston, six miles south-west of the city, and now had their sights set on securing a lucrative government contract to train Royal Air Force volunteer and reserve pilots, in readiness for the war that was brewing in Europe.[1]

The chairman, managing director and driving force of the new company was Captain Roy Harben (1887–1947), a veteran of the Royal Flying Corps and winner of the Distinguished Flying Cross.[2] Harben had seen for himself the build-up of Germany's flying clubs and the re-formed Luftwaffe[3] and had taken his concerns to the Air Ministry, who were already annexing small airfields as operational bases for their squadrons-in-waiting.

Wing Commander Roy Harben founded Air Schools Ltd, the company that later became Derby Aviation, in 1938.

With the contract signed Captain Harben delegated the task of setting up the flying school to Edward Philips, who until recently had been part of the team responsible for organizing the legendary Royal Air Force Flying Displays at Hendon.[4] Over the summer months Air Schools Ltd took delivery of twelve De Havilland Tiger Moths, four Hawker Hinds, three Fairey Battles and one Hawker Audax from the RAF in readiness for their first military contract, which began instruction in the autumn of 1938 as Number 30 Elementary and Reserve Flying Training School.[5]

As political events escalated the pace of pilot training increased and the complement of Tiger Moths soon swelled to 72, with Air Schools' civilian staff working a two-shift regime seven days a week and flying continuing well into the early hours of the morning.[6] With an operation dealing with 180 trainee pilots at any one time the Royal Air Force were soon obliged to expand the limited facilities at Burnaston. The new buildings included a large hangar (Big Hangar) for storing and maintaining aircraft, together with a selection of transportable hangars, a parachute packing shed and a Link Trainer shed to house an early type of flight simulator. Burnaston House, the airport's dilapidated 19th-century mansion, was cleaned up for use as staff living quarters with an officers' mess on the ground floor.[7] Prefabricated timber huts were

Levelling the site for the new grass airfield at Burnaston, April 1938.

built behind the flying strip as the administrative base for ground and air crews. The training of pilots and engineers was well under way when Burnaston Airport was officially opened on 17 June 1939 with a grand flying spectacle dominated by RAF bombers.[8] Trading during the financial year of 1939 was 'very successful' with contracts for the Link Trainer, the most profitable component of the company's business.[9] By developing a number of enhancements for the Link trainer, including wrap-around scenery, Air Schools made an important contribution to the wartime training effort.

Derby Aviation's original offices at Burnaston Airfield, 1947–65.

When war broke out in 1939, Captain Harben was recommissioned as a serving officer for the Air Ministry. As the law demanded, he resigned from the board of Air Schools Ltd and sold his shares. In order to continue his crucial role as the motivation behind the development of the company, he became responsible for non-service matters as commanding officer and general organizing manager at Burnaston.[10] He went on to establish a second flying school at Wolverhampton[11]

Staff Refreshments (Tea). No. 112

DERBY AIRPORT - BURNASTON
OFFICIAL OPENING CEREMONY
by
The Right Honourable SIR KINGSLEY WOOD, M.P.
(His Majesty's Secretary of State for Air)
Saturday, June 17th, 1939

The holder of this ticket is entitled to receive Refreshments (value Sixpence) in the Marquees in any Enclosure other than the Official Enclosure.
This card must be surrendered on receipt of afternoon tea refreshments, which will be available only between the hours of 3.30 p.m. and 6 p.m.
All drinks must be paid for when ordered.

Burnaston Airport in 1956, looking westwards along Runway 27. Burnaston House is the white building amongst the trees to the right.

and create a flying training programme unsurpassed in its day.[12] By the end of the war Air Schools' operations at Burnaston and Wolverhampton had trained in excess of 14,000 pilots from civilian life to RAF 'wings' standard. With more than a hundred Air Ministry aircraft in their care during peak years, the company had the best maintenance and lowest accident rate of any school in the Royal Air Force Flying Training Command.[13]

Despite the handsome profits achieved by Air Schools Ltd in the early years, even before the end of the war Edward Philips, the new chairman, realized that the demand for military pilots would eventually dry up. In the very short term the business was saved by government-sponsored courses to provide refresher training for the RAF Volunteer Reserve, together with a short-lived initiative to train pilots to officer status to replace wartime crews who had returned to civilian life. Training courses were also commissioned by the

Wartime trainees help each other prepare for thier first solo flights.

army for established pilots and navigators, focusing on fighter control to support a new arena of war in Korea.[14] Air Schools employed nine Tiger Moths and two Avro Anson Is at Burnaston for this work, and a further twelve and two at Wolverhampton. The new courses included aviation law,

Three RAF Tiger Moths flying over Burnaston in 1947.

Air Schools' facilities at Burnaston after the Second World War: Engine and air frame instruction (top left), training aircraft (top right), Link Trainers (bottom left) and the control tower (bottom right).

flight procedures, aeronautical charts, aircraft instuments, radio aids, meteorology, signals and flight theory. They were slow to attract trainees so the company invested in an advertising campaign to stimulate recruitment and staged small air displays to promote the services on offer. Although every effort was made, pupil numbers and flying hours never quite reached expectations. When the Air Ministry announced in 1953 that future programmes would not operate from grass airfields, both flying schools were forced to close. As turnover crashed and profits dried up, many of the company's pilot trainers lost their jobs. To keep the business alive income was generated by leasing the in-house fleet (a 3-seater Miles Messenger and four ex-airforce Austers) for ad-hoc charters and by renting out unused premises on the airport complex to willing tenants.[15]

By 1957, Air Schools had resurrected the training side of the business by acquiring the London School of Flying and moving activities to Elstree Aerodrome, one of the best-equipped schools in the country.[16] In the same year the company purchased Photo Flight Ltd, a business engaged in aerial photography and surveys.

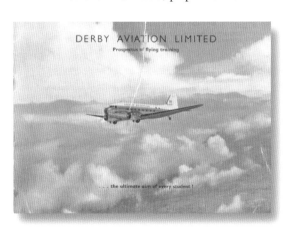

Derby Aviation offered flying tuition for those wishing to secure a professional pilot's licence. Basic training was carried out on Chipmunks though conversion courses on other types of aircraft could be arranged, up to and including DC-3s.

Derby Aviation

With military-related activities at an end Air Schools had to explore new business opportunities to survive. In 1947, a separate company, Derby Aviation, was formed to attract and handle aircraft brokering and civilian light aircraft activities including maintenance and cargo transportation. Business was found from the most unlikely sources. Two short-term contracts were secured from the Ministry of Supply: one to overhaul and repair mobile cranes and earth-moving equipment, and another to preserve, identify and package military equipment that since the war had been lying idle. Non-military activities were far and few between but did include rebuilding four crashed Miles Messengers (liaison aircraft) for Miles Aircraft, surveys of electrical power lines and trials with the police for traffic control.[17] The first year's profit for Derby Aviation was £99, disappointing but not crushing for a company who were making long-term plans to move into the serious business of passenger aviation.

Following Captain Roy Harben's untimely death in February 1947, the board of Air Schools broadened its horizons by inviting personnel to join the company, each with particular and relevant experience. New energies were needed to consolidate what Harben had begun and generate future expansion in the commercial and domestic market place. Group Captain C A B Wilcock was invited to be chairman;[18] Edward Philips was appointed managing director and Wing Commander Alan Roxburgh became chief flying officer.[19]

Avro Anson (G-AMDA) in front of the municipal hangar at Burnaston. Derby Aviation undertook aerial surveys over the Midlands with this model as part of a project to produce magnetic maps of the entire UK.

With the new team in place discussions began about how to secure working capital, how to deal with debtors and creditors, and which aircraft to buy. Money was raised by the issue of new shares and investment was made in equipment and tools so engineers could obtain the necessary Certificates of Approval to work on civil aircraft. Despite the government ban on travel abroad, the board were determined to purchase new Messengers and Geminis as soon as the business could afford the necessary deposits. Serious thoughts focused on attracting general charter work, particularly excursions and holiday flights to meet the post-war aspirations of the travelling public. Business would be split between taxi charters and regular scheduled services to selected destinations from both Derby and Wolverhampton. Amongst the innovative ideas debated in the late 1940s to widen the company's activities was the setting up of an air college in Derby, opening a travel business serving the Midlands and acquiring an agency to sell helicopters, despite the enormity of the financial implications. In the meantime the chairman suggested a company livery together with smart uniforms and badges as a start to bringing the names of Air Schools and Derby Aviation before the general public. Hopes were high in these heady post-war years though sadly profits remained noticeably low as taxes soared and overheads crept upwards.

Commercial passengers

In the post-war era flying was poised for new peace-time applications with both freight transportation and passenger travel. Following the success of the Berlin Airlift, which dropped supplies of food and fuel into Berlin in the late 1940s, flying was established as an effective mover of cargo. Derby Aviation was soon picking up lucrative jobs. No contract was too small or too large as pheasants were brought from Denmark to breeding farms in Warwickshire and night-time newspaper flights carried thousands of copies of the morning editions to Exeter and Cardiff.

Passenger services were slower to materialize. The public were not yet ready to embrace flying as an alternative to road and rail travel. The company's first commercial passenger venture took place

Air Schools' first passenger service used Miles Messenger (G-AILL) on a charter flight from Burnaston to the Isle of Man on 21 August 1947.

Miles Gemini (G-AJZJ) was an early member of Derby Aviation's charter fleet and one of several aircraft acquired from Kenning Aviation when it ceased operating in 1948.

on 21 August 1947 when a Mr Turner and two fellow motorcycle enthusiasts chartered Derby Aviation's 3-seater Miles Messenger (G-AILL)[20] to fly them to the legendary TT races on the Isle of Man. This 320-mile round trip, at speeds reaching 135 mph (217 kph) was followed by other ad-hoc contracts using the Messenger and a Miles Gemini (G-AJZJ),[21] another twin-engined 3-seater touring aircraft. So encouraged was the company for the future of commercial aviation that within the year

Group Captain C A B Wilcock was chairman from 1947 until his sudden death in January 1962.

Derby Aviation had acquired the first of four 8-seater De Havilland Rapides (G-AIUK).[22] This ex-Air Force model, with its range of 573 miles (922 km) and top speed of 157 mph (253 kph), was an effective addition to the fleet. As in other aircraft of its day comfort was lacking and it was sparsely equipped for its new commercial role, with only basic landing aids and a simple instrument panel. Rapide pilots had to rely on their map-reading skills to navigate their way around the country, together with bearings supplied by VHF radio from ground stations with direction-finding equipment.

During the early 1950s passenger work was scarce but requests were forthcoming, with brewers needing to be flown to Copenhagen to check on the quality of their imports, businessmen having to get to Amsterdam for meetings, and couturiers and models wishing to travel to Paris and Milan for catwalk shows. The demand for

Loading a cargo of 2,000 pheasants in Denmark, 1959.

Derby Aviation's air hostess Jean Merritt welcoming passengers on board for a flight to Jersey in the early 1950s.

passenger services grew slowly but steadily, particularly with holiday-makers bound for the popular Channel Islands. As a mark of their success Derby Aviation acquired three further Rapides (G-AKOV, 1950; G-AEAL, 1953; and G-AIUL, 1954) and applied for licences to operate scheduled services from Burnaston and Wolverhampton to Jersey. It was a momentous day when the first scheduled passenger service took off from the grass of Burnaston on 18 July 1953. The following year a further passenger service began from both bases, this time to Ostend. On both these routes the journey had to be broken by stops at Birmingham, in both directions, for the obligatory customs clearance.

With the final demise of the Flying School in 1954,[23] the training personnel left en masse, leaving a depleted staff of 14 to cope with every aspect of the company's new business adventures with passenger and freight aviation.

The fuselage of the DH89A Dragon Rapide was a wooden box with plywood covering. Fabric was stretched over the wings and tail surfaces, which were then strengthened with dope before spray painting. With a cruising speed of 132 mph this popular 8-passenger airliner was operated by the company between 1948 and 1957. Derby Airways eventually owned four De Havilland Rapides. G-AIUK was Derby Aviation's first Rapide, originally built for the RAF.

Scheduled services with DC-3s and Marathons

Scheduled services were an instant success for Derby Aviation as a new generation of travellers looked for speed of communication and aspired to the glamour of flying. To keep up with demand the board of Air Schools Ltd made the massive jump to the 36-seater, twin-propeller, Douglas DC-3, which could operate from any rough airstrip and fly up to 10,000 feet, the limit without pressurized cabins. The DC-3s with their large square windows were a relatively modern type and irresistible with so many former military models available in tip-top condition at knockdown prices. Healthy profits from a subsidiary company, Derby Aero Surveys, were used to finance the new fleet.[24]

The first DC-3 (G-ANTD) was purchased in April 1955 for £22,000, having already been converted from military use. It was named *Dovedale* after a Derbyshire river valley and entered service on 3 May, carrying a party from Manchester to Amsterdam. The following year General Montgomery's former personal DC-3 was acquired from the Air Ministry for £31,000.[25] The quality mahogany interior fittings were removed and replaced with maximum capacity passenger seating in smart royal blue leather with paler blue headings and carpets. Derby Aviation's pale and dark blue house colours were promptly painted on as the company's first official livery – white body with slender bold horizontal stripes and upper-case lettering.

Almost every year throughout the 1950s another DC-3 or high-wing 20-seater, 4-engined Handley Page Miles Marathon was acquired to meet passenger and cargo demand, until the company owned eight models.[26] The Marathons were unfortunately no better equipped than the Rapides they replaced. They too lacked auto-pilots, de-icing systems and any form of heating. Regular customers soon learned that it was prudent to bring along extra clothing – and even umbrellas to deal with leaks from the overhead hatch and cockpit canopy, a known hazard with Marathons. The airline's remedy for the draughty cabin was hot drinks throughout the flight. Despite any inconveniences, business thrived as the energies of Derby Airways' engineering division, experienced technicians, ground staff and crews were pushed

The Miles Marathon (G-AMGW) *Millers Dale* was the first of three of this type operated by Derby Aviation. The Marathon was a primitive aircraft but served the company well.

Warmly wrapped-up passengers being served hot drinks on board a Derby Airways Marathon in 1956. Dripping rain was a typical hazard within the cabin, so regular customers brought umbrellas for the journey.

This DC-3 (G-AOGZ) was the personal transport aircraft of General Montgomery during the Second World War. When acquired by Derby Airways in 1956 it was repainted in the airline's livery, stripped of its plush mahogany furnishings and refitted with commercial passenger seating.

to the limits. As services moved back and forth from passenger to freight the seats were promptly removed or replaced as needs demanded.

By the mid-1950s the company had begun to expand their programme of scheduled services to include routes that offered year-round opportunities. A new destination for 1956 was the Isle of Man. The following year the company secured another important route in response to Rolls-Royce's announcement that it would be moving a large proportion of its aero-engine overhaul and manu-facturing operations from the Midlands to Hillington, on the out-skirts of Glasgow. With a guaranteed contract of 16 seats per day Derby Aviation began their new scheduled service from Burnaston to Glasgow in March 1957.[27] Public awareness of Derby Aviation's scheduled service operation was further enhanced when seasonal flights began out of Northampton and Oxford to Jersey, and to a variety of destinations from Luton.

Ad-hoc charters during the later 1950s ranged from straightforward revenue-generating jobs to humanitarian missions on behalf of the government. In the early months of 1957, the DC-3s were deployed in transporting troops from Malta back to Britain following the Suez crisis. This was followed by an assignment to carry refugees from Linz in Austria to England in response to the crisis in Hungary.[28] The most lucrative commercial customer for charter services at this time was Rolls-Royce, who signed an ongoing contract to transport their engines

An advertisement from the official programme that marked the opening of Burnaston Airport on 17 June 1939.

Derby Aviation's original air-hostess uniform was a belted dark blue pinafore dress worn with a crisp white blouse which was designed with deep cuffs. The hat was a traditional airline pill-box displaying the company badge. A co-ordinated coat with a check lining was standard issue for warmth both out of doors and on board. The aircraft used by the company during the 1950s lacked any means of cabin heating.

to RAF military units as far away as Aden, Bahrain and Karachi. Closer to home Derby Aviation transported a total of 254 Rolls-Royce Avon turbo-jets to Toulouse in France for Sud-Aviation's Caravelle airliner programme. The engines were shipped in pairs and frequently arrived warm from the engine-maker's nearby works, requiring very careful handling when being loaded aboard the Douglas DC-3s on special roller-equipped cradles.

Further expansion during the late 1950s was into the area of package holidays, bringing cheaper and more affordable travel to an untapped market. Derby Aviation flew its first inclusive tours (IT) service from Birmingham to Palma on 18 May 1957, having already formed a new subsidiary, Inclusive Air Holidays, to handle this potentially exciting work. Opportunities snowballed with flights, mainly in the DC-3 fleet, operating from Derby, Manchester, Birmingham and Gatwick to all the popular summer holiday resorts around Europe. During the cold winter months the company flew winter sports enthusiasts to the mountains for pre-organized trips. In 1958, the Lourdes centenary year, eight-day pilgrimages were organized to the Pyrénées for 35 guineas per person, each tour accompanied by a spiritual leader. Another initiative was the introduction in 1959 of Winter Sunshine Cruises, the flying version of a sea cruise. Operated on behalf of Lord Brothers Tours, each holiday took a DC-3 away for two weeks. Stops were made in Madrid, Marrakech and Agadir, with seven nights on Tenerife, the largest of the seven Canary Islands. Derby Airways was one of the UK's pioneers in the package-holiday industry that would capture the public's imagination for years to come.

Despite the support and enthusiasm for Derby Aviation's services and its dominance at Burnaston throughout the 1950s, the company struggled to finance the growing pay-roll and make profits. Cash flow was an on-going problem, aggravated when the government laid down new restrictions on bank overdrafts. The airline business was a precarious one, but Derby Aviation were determined to survive and prosper.

Derby Airways

On 12 March 1959 Derby Aviation were renamed Derby Airways and registered as an airline company. Although they were already an established carrier it was thought that the new name would promote to the public an image of a business that focused on passenger flights. The choice of the new identity posed an unexpected problem as two local pilots had already applied for the same name. After a persuasive chat they agreed to reconsider and used an amalgamation of their personal names, AsCoop Airways (Ascott and Cooper), instead.

In 1957 a modern Instrument Landing System (needle on a dial) was installed in the Marathon fleet to replace the outdated Morse code landing system.

In the summer season of 1959, Derby Airways carried in excess of 16,000 passengers in its fleet of five DC-3s and three Marathons. The scheduled network now flew to a total of 15 popular destinations across the length and breadth of the UK.[29] As each of the company's aircraft went through the hangar on routine maintenance it emerged with the new name in a solid serif typeface. Before the year was out the original company, Air Schools Ltd, had gifted some of its assets to the

Derby Airways based their success in the early 1960s on their DC-3 fleet which was fitted with state-of-the-moment navigational equipment (V.O.R.). G-AOFZ seen here in the original distinctive company livery served from 1960 to 1966.

Derby Airways hangar at Burnaston during the late 1950s.

The engine workshop at Burnaston was kept very busy during the 1950s. The two Marathons purchased from West African Airways in 1956 were practically rebuilt.

newly named airline, now a financially separate and independent entity.[30] Air Schools would concentrate solely on the business of being a finance company and the lessee of Burnaston Airport.[31]

This was also the year when the company were at long last granted limited customs clearing facilities from their home hub at Burnaston. International business travellers and holiday-makers were now permitted to fly direct to the Channel Islands and the continent without lengthy and time-wasting stops at other British airports for customs clearance. To handle this advantage a customs clearance room had to be built at Burnaston Airport.

In 1959, the company reached 'Twenty One Years' in the business of aviation. A celebration dinner including roast turkey and iced wonder cake marked the occasion, together with an illustrated booklet which highlighted the achievements of the business and introduced the key personnel. Ron Paine, a gifted engineer and racing pilot, was the director in charge of engineers and technicians. Wing Commander Alan Roxburgh was singled out as having developed the company's many activities.[32]

As the airline industry as a whole necessarily become more rigidly controlled and organized, Derby Airways took it upon themselves to address the need for formalized training for their air crews, ground engineers and cabin staff. In the post-war years, a 16,500 lb

Derby Airways celebrated their 21st anniversary with a commemorative booklet illustrating their achievements and with a six-course dinner on 19 November 1959.

aircraft such as a 22-seater Marathon needed just one pilot to secure a Certificate of Airworthiness. From 1959 the Ministry of Civil Aviation insisted that a captain's assistant was available to navigate and generally help when needed in aircraft heavier than 12,500 lb. These apprenticeships were invaluable to young pilots. In the early days it was acceptable to hand a girl a uniform with a few words of encouragement and she became a *bona fide* air hostess. From 1959, Derby Aviation's Hostess Training School offered a compulsory three-week training programme teaching the rudiments of flight and meteorology, bar procedures and stock control, and the basics about health and immigration requirements. The BBC heard of the efforts being made and came to film the trainees in a move aimed at providing the general public with an insight into the standards being set in the world of passenger aviation. Travel was a sexy and exhilarating business, and with its proven track record Derby Airways had a choice of applicants. Following the 1961 Aviation Act, Derby was one of the first carriers to be approved for the grant of an Air Operator's Certificate, signifying high standards of aircraft maintenance and flight operational facilities. In 1962, Captain Bert Cramp established the company's first Pilot Training School, offering practical instruction in a classroom setting for the new intake of pilots and existing crews as they were introduced to new models in the fleet.

The momentum of expansion continued unchecked in the early 1960s as the flood-gates opened and reservations came pouring in after 1 April each year for the summer season. To ease the load and share the burden Derby Airways granted Mercury Airlines in Manchester a sales agency to promote their flights. Passenger demand, particularly for IT, meant that the company were repeatedly looking to increase fleet capacity. In 1960 and 1961 three 36-seater DC-3s joined the fleet – G-AOFZ *High Dale*, G-AGJV *Millers Dale* and G-AKJH *Monsal Dale* – the later two names taken from the recently retired 22-seater Marathons.[33] With these extra seats on offer the airline reached unprecedented activity, carrying over 32,000 passengers in the summer of 1960, an increase of 100 per cent on the previous year. On 14 July 1961 Derby Airways carried its millionth passenger. The

G-AKJH was the last Douglas DC-3 to join Derby Airways in 1961. It is seen here serving as a freighter. In the background are the Argonauts acquired from Overseas Aviation in 1962.

scheduled flight timetable for 1963 was packed with choice – eight continental destinations, thirteen domestic routes and daily services to the Channel Islands from seven UK regional airports. A return fare from Derby to Belfast cost £11, any day of the week, while a long weekend to and from Barcelona from Cardiff or Bristol would set you back just £34. Despite the outward appearance of real progress, the work pattern was too summer-holiday orientated, with a very low trough in the winter months. Future needs would need to focus on an all-year-round policy. In 1963, the company issued their first Business Services Timetable, a dedicated year-round schedule aimed at the business community and forming a framework for later growth.

In 1964, Derby Airways became a signatory to the International Air Transport Association (IATA) Multilateral Interline Agreement that allowed the mutual acceptance of tickets with other signatories to that Agreement.[34] By becoming a participant with IATA, Derby Airways grew to be a recognized international carrier, which in turn brought its own rewards when larger members fed the smaller independent valuable customers. Turnover increased by 25 per cent with the added business secured from other airlines. The company became a full member of IATA in 1984.

Ron Paine joined Derby Aviation as director of engineering in 1940. He was a driving force during the early years and rose steadily through the ranks to become the joint managing director. He left in 1970 when Minster Assets insisted on putting a new management team in place.

Derby Airways brochure, 1960.

Argonauts and a banking partner

With a well-established network of routes and growth in IT services, the company were quick to recognize that their 36-seater DC-3s were too small and lacked the performance and comfort to exploit fully the growth they aspired to. The airline would become paralysed if the fleet were not updated. Customer awareness demanded more visibly modern aircraft plus basic extras such as controlled cabin pressure and state-of-the-art tricycle landing gear for more comfortable landings.

In an increasingly competitive business and with tour operators negotiating cheaper and cheaper prices, larger machines with increased seating capacity were needed to bring down passenger costs per mile. Derby Airways' fleet in 1961, of eight twin-propeller DC-3s, was simply unsuited to future growth and survival.

Cabin service on board a Derby Airways Argonaut in 1962.

With limited funds the board of Derby Airways had little choice when deciding how best to update their fleet. The preferred option was for the pressurized 4-engined Douglas DC-6, a superb aircraft offering attractive seat-mile costs. Two were being sold by American Airlines and the company began the process of selecting and licensing flight crew members. There was great anticipation at Burnaston over the proposed arrival of the big Douglas aeroplanes, but circumstances intervened and they never came.

At the end of September 1961, a Gatwick-based IT operator, Overseas Aviation, went into liquidation and their fleet of 70-seater Canadair C-4 Argonauts was repossessed by the leasing bank, Lombard Ltd, who duly offered them to Derby Airways.[35] In a moment's madness the management accepted an exceptionally attractive deal that included five aircraft (two for spares) at a very low price in exchange for a sizeable investment in the company by Lombard, who with their international reputation would guide the board with their business advice. Unfortunately the Argonauts had neither the range, nor

Derby Airways Canadair C-4 Argonaut. This model was fully pressurized, cruised at 225 mph (362 kph) and carried 70 passengers with a crew of five.

the capacity nor the cargo doors of the DC-6, and being tail-heavy, they were ill suited to the short grass runways of Burnaston.[36] The Argonauts proved to be uneconomic to keep in the air and their unreliability cost the company many contracts, even threatening the airline's continued existence.

Following the arrival of the first Argonaut (G-ALHS) in a bellow of reverse pitch on Burnaston's small grass airfield on 5 October 1961, work started immediately to bring the aircraft up to Derby

Derby Airways' maintenance staff wrestle with a wheel and brake assembly as Argonaut (G-ALHS) awaits attention inside the former RAF hangar at Burnaston, 1950s.

Airways standards. Passenger seating was increased with five extra seats and two more cabin windows were cut into the forward section of the fuselage. The new company livery with its bands of grey, white and two tones of blue was promptly painted on, together with bold 'DA' letters on the tail fin. Despite the disappointment of not acquiring the DC-6s, employee morale was high. In the short term the piston-engined Argonauts proved a worthwhile asset as the airline sought to challenge the boundaries of the business with experimental ventures, both in passenger traffic and freight contracts. The fleet was based at Birmingham, a larger airfield than Burnaston, but with the appropriate licences in place was soon heavily engaged in charter work and IT services – notably for the growing market in the south-west, transporting holiday-makers from Cardiff and Bristol to Nice, Palma, Perpignan (for the Costa Brava), Ostend and Rotterdam.

Wing Commander Alan Roxburgh, chairman from 1962 until poor health hastened his retirement in 1965.

The future looked extremely promising. As business grew and cash accumulated, investment was made in promoting the airline. A country-wide sales team was set up with allocated boundaries and responsibilities to sell Derby Airways as a brand to both travel agents and personal travellers.[37] To meet marketing needs an advertising budget was made available to promote the wide-reaching network of services that now extended from Glasgow and Belfast to Majorca and Barcelona.[38] With a staff in excess of a hundred employees, business was hectic and the company were surviving, unlike some independent British operators who were falling by the way.

The largest portion of the company's business in 1964 was summer charter work for established tour companies, followed closely by holiday flights booked directly by individual travellers. The other lucrative arm of the business was seasonal IT services with routes now operating from six British airports to exotic holiday destinations around Europe and the Mediterranean.[39] The smallest sector of the business in the early years was the year-round scheduled services aimed at the business customer. Despite the obvious success in breaking into the heady realms of passenger aviation, Derby Airways was still perceived as a small local airline operating from a provincial grass airfield in the early 1960s.

Plans to leave Burnaston

By 1960, the number of passengers 'flying Derby' and passing through Burnaston Airport had reached the encouraging figure of over 45,000 a year. Traffic to the Channel Islands alone had more than doubled in the previous 12 months. Freight traffic was also healthy with a pleasing uptake and potential for growth following the granting, the year before, of customs freight clearance facilities at the Derby hub. Plans were already underway for further increases in activity, but the board realized that increased traffic would create its own problems. The grass surface at Burnaston was starting to break down under the continual pounding of aircraft wheels, and although remedial work had been undertaken to stabilize the soil the surface was inadequate for modern, heavier aircraft. The constraining perimeter was also challenging for even the grass-loving DC-3s, which occasionally clipped the fence posts with their wheels on approach. With only gooseneck flares for after-dark operations, night flying was still a primitive affair and generally considered to be a nuisance. Burnaston was falling way short of expectations as the board looked seriously at their future needs.

It came as no surprise when Derby Town Council announced remedial plans for a brand-new airport for the East Midlands that would replace the inadequate facilities and hotch-potch of buildings on the old RAF base at Burnaston. The site chosen was a neglected wartime airfield at Castle Donington, just a few miles from the proposed continuation of the M1 motorway[40] and the prosperous industrial centres of Derby, Leicester and Nottingham.[41] The public enquiry heard objections that there was no need for a new airport facility in the area but the facts spoke for themselves. After months of deliberation the idea was upheld, to the relief of Derby Airways, who realized that their future depended on the move. With improved transport links to and from the new airport, stretching to an ever growing catchment area, more passengers and freight business would inevitably follow. Derby Airways would be the only airline based at the new airport.

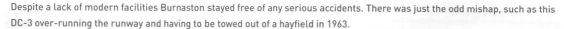

Despite a lack of modern facilities Burnaston stayed free of any serious accidents. There was just the odd mishap, such as this DC-3 over-running the runway and having to be towed out of a hayfield in 1963.

The directors of Derby Airways in 1963. Left to right: Wing Commander Alan Roxburgh, chairman; Mary Agar, secretary; Denis Sullivan, financial director; and Ron Paine, director of engineering.

The dilapidated airport premises lying to the north of Castle Donington village were finally acquired in 1963 with a price tag of £37,500. A year later planning permission was in place and the bulldozers had been sent in. The £1.4 million redevelopment created an up-to-date facility boasting a basic requirement 5,850-foot tarmac runway, a 60-foot taxiway with lighting for the hours of darkness, a new hangar, basic Decca radar to 'talk down' pilots on their descent, a dedicated terminal building and parking for 850 cars.[42]

With the transfer from Burnaston to the new East Midlands Airport imminent it was clear to the board that it must address the mistakes of the past and consider its fleet capacity needs for the future by re-equipping with modern turbo-prop aircraft.[43] The Argonaut had been a difficult aircraft to sell with its high operating costs per seat, limited range and unsuitability for transporting cargo. The Hawker Siddeley 748 was considered as a replacement, but after careful evaluation the British-built Handley Page Herald 200 with its Rolls-Royce engines was the board's choice. Two second-hand models were sourced at a cost of £600,000.[44] On 1 February 1965 the first 56-seater Herald (G-ASKK) touched down on the sodden surface at Burnaston in a shower of mud and was promptly washed down by the waiting team of engineers. Derby Airways would eventual acquire six models in the Herald series. All of these boasted large windows providing passengers with unobstructed views of the countryside below and wide doors ideally suited to loading cargo. The Herald was a worthy aircraft in the fleet of the 1960s, serving on freight runs, regional scheduled flights and week-end excursions to the continent.

Behind Derby Airways' modern and optimistic façade the need for serious financial investment was ever present. The airline's second-hand fleet understandably generated problems, mostly unpredictable ones. Older piston-engined aircraft were noisy and exceptionally labour intensive to keep in the sky. The newer jets and turbo-props were attractively quieter, designed to fly for longer periods with minimum attention and therefore capable of increasing revenue-earning opportunities. The old Douglas DC-3s were finally sold off (1965–7) as the cost of keeping them airborne outweighed any profits that could be made from flying them. With their withdrawal passenger services to airports with grass runways, such as the long established route to the Isle of Wight, had to fold.

The type of operation offered by Derby Airways in the early 1960s was rapidly becoming outdated and financially unsustainable. Derby Airways, an independent airline, struggled to secure much wanted route licences. Although some international short-haul routes were identified and claimed, the company was not as yet in fierce competition with British Airways and other European state-owned carriers. Derby Airways had traditionally focused on providing a feeder service enabling long- and medium- haul passengers to fly from their local airport to the major airports without the need for surface transport.[45] Attitudes were poised for change.

British Midland Airways

New name, new hub

As work was nearing completion at East Midlands Airport, Derby Airways announced that from 1 October 1964 it would change its name to British Midland Airways. The old name was considered provincial and inappropriate for an airline with aspirations to become a national and international carrier based at a stylish new airport in the centre of Britain. The new company name and distinctive tail fin 'BM' lettering was soon to be seen on the upper white fuselages of the DC-3 and Argonaut fleet.[46]

In November 1964, a modest but significant deal was struck when the newly named company acquired the assets of Mercury Airlines of Manchester, a small operator already known to the company,

who before their liquidation had run services from Manchester to the Isle of Wight and Newcastle. British Midland comfortably absorbed these routes into their timetable while also taking over valuable check-in and office facilities at Manchester Airport. In addition they gained the services of Mercury's station manager, Michael Bishop.

On 1 April 1965 an entourage of trucks and cars began moving engineering equipment, reservations boards and typewriters to British Midland's new home at Castle Donington. The following day the company's

Douglas DC-3 *Darley Dale* (G-AOGZ) in front of the Bellman hangar at Burnaston Airport shortly after Derby Airways changed their name to British Midland Airways in October 1964. The interim BMA livery was restrained, echoing the classic design of the old Derby Airways livery.

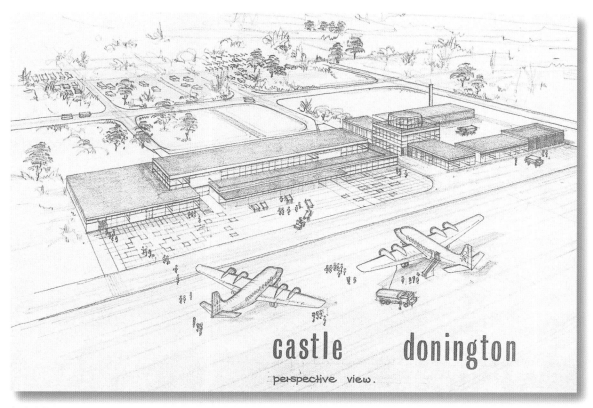

Artist's impression of the new East Midlands Airport, 1964.

As part of the new BMA image a fresh uniform was introduced for ground and cabin crews: black tailored two-piece suits with kick-pleat skirts and single-breasted jackets with crested buttons. This was complemented by a white blouse and traditional black airline hat adorned with the new British Midland logo badge. The summer uniform, seen here, was worn from 1 June to 29 September and featured a belted shirt-waister dress in pale blue cotton.

first Handley Herald 211 (G-ASKK) took off on its maiden scheduled service to Glasgow from the grass of Burnaston, arriving home to the tarmac runway of East Midlands Airport. The return fare on this most profitable of routes was £14 12s 0d (£14.60). The total relocation from Burnaston took place over the next six months.[47]

Winter Timetable
1965-1966

Effective 1st Nov 65-31st Mar 66

Passenger numbers soared to 86,000 in the first year of operations at East Midlands Airport. The volume of IT work and freight business doubled.[48] Attention focused once more on the fleet and the future needs of the business, as the world of aviation was moving into the jet age. In the autumn of 1965 the board of British Midland made a rash decision, agreeing to purchase three new BAC One-Eleven jets for the recommended retail price of £4 million. The bank was predictably reluctant to lend the fledgling airline such an enormous sum. The management questioned the wisdom of its decision and caution prevailed. Nevertheless with only four outdated DC-3s, three ailing Argonauts and three promising turbo-prop Heralds in use, important choices needed to be made.

Michael Bishop was born in Bowdon, Cheshire, on 10 February 1942. He was the only son of an Australian-born soldier who was injured in France and sent to England to recover from injuries sustained during the First World War. During the 1930s his father set up a crane maintenance business on Liverpool Docks together with a specialist vehicle-building firm creating ambulances and brewery lorries. As a young boy Michael Bishop was an enthusiastic aircraft spotter, his interest stimulated when he secured a holiday job at Manchester Airport at the age of 16, working for Airviews, a small aerial photography and charter business.

On leaving full-time education Bishop went into business with his father, quickly establishing his own commercial ability by starting, building up and selling a paint distribution business, all within four years. With a longing to move into civil aviation and eventually invest in a small local carrier, he joined Mercury Airlines in 1963 to manage their airport traffic office at Manchester Airport. With his obvious ability and enthusiasm Bishop progressed quickly and soon established a passenger-handling agency. After the British Midland take-over of Mercury Airlines in 1964, Michael Bishop remained in Manchester and built up a significant handling business for his new employees. At the age of 27, in 1969, he was catapulted overnight to director and general manager of the whole airline, becoming managing director when he was 30.

The Vickers Viscount

The disappointment of backing out from acquiring the British Aerospace jet was short lived, for six months later a contract was signed for three second-hand Vickers Viscounts from British United. The first 64-seater Viscount Series 736 (G-AODG) cost £175,000 and was handed over at Jersey Airport on 10 January 1967. It was promptly followed by a second (G-ASED), a 73-seater Series 831, which arrived at East Midlands on 15 February.[49] The new British Midland livery was hastily painted on both turbo-props. The Viscounts were put to work on scheduled flights around the UK with pilots and cabin crews working an average of six flights a day. No routes were more challenging than those to the Channel Islands, where weather conditions were often unpredictable.

The 4-engined turbo-prop Viscount fleet proved to be an exceptionally reliable choice for British Midland, providing the airline with a year-round service. The seating capacity and overall speeds were far greater than those of the DC-3s or Argonauts and as such dramatically increased the profitability of the service on offer. Passengers enjoyed the benefits of a panoramic view from heights of 17,000 feet out of large windows and the comfort of a vibration-free ride. Air conditioning was an added bonus in the blistering summer heat and on-board bucket toilets were much appreciated. The cabin crew had the benefit of spacious galleys for the preparation of hot drinks and meals in foil trays. The only hiccup with the turbo-props was a need for long paved runways, something not always available in the 1960s. The attractiveness of the Viscounts was such that over the next 11 years British Midland Airways acquired another 27 models.

To mark the arrival of the new Vickers Viscount (1967) whilst also celebrating the 30th anniversary of the company (1968), cabin crews were issued with a new made-to-measure uniform. This was designed in house by Mary Agar, the financial director, and produced by the Derby Co-op. A turquoise-blue two-piece suit with straight knee-length skirt and collarless jacket was worn with a beige blouse and navy accessories. The pill-box hat was reshaped and adorned with a revamped company badge in turquoise and gold. In case of inclement weather, a raincoat was regular issue together with a white scarf to hold the hat in place. The complete uniform, costing £50, included a jacket, two skirts, four blouses, a hat, two pairs of shoes, a handbag, a raincoat and gloves. Men continued to wear more traditional pilot-style uniforms that included rank markings and narrow gold bands.

This Vickers Viscount 760 (G-AWCV) was British Midland's sixth model of this type to join the fleet. The large oval windows were characteristic of early Viscounts. G-AWCV is seen here wearing the company's new livery in 1968.

Externally the Viscounts looked almost alike but internally they differed drastically from one sub-type to another.[50] The pronounced differences in the cockpit were potentially problematic though a three-week training course ensured that all pilots were familiar with at least four of the sub-types.[51] The ground instructor for the Viscount fleet was the legendary chain-smoking Peter Hill, whose school was a Portacabin belonging to East Midlands School of Flying and whose knowledge was instilled in every young pilot who came through his door. The British Midland Viscount simulator housed in Hangar T2 at the airport had no visual system but provided many hours of invaluable training for new recruits. On-board training instruction was the responsibility of Jim Snee, who served the company for 35 years.[52]

The arrival of the all-promising Viscounts led to the immediate demotion of the DC-3s to freight work until their eventual retirement. The Argonaut fleet continued with IT work around Europe. Sadly, on 4 June 1967, British Midland Airways experienced a tragic loss when Argonaut G-ALHG crashed whilst approaching Manchester on the return leg of a flight to Palma. Sixty-nine passengers and three of the crew lost their lives. Due to a failure of fuel transfer one of the aircraft's four engines had drained in flight, resulting in the loss of that engine. In attempting to feather the offending prop a second engine was closed. Lacking the power-assisted control systems fitted to more modern aircraft, it became impossible to maintain height and the Argonaut eventually crashed on a building site at Stockport, five miles short of Manchester's Runway 24. The two remaining Argonauts in the fleet continued to fly for a short period, after a brief grounding, but were eventually sold for scrap. Extensive investigations by the Board of Trade identified the cause of the disaster and the inquest that followed exonerated the airline from any blame.

The British Midland fleet now consisted exclusively of second-hand turbo-prop Viscounts, a popular aeroplane ideally suited to regional and short-haul traffic.[53]

Frank Marshall, joint managing director, 1966–9.

Minster Assets on board

The year 1968 had far-reaching consequences for the UK's airline industry. The steady growth that had characterized the previous decade collapsed and was alarmingly replaced by a downturn. Two independent British carriers, British Eagle and Transglobe Airways, fell victim to rising fuel prices and the changed circumstances, sending a wave of fear across the industry. British Midland could have gone the same way when Lombard Banking, their business partner since 1962, withdrew their support. The directors of British Midland were left with a working capital of just £25,000 until Ron Paine, the company's chairman, joint managing director and driving force, negotiated a life-line.[54] Help came from Minster Assets, a small City merchant bank with interests in shipping and the motor insurance industry, who invested £150,000 in the company.

Peter Cannon, managing director of Minster Assets, had a personal enthusiasm for airlines, having some years earlier rescued another independent carrier, Invicta Airways, with an injection of cash.[55] Following the initial investment, making Minster Assets the principal shareholder in British Midland, it was no surprise to the business world when the two airlines amalgamated in March 1969 with a further injection of £450,000 of capital from the merchant bank. The name British Midland Airways was retained, as was the basic livery of the fleet. One small concession was the inclusion of Invicta's rampant horse symbol on the fleet fuselage. Within months this mark was removed when Hugh Kennard, the former managing director of Invicta, bought back the business and set up again as an independent freight operator using the name Invicta Air Cargo and his old logo.

The merger was welcomed, but inevitably there followed redundancies and forced resignations in both airline companies. These were hard and painful to bear. Ron Paine, who had secured Minster Assets' support in the first place, left along with other directors in the clear-out. The management of Minster Assets were determined to protect their investment and ensure that the new company realized their potential for success, but to do that, they wanted fresh talent. The new British Midland Airways would be tightly controlled and run by qualified personnel. James Hodgson, another director of Minster Assets, became chairman. Stuart Balmforth, whose background was in accountancy, took on

James Hodgson of Minster Assets, chairman of British Midland Airways from 1969 to 1972.

Peter Cannon of Minster Assets, chairman of British Midland Airways from 1972 to 1973.

A R G McGibbon, deputy chairman of Minster Assets and chairman of British Midland Airways from 1973 to 1978.

the role of company secretary and financial director. Michael Bishop, with his proven entrepreneurial skills, became general manager (1969) and later managing director (1972). In 1968 John Wolfe, who was to have a pivotal role in the airline's future development, was brought into the executive team running the business.

The merchant bank's confidence and belief in the company had no bounds. Their support was cemented when more money was made available to take the airline into the jet age. An order was placed in June 1969 for three brand-new BAC One-Eleven 523s, a British-built jet that would transform the image of the airline. The interior specification for these single-aisle aircraft was for 119 one-class tourist seats, all with seat-back catering tables set into mustard and orange upholstery. Payment would be made by leasing agreements, normal practice for aircraft purchases – two with the manufacturer and one with a subsidiary of the Norwich Union.[56]

A cargo of cigarettes being offloaded from an Argonaut (G-ALHY).

With the on-going encouragement of Minster Assets, plans to expand the fleet even further were actioned with orders for two second-hand Boeing 707-321s from Pan Am.[57] These single-aisled jets carried 189 passengers and flew at 550 mph with a range of 4,000 miles, the equivalent of London to New York. They were capable of taking British Midland into the long-haul charter market, a largely unexploited area. The necessary foreign carrier permits were obtained from the US Civil Aeronautics Board to tie in with delivery of the jets in 1970.[58]

The 1960s and 1970s were a fun time for British Midland. Management were fiercely determined to succeed but were less commercially minded than they necessarily became in later years. Staff performed with great efficiency, their reputation was founded on friendly service, and yet they behaved as one large family team, as suited a company of just a couple of hundred employees. The reservations team had the enormous breadth of knowledge to remember the routes and flight times before computerization. Cabin crews would think nothing of entertaining passengers with songs and jokes when flights were delayed. At Christmas there was always time to dress up and distribute presents to younger travellers. Everyone mucked in, when and wherever needed. But the airline industry was a precarious one, and with world recessions and other disasters in the years ahead BMA had to adapt quickly to survive. As the company grew and modernized, tighter commercial restraints were understandably introduced and the early experience of family unity was unavoidably lost.

First routes from Heathrow

In July 1969, Michael Bishop secured BMA's first service into London Heathrow, marking an important milestone in the company's history.[59] This came about when another carrier, Autair International Airways, announced an intention to suspend and abandon all their scheduled routes in favour of relaunching their business in the fast-growing package-holiday market.[60] Recognizing the potential value of a presence at Heathrow and its slots years before other entrepreneurs did, Michael Bishop seized the opportunity by applying for the unwanted licence out of Teesside to Heathrow.[61] With the necessary approvals in

Michael Bishop, general manager, receiving the lease documents for the new London Heathrow accommodation in 1969.

place BMA claimed their first slots to the London hub and began their twice-daily weekday Viscount service from Teesside to Heathrow on 3 November 1969.[62] The airline established their presence in the newly built Terminal 1 at Heathrow (1968) with two uncomputerized check-in desks on island D and a partitioned space, known fondly as the office, and three uniformed ground staff.

Minster Assets welcomed this expansion, and in early 1970 advanced the airline a further £1.5 million, bringing their total outlay to £6 million and their holding in the company up to 90 per cent. The investment bankers were impressed with the new management team that had been put in place and confident in the great strides that were being made.

Fuelled with working capital, the company sought to increase their scheduled services from Heathrow. In 1973, a new route was inaugurated to Newquay and two years later another to Birmingham in association with British Airways, the national flag carrier. In 1974 the airline made a route application which would later prove vital to its future. The service requested was a route from Heathrow to Strasburg, the home of the European Parliament. The new service was inaugurated in April 1974 though as a European destination Strasburg was never popular. Despite every effort to fill empty seats, with measures such as offering long-weekend ski breaks, Heathrow to Strasburg never reached expectations and was a short-lived operation. However, the company was now an established international operator, as laid down in Heathrow's Traffic Distribution Rules (1977), and after 1986 British Midland Airways had an important advantage when it came to battling for scheduled flights to European destinations.

Terminal 1 at Heathrow nearing completion in 1968.

Moving into the jet age

The first of British Midland Airway's three BAC One-Elevens (G-AXLL) was handed over to the chairman, James Hodgson, at East Midlands Airport on 5 January 1970.[63] British Midland now had 'a sting in its tail', a reference to the One-Eleven's tail-mounted auxiliary power unit.[64]

By the end of March the new jet fleet had taken over the important scheduled routes from East Midlands to Glasgow and Dublin, together with a major portion of the company's rapidly expanding IT operation. By May 1970, the new BAC One-Elevens had replaced the company's Viscounts on the Teesside to Heathrow scheduled service, cutting the journey time from 80 to 50 minutes, to the delight of the travelling public.[65] As the summer season developed the One-Elevens became increasingly evident at many of the UK's regional airports: British Midland took advantage of the speed, capacity and flexibility of their new jet fleet to penetrate further into the IT market. Operating on behalf of Clarksons, Horizon and Global Holidays, the three jets flew from London, Manchester, Glasgow and Belfast to popular Mediterranean resorts. Unfortunately few tour operators offered their customers package holidays starting from East Midlands Airport; nevertheless, in 1970, this market represented more than 55 per cent of the company's business.

Sir Geoffrey Tuttle, air marshal and aerospace consultant (left), hands over a new BAC One-Eleven jet to James Hodgson, chairman of BMA, 5 January 1970.

In addition to these lucrative short-haul contracts, the board were focused on establishing the airline as a reliable transatlantic carrier. Towards this end, the company took delivery of their first 4,000-mile (6,400 km) range, second-hand Boeing 707-321 (G-AYBJ) in April 1970. After four weeks of crew training in Miami the ex-Pan Am 189-seater jet was flown back to Britain for duty. With a foreign carrier permit in hand and facilities established with worldwide host airports, British Midland were poised for long-haul IT and transatlantic charters. A second ex-Pan Am Boeing 707-321 (G-AYVE) was introduced in March 1971, starting work with long-haul charters from Gatwick, Stansted, East Midlands and Prestwick to destinations including New York, Toronto, Seattle, the Caribbean and Hong Kong.

British Midland's first long-haul Boeing 707 jet, a Series 321, was purchased from Pan Am for £1,600,000. Before delivery in April 1970 the board sought approval from the US Civil Aeronautics Board to operate transatlantic charters. Later the airline acquired improved versions of this aircraft.

To mark the introduction of the BAC One-Eleven in 1970 a trendy uniform was commissioned from Teddy Tinling, a fashion designer who specialized in celebrity tennis outfits. His bright orange A-line Courtelle dress was worn above the knee with a matching loose-fitting mandarin collared jacket, black accessories and white gloves. The large high-crowned hat was created in orange felt and worn with a wet-look scarf in winter. This chic uniform, introduced in 1970, was never popular with the cabin crew as the fabric perished when washed. It was soon replaced by another orange two-piece suit, this time in gabardine with a zipped jacket, worn with a peach-coloured blouse.

British Midland Airways
Winter Timetable and Fares

Valid 1 Nov 1973 – 31 March 1974

One of the more unusual, but successful, charter opportunities in the 1970s was Hadj flights carrying Muslim pilgrims, in neutral livery 707s, from Indonesia and the Middle East to Mecca for their annual pilgrimage. Another was a freight contract from a Canadian fishery, moving their produce around the world. As a whole, charters represented just 10 per cent of the company's business during this decade. They were fun opportunities welcomed by the crews involved, even though they had to source their own accommodation on arrival at unfamiliar destinations. In the years before sophisticated methods of money transfer it was quite normal for the pilot to take a briefcase of cash on board to settle landing fees and pay for fuel for the return journey. Flying for British Midland was a glamorous and prestigious career, and quality staff were never lacking.

Outwardly the airline was flying high as a regional carrier, but behind the scenes it was still a constant battle to survive in this high-risk business. Before credit card transactions became commonplace travel agencies held on to customer payments for months, creating serious cash-flow problems for the carrier. By 1970, the total fleet had shrunk to eight aircraft, barely enough to maintain scheduled services and meet the IT and charter demands. With only four Viscounts in service the Leeds to Glasgow route was axed, and when the airline's principal customer, Rolls-Royce, crashed in February 1971, the East Midlands to Glasgow route was inevitably affected. Although passenger numbers increased when the One-Elevens were introduced on the Teesside to Heathrow route, these 119-seater jets were hard to fill and the company had to revert to the older 80-seater Viscounts to make the route profitable. To sustain the scheduled services, which now represented just 35 per cent of the company's activities, the board willingly agreed to purchase additional turbo-props.

It was in November 1971 that the 29-year-old general manager, Michael Bishop, read in the trade press that South African Airways were offering for sale their entire fleet of seven Viscount 813s. With a budget of just £135,000, enough to secure two aircraft in the current market, he flew to

Johannesburg with the company's chief engineer, Tony Topps, to inspect the aircraft.[66] Extensive modification and maintenance would be necessary, but not beyond the capabilities of BMA's engineers. To Bishop's astonishment, a deal was agreed for the whole fleet plus spares, within his specified budget. Two years later another four Viscounts were acquired to meet growing passenger demand, this time from Nora Air Services of West Germany. With the fleet now sorted, the airline's popularity grew in leaps and bounds as more and more people experienced BMA's friendly service and competitive fares. A new and popular service was introduced in 1974 when the company took over a thrice-daily Belfast to Gatwick route previously operated by British Caledonian Airways. With value fares and a reputation for reliability BMA carried 10,000 passengers on their successful Heathrow to Teesside route in January 1974 with a one-way fare of just £10.

Despite internal prosperity there were three unrelated happenings at home and abroad during the early 1970s that brought the travel industry to its knees. First came the 1973 fuel crisis, when the Organization of Arab Petroleum Exporting Countries restricted world oil supplies, an action that resulted in a world economic depression.[67] Secondly, the new InterCity 125 train was introduced across the UK in 1973, offering the travelling public a serious alternative to flying.[68] And thirdly, the miners' strike of 1974–5 crippled Britain and curbed all unnecessary travel.[69] Although British Midland Airways fought hard to maintain their position in the market, they were understandably affected by these events.

The Boeing 707 charter work had begun so well, with a strong concentration across the Atlantic, but the level of success could no longer be maintained. The company struggled to offer competitive charter rates with rising fuel prices to absorb and expensive repayments to make to their leasing companies. A further factor that brought about the demise of transatlantic charter operations was the competition from larger airlines who, in order to fill their new 350-seater Boeing 747s, introduced a low Advance Purchase Excursion (APEX) fare to fill their seats and offered contract fares for tour operators which were unfortunately as cheap as the charter rate offered by British Midland. The final blow fell when the airline ran into a potentially damaging legal situation with the USA, their

The second edition BMA livery, introduced in 1970, adorned the company's fleet (Viscounts, One-Elevens, Boeing 707s, Shorts 360s, Fokker F-27s and DC-9s) for 16 years. The palette of white, blues and silver was maintained but with greater emphasis on pastel blue and lightness, and the introduction of a more modern stylized logo for the tail fin.

single most important market. The US Civil Aeronautics Board (CAB) had declared that BMA passengers on group charters were supposed to be fully paid-up members of the club or society with whom they were travelling for at least six months before flying. Considering the nature of BMA's charter business this was an impossible ruling for the airline to comply with or enforce, and one that stifled opportunities for doing business with the USA. In an unprecedented move British Midland Airways obtained an injunction against the US CAB, knowing full well that the discrimination was politically motivated. However, the US government was determined to purge charter carriers to protect scheduled airlines and at the hearing in 1973 the company were judged guilty of carrying illegal passengers and duly fined.

By 1972, it had become clear that profitability with the jet fleet was falling considerably below expectations. Although British Midland Airways (and previously Derby Airways) had led the way in the UK IT business, they were now losing ground to the specialist companies who themselves were struggling. The market was very competitive and British Midland had to acknowledge that their involvement was of dubious value as the charter rate became less and less attractive. A sound decision was made in 1972 to make the summer season of 1974 the last for this sector of the business. Others were not so shrewd. The fuel crisis and other financial pressures pushed Clarksons, the leading operator, into liquidation in 1974.

As far as the fleet was concerned this inadvertently brought about the demise of British Midland's One-Elevens when it was decided to standardize on the Viscount fleet. In the short term the three One-Eleven jets were used for scheduled work or leased. The second-hand market for these short-haul jets proved challenging, but they were eventually disposed of to TransBrasil in an exchange for three Heralds.[70] As the 1972 summer season tailed off alternative options were sought for the 707 long-haul jets rather than face the option of their disposal too.

British Midlands' first turbine-engined aircraft was a Handley Page Herald 211 introduced into the fleet in 1965. This model, Herald 214 (G-ATIG), flew scheduled services between 1973 and 1977.

Instant Airlines

In May 1972, an airline from the Middle East wet-leased one of BMA's 189-seater Boeing 707s, to make up for a temporary shortfall in its own capacity on a short-term contract, complete with flight and cabin crew. This marked the beginning of a new and lucrative line of business, the Instant Airline.[71]

The era of the Instant Airline began in earnest in November 1972 when Mohammed Abdel Bagi, chairman of Sudan Airways, chartered two Boeing 707s to take over the operation of all his airline's long-haul routes with an initial contract for one year valued at £3.3 million. The two jets were painted in the host livery within ten days and put into service on Sudan Airway's Blue Nile international route between Khartoum and Heathrow. As part of the deal British Midland would train the Sudanese flight and cabin crews in readiness for them to handle the entire operation themselves.[72] The Sudan Airways contract eventually came to an end in July 1974, but was quickly replaced with a similar deal with Iraq Airways. The obvious demand for Boeing 707s to be made available for short-term leasing throughout the world led British Midland to set up a separate leasing division, BMA Leasing, to deal specifically with this type of work. John Wolfe and Stuart Balmforth handled the business side of this successful and profitable venture.

Signing the Instant Airline contract with Sudan Airways in November 1972. Seated: Peter Cannon, BMA chairman, and Mohammed Abdel Bagi, Sudan Airways. Standing: C Murland, BMA, Michael Bishop, BMA, and El Amir, Sudan Airways.

In 1975, three more 707s were added to the leasing pool and promptly assigned as Instant Airlines to Bangladesh Biman, Kuwait Airways and Syrian Arab Airlines. To maximize profits the company systematically upgraded the comfort and facilities on board their 707s with additional galleys, freshly upholstered seats with a chevron designer fabric, and two extra emergency exits with slim-line escape slides. Unfortunately, the 1973 fuel crisis badly affected the operating costs of the original version Boeing 707-321, which had a high fuel consumption.[73] The company's later turbofan models performed considerably better and were far more efficient.[74] In 1979, an all-cargo 707 joined the leasing pool; its first freight leasing assignment was for Pakistan International Airways.[75]

Aircraft other than 707s were also made available for leasing when temporarily surplus to British Midland's own requirements. In 1975, British Midland's Heralds flew for Air Anglia and British Island Airways. In the same year two Viscounts flew as dry-leases on behalf of Cyprus Airways, who had recently suspended all operations following the destruction of three of their five Trident jets. The Cypriot airline's planes had

Repainting a British Midland Boeing 707 in readiness for an Instant Airline contract with Syrian Arab Airlines.

Boeing 707 (G-BFLE), wet-leased to Gulf Air in the 1970s.

been bombed on the ground at Nicosia Airport by the Turkish Air Force during their invasion of Cyprus in July 1974. In a valiant attempt to rebuild their national carrier, Cyprus Airways restarted limited operations. These were not from Nicosia Airport as it was out of action, but from Larnanca, a new airport opened in February 1975 on what remained of an abandoned 1930s airfield. Larnanca with its short runway was unsuitable for jets but quite adequate for BMA's Viscounts. This long-term contract served routes to Athens, Heraklion (Crete), Beirut and Tel Aviv. One unfortunate outcome of the leasing of the Heralds and Viscounts was that fewer maintenance staff were required. It was hard but made economic sense to let more than forty engineers go.

The demand for Instant Airline aircraft understandably fluctuated. Sometimes the 707s were in-active for weeks, but then a new instruction arrived and within 36 hours a new livery had been painted on. When Libyan Arab Airlines demanded a particularly speedy turnaround they were surprised, but thankfully amused, when the new paintwork melted in the blistering Mediterranean heat on arrival in Tripoli, revealing the livery of the previous contract which had been for the Israeli airline El Al. After every repainting the plane had to be reweighed to check the centre of gravity, for against this the loading was established. In order to satisfy the needs of Instant Airline customers British Midland Airways frequently had to supplement their own 707 flight engineers and pilots from outside the company. This was normal practice across the industry.

In the early hours of 9 July 1977, British Midland's Boeing 707-321 (G-AZWA), flying in the colours of Kuwait Airways and with a locum pilot, was hijacked by five Palestinians while en route

An Instant Airline contract with Uganda Airlines, August 1976.

Cyprus Airways leased BM's Viscount 813 (G-AZLR) when their own fleet was grounded in 1974. The Viscount 813 fleet was purchased by Michael Bishop from South African Airways in 1971, doubling the size of the airline overnight.

A British Midland Airways Boeing 707 undergoing a lightning livery change from Syrian Arab to Tunis Air in readiness to fulfil a new Instant Airline contract, 1977.

from Beirut to Kuwait. On arrival, a relief crew led by Captain Ron Hardy was substituted and the passengers were exchanged for five hostages, Kuwaiti government representatives. The gunmen demanded the plane be flown to Aden but the Yemenis had other ideas – as did the Bahrainis and the Dohanese in Qatar, the other destinations suggested by the hijackers. Eventually, with no fuel to spare and with a Kalashnikov assault rifle at his head, Hardy negotiated with the Syrian authorities and landed his aircraft safely at Damascus. Negotiations on the ground were unresolved so the armed hijackers demanded to be flown on to Tripoli. While moving slowly down the runway a skirmish occurred on board and the hijackers disarmed their erratic leader. The take-off was calmly abandoned by the hero of the day, Ron Hardy, allowing Special Forces to board the aircraft.[76] Back at East Midlands Airport the BMA team listened in disbelief to the whole episode.

Not all Instant Airline agreements were straightforward and without complication. In the autumn of 1977, British Midland were approached with a very attractive proposition by Yemen Airways Corporation for two 707-320 jets with a wet-lease contract for 21 months. Negotiations appeared to have been concluded when both parties signed a binding agreement in January 1978. Without delay British Midland Airways committed themselves to a $13 million leasing agreement to secure the necessary aircraft to tie in with the contract dates. However, Yemen Airways tried to back out of their obligation and British Midland had to mitigate their losses by entering a lower-valued agreement with DETA (Linhas Aéreas de Moçambique) to place the two jets. Not prepared to let the matter lie, British Midland Airways sought help from the British government, took legal advice and finally, with great secrecy, initiated some drastic action. The prime minister of the Yemen Republic was due to arrive at Heathrow on a personal visit to meet with the new prime minister of the UK, Margaret Thatcher. As soon as the aircraft was down in the VIP area, British Midland personnel seized the moment and obtained an injunction to detain the aircraft before informing an astonished BAA duty

British Midland's Boeing 707 fleet was used throughout the 1970s as Instant Airlines. Each wet-lease contract came complete with pilots and cabin crew to operate the service.

officer, who immediately acted by positioning heavy construction vehicles in front of the plane to prevent it from moving.[77] The British government was furious and arranged for the Yemeni prime minister to travel home by other means. To minimize the embarrassment the aircraft was released some weeks later, but there followed a gruelling court battle after which the Yemen government paid compensation of £3 million for reneging on a legally binding agreement.

By 1979, Instant Airlines had been supplied to 25 carriers and earned the company £40 million in foreign exchange. In recognition of this remarkable achievement British Midland Airways were granted the Queen's Award for Export Achievement. As successful as the Instant Airlines business had been, by 1985 the venture had come to its natural end. Existing customers had now re-equipped their fleets with their own wide-bodied jets and knew how to operate them, having been trained by British Midland personnel. New customers did not materialize as world markets now offered attractive opportunities with more cost-effective aircraft for those hoping to establish or supplement their own fleets.[78] BMA had the foresight to remove themselves promptly from this sector of the industry.

Ron Hardy, chief pilot, photographed at the Oxford Air Training School where BMA sponsored an annual course for *ab initio* trainees during the 1980s.

During the 1970s BMA also operated a successful charter business with its adaptable Boeing jets. On 4 April 1975, just weeks before the end of the Vietnam War, the *Daily Mail*, on behalf of the charities Project Vietnam Orphan and the Ockenden Venture, chartered a British Midland 707 to rescue in excess of a hundred children from the raging heat of Saigon. With fuel donated by BP and the unflinching support of British Embassy staff on the ground in Saigon, who dealt with laboured negotiations over emigration quotas, the children were airlifted to safety. A team of doctors and nurses dealt with many cases of dehydration on the journey to Britain. This was the final rescue of any nation before the North Vietnamese claimed victory and the last US soldier left the country on 30 April 1975.

By the mid-1980s British Midland's diminishing Boeing 707 fleet was employed mainly in conventional holiday charters from UK airports including Gatwick, Manchester and Belfast to destinations such as Vancouver, Toronto and Los Angeles on behalf of tour operators on both sides of the Atlantic. New noise regulations introduced in 1985 pushed the 707s out of practical use as the modification of each plane was simply too costly. With fuel prices soaring again in the wake of the Iran–Iraq War, the 707s with their crippling fuel burn had become virtually obsolete. All 11 were subsequently sold.

Bringing the Vietnam orphans aboard a BMA 707, the last aircraft to rescue refugees from Saigon.

Arrival of the DC-9

In June 1976, Michael Bishop, now managing director of British Midland, negotiated a deal to refresh the fleet with four second-hand DC-9 jets from the American firm McDonnell Douglas. Within the industry this was a surprising choice, for no British carrier operated this medium-range (1,500 miles / 2,400 km) type which, to date, remained uncertified in the UK. But Bishop had secured a deal that was sufficiently attractive to make the costs associated with certification worthwhile. The DC-9 with its graceful lines and distinctive high-level horizontal stabilizer or 'T' tail offered speed, reliability and comfort as it flew at the high altitude of 27,000 ft (8,000 m). This was high-performance luxury

By 1979, BMA had acquired four DC-9s. Many were astonished when the company invested in this uncertified US aircraft.

when compared with the old Viscount fleet, and promised to be far more economically viable than keeping the unsatisfactory One-Elevens airborne. Until such time that BMA had built up their own expertise, tools, spares and test equipment for the DC-9 fleet, crew training and major maintenance work were undertaken by KLM, and later by Finnair.[79]

The first DC-9-15 series jet (G-BMAA), which initially retained its US registration (N65358), was fitted out with an 85-seat configuration and put into service four times daily on the Heathrow to Teesside scheduled service.[80] The flight time was just 55 minutes, 15 minutes shorter than the same

British Midland Airways
SUMMER TIMETABLE

Valid April 1st 1977-
October 31st 1977

British Midland Airways
WINTER TIME TABLE

Valid November 1st 1976-
March 31st 1977

British Midland Airways' passenger check-in desks at East Midlands Airport, 1976.

journey by Viscount turbo-prop. The second DC-9-14 series (G-BMAH) was leased from Finnair, and took over the Gatwick to Belfast route. To the delight of business travellers, the new jet cut the 95-minute journey time by a third and before long the airline had increased the route frequency with four flights each weekday and two at weekends. The third DC-9-15 series (N-48075) arrived in early 1978 and was immediately put into service from Heathrow to Liverpool and the Isle of Man, freeing the Viscount fleet to fly services from East Midlands Airport to Palma, and Frankfurt via Birmingham and Brussels, routes secured in 1972, and from East Midlands to Amsterdam and Paris, licences also granted in 1972. British Midland Airways were so enthused by the DC-9s' keen reception that they resurrected the old Derby Airways tradition of naming their aircraft after beauty spots in the Midlands. Having found in the DC-9s and the Viscounts the fleet for the immediate future, the remaining three Heralds were sold in 1977.[81]

By 1976, the orange uniforms had disappeared in favour of what became known as the Maid Marion look. This was an in-house design in a palette of greens that focused on comfort and practicality.

British Midland were the first UK airline to use the American-built McDonnell Douglas DC-9. This welcome addition to the BMA fleet began work on the Heathrow to Teesside route in July 1976.

A management buy-out

After nearly a decade of unwavering support Minster Assets became apprehensive about continuing the relationship with British Midland Airways. The airline industry was a high-risk roller-coaster of a business. The company's profits were at best minimal and at worst there were hefty losses. The merchant bank made it known to Michael Bishop, the company's managing director, that as soon as the business was showing a respectable profit they would seek a buyer.

In April 1978, BMA registered their financial return for the previous year, showing a turnover of £26.3m with pre-tax profits of £1.47m. This encouraging trend, attributed to the success of strong scheduled services from East Midlands and Birmingham, was the perfect opportunity for the 35-year-old Michael Bishop to make a move. With his sound knowledge of the business of aviation Bishop sensed an upturn in the industry and knew instinctively that the moment was right to buy the airline. The travel trade was in the process of significant change as ticket purchases were moving towards credit card payments and agents now performed on-line transactions, providing money in advance and avoiding problems of cash flow.[82] Michael Bishop wasted no time in beginning negotiations with Minster Assets to acquire BMA outright. He was supported by Grahame Elliott, a chartered accountant and friend of long standing, and two of his co-directors, Stuart Balmforth, chief accountant, and John Wolfe, general manager.[83]

Michael Bishop joined BMA as northern regional manager in 1965. He became general manager under Minster Assets in 1969, and managing director in 1972. Following the buy-out in 1978 he became chairman and managing director.

Stuart Balmforth was appointed company secretary in 1969 when Minster Assets reorganized the board of BMA. In 1978 he became financial director.

John Wolfe joined BMA in 1965 and in 1968 was appointed manager of commercial services (cargo, charter and traffic). In 1975, he became general manager and a director.

Bishop, Balmforth and Wolfe (the BBW Partnership) were very different men but they respected each other's opinions and together had the right ingredients to run and develop an airline. Michael Bishop, the driving force, raised finance and had the vision, determination and tenacity to expand the business. John Wolfe, the organizer, handled all aspects of engineering, operations, licensing and standards. Stuart Balmforth, the most cautious member of the team, was responsible for the financial side of the operation, which involved not only day-to-day business but the introduction of new systems and premises. Grahame Elliott, with his invaluable background in structuring deals, became a non-executive director.

As a vehicle to release the merchant bank from their investment, a company was formed in the name of British Midland Holdings with Michael Bishop holding 51 per cent of the share capital.

Grahame Elliott, accountant and life-long friend of Michael Bishop, became a non-executive director of BMA following the management buy-out in 1978.

The business name was registered as British Midland, while the trading name remained British Midland Airways (BMA). The next step was to find a financial partner, not an easy task in the economic climate of the late 1970s when the City was uninterested in volatile airlines and the banks were not comfortable with management buy-outs. A chance meeting in Los Angeles led Michael Bishop to a prosperous Californian entrepreneur, Dr Robert Beauchamp, a successful dentist with practices stretching across California and employing more than six hundred people. 'The Doctor' had generated his great wealth from property investments, including boat slips along the Californian coast line, and from a shipping business that moved cargo. Following nine months of delicate negotiations and a couple of hiccups involving media rumours, Dr Beauchamp agreed in principle to lend the three partners enough money to pay Minster Assets £2.8 million, the calculated value of the airline.[84] He privately hoped that one day the company would be floated on the stock market. To secure the loan, Michael Bishop agreed to lease from Beauchamp three Boeing 707s (one cargo and two passenger), which Beauchamp had recently acquired as a tax shelter.[85] As UK citizens the three working directors held the controlling 75 per cent of the equity while Beauchamp, a US citizen, held the remaining 25 per cent.[86]

By 1984, the US was in a deep recession and Beauchamp, having lost heavily with his property investments at home, was keen to liquidate his speculative investment with British Midland. By July that year, the BBW Partnership had raised the necessary finance with Chemical Bank and Beauchamp, now 70 years old, was repaid with interest. His 25 per cent shareholding was absorbed back into the company.

Route swapping

By January 1978, British Midland Airways had become a privately owned independent airline. With 850 members of staff, it was considered a small carrier by the standards of the industry, but with the new management team in place thoughts turned to future growth and fresh business opportunities. Michael Bishop was focused on more than mere survival within an unpredictable industry that by 1979 was suffering badly from the clutches of world recession and the soaring fuel prices of the second oil crisis, following the Iranian Revolution.[87]

Top of the list of priorities were new scheduled services to add to the route network. The BBW Partnership recognized from the outset that this would involve competing with the state-controlled flag carrier British Airways, which to date held unfair monopolies on most national and international routes. For the company to contemplate long-term survival, various practical issues would have to be addressed. The Boeing 707 fleet would require updating with turbofan models that would be more economical to operate.[88] A computerized revenue accounting system was urgently needed to improve many aspects of business efficiency and, in particular, to deal with the complex problem of costing flight coupons from transactions with interline partners.[89] The question of accommodation would have to be looked at too, for the inherited facilities at East Midlands Airport were less than satisfactory. The latter three difficulties were tackled in the coming months and years using the talents and competence of Stuart Balmforth and John Wolfe. The problem of acquiring routes was to become Michael Bishop's personal vendetta, handled with resolute determination and patience over the next 30 years.

In 1979, the Conservative party under Margaret Thatcher won the general election and within months rumours were being voiced that some of the restrictive measures that gave British Airways their route monopolies would be lifted. If the governments of other European countries considered deregulation too, the door would finally be open for healthy competition, lower fares and new destinations for UK and European travellers. The newly independent BMA were hopeful of expanding their network of scheduled flights.

To mark the 40th anniversary of the company and the management buy-out from Minster Assets, a new uniform was commissioned in 1978. This came from Garroulds, one of Britain's leading designers and manufacturers of 'career clothing for the professions'. The uniform they produced was an A-line skirted suit with a hip-length single-breasted jacket in a mink colour easy-care fabric. This was worn with a matching hat designed with a deep soft brim dipping at the front, and a white, brown and rust striped blouse. The outfit was accessorized with smart brown patent shoes and bag, and brown leather gloves.

Within months of taking over the reins of British Midland, Michael Bishop negotiated a major route swapping operation with British Airways, who were coming to terms with enormous financial losses.[90] British Midland agreed to relinquish continental licences from Birmingham to Brussels and Frankfurt in return for BA handing over all their routes originating from Liverpool (Speke).[91] The deal, which cost British Midland Airways £4 million, gave the company a total of six new routes from Liverpool (to Belfast, Dublin, Jersey, the Isle of Man, Glasgow and Heathrow) together with promises of others to follow to more UK and continental destinations. In 1980, BMA were handed two routes from Heathrow, to the Isle of Man and Leeds.

BMA's first computerized reservation network was introduced in 1978.

The new services were flown by the Viscount fleet with the exception of the Heathrow to Liverpool route, which used the more powerful DC-9 five times daily. To commemorate the new venture the airline's third DC-9 was named *Merseyside*. The new Liverpool service increased traffic manyfold and pushed the number of passengers carried by British Midland to over a million a year. Marketing the new scheduled service network was the responsibility of Colin Roberts, a forceful member of the team whose ability and single-mindedness were crucial to the company. Staff across the company were inspired by the passion, drive and energy of the new BBW Partnership.

Further swaps took place in 1979 when British Airways axed no fewer than 26 loss-making routes from their domestic and regional network and pulled out completely from six UK airports. Among these airports were Leeds/Bradford and the Isle of Man, from both of which BMA secured

AIR SERVICE AGREEMENTS

From 1946 to 1976 world air travel was controlled by an agreement known as Bermuda I which took its name from the island where British and American transport officials met to negotiate a post-war accord aimed at stopping the global domination by US airlines of the air transport industry. The 1946 agreement established the principle of dual designation – that is the right to designate airlines, one or two from each country, as flag carriers on the same routes. It established a precedent for the signing of approximately 3,000 bilateral agreements between countries worldwide. In 1976, the UK renounced Bermuda I on the grounds that US carriers had a disproportionate share of the traffic, which was contrary to the terms and the spirit of the original agreement. Fearful of a complete breakdown in commercial activity with the UK, the Americans signed Bermuda II in 1977.

The Bermuda II legislation of the late 1970s was more restrictive than its predecessor and complex in its detail, but in reality it advocated bilateral agreements that inevitably controlled competition on the long-haul trunk routes of the world and severely limited access to Heathrow. This was a harsh blow to BMA's aspirations, for British Caledonian claimed priority as the UK's largest independent scheduled service airline at the time, leaving British Midland's transatlantic and European dreams temporarily crushed. In response, the company prudently decided to change their focus by concentrating initially on winning the prestigious UK trunk routes out of Heathrow. The battle was hard fought but eventually successful. The fight to break European monopolies was tougher still but this too was eventually achieved after years of campaigning.

British Midland's DC-9-14, *Merseyside*, taking off from Speke Airport, Liverpool, in 1980, still wearing its Finnish registration. The name of the aircraft was changed to *The Florentine Diamond* in 1986, to mark the introduction of the new Diamond Service. This model (G-BMAH) was a short-bodied version of this long-time popular jet airliner.

licences and slots to fly to Heathrow.[92] Another service won at this time was the popular business and leisure route from Glasgow to Jersey which came into operation in April 1980. Two additional DC-9-15s were acquired in late 1979 and early 1980 to supplement the expanding regional network. By 1981, British Midland Airways had established itself as the second busiest operator out of Heathrow with a high-profile presence in Terminal 1 and a large portfolio of take-off and landing slots.

Despite the satisfaction of picking up British Airways' discarded domestic routes and the great strides made by the company, Michael Bishop remained frustrated. British Airways still held a monopoly on the major UK trunk routes out of Heathrow that guaranteed them significant revenues and offered the public no choice. It was unreasonable that the government should allow such dominance by the national flag carrier and not allow independent airlines to compete for these profitable routes in and out of the London hub. The ridiculous argument put forward by the British Airports Authority (BAA) for such discrimination was the lack of aircraft parking spaces at Heathrow to meet any additional movements. The fight to break this unfair domination was about to begin in earnest.

Colin Roberts began his career with British Midland briefly in 1967, but then returned in 1971 as sales representative for the Midlands. He rose steadily through the ranks to become sales and marketing director in 1978, a post he held until his retirement in 1989.

Donington Hall

As British Midland Airways looked towards winning new routes they realized that business growth would be rapid when the legislation allowed. It was time to address their administrative set-up, which in 1980 was still housed at East Midlands Airport, in prefabricated buildings scattered around the airport complex. Such modest accommodation was quite inade-quate to meet the company's future needs. A permanent head-quarters building was required, preferably a freehold property that would be an asset to the business. Any new premises would need to house an expanding reservations department, the oper-ations division and a full back-up team who would liaise and work together. City centres were the first consideration so long as the position offered easy access to East Midlands Airport – possibly an older property with spacious rooms, which could provide flexibility of use and additional land for further expan-sion when necessary. The choice would need to reflect the style and quality of British Midland's service, and the philosophy and growing aspirations of the management.

The search during the spring of 1980 was extensive but did not take long. Donington Hall, an abandoned stately home lying just off the airport boundary, was on the market with a price tag

The Gothic decoration in the Donington Chapel was mostly beyond repair when BMA purchased the premises in 1980.

Donington Hall stood empty and neglected for more than a decade before a small management team from British Midland Airways came to view the premises in 1980.

The lofty space of the old Donington Chapel was refurbished as British Midland's staff restaurant.

of £200,000. Following initial doubts about the scale of the project, the idea gathered momentum and, with Dr Beauchamp's support, a price of £185,000 was agreed and the necessary finance was secured with the Security Pacific Bank in Pall Mall. Over the next 18 months a programme of total restoration and refurbishment was carried out to convert the historic 18th-century mansion, home for centuries to aristocrats, prisoners-of-war and wartime refugees, into a commercially viable office building. Stuart Balmforth handled the project that necessarily embraced the historic nature of the building and cost in excess of £1.7 million. The end result was a fully integrated and computerized business headquarters worthy of being voted the outright winner of the 1983 Business and Industry Premier Award, which was designed to identify environmentally conscious companies.

In September 1982 the company moved into Donington Hall and within six months the prestigious UK trunk routes from Heathrow to Glasgow and Edinburgh had been won. The surplus accommodation at Donington Hall was soon absorbed even though, at the outset, it was planned to lease a third of the space to tenants. The library became the home of Central Reservations, where a large team of staff equipped with personal computers coped with more than a million ticket sales per year. The bedroom floor was refurbished as offices for the main board and administrative staff. The billiard room and oval bedroom in the belvedere were converted into boardrooms for meetings and private luncheons. The basement floor, unsuitable as prime administrative space, was utilized for general storage, the post department and depositing archives. The Chapel, with some of its original features intact, became the staff restaurant.

An aerial photograph of Donington Hall (left) with the new Hastings House (right) built behind the original 18th-century mansion, stable block and service wing.

One of the more visual departments in Donington Hall was Operations, which provided daily information relevant to all aspects of flying a fleet of aircraft around the world. By the early 1990s, this information, which included planning, departures, arrivals, crewing and maintenance, was computerized for instant access by all members of the management team.

Hastings House, completed in 1990, offered an additional 40,000 sq ft of office space to meet the needs of the growing company.

In 1987, plans were approved to utilize land behind Donington Hall that was surplus to British Midland's original requirements. The new purpose-built 40,000 sq ft (3,700 sq m) office building, designed by Trevor Pargeter architects of Leicester, provided the airline's growing administrative operation with a comfortable and flexible working environment. It was opened in the autumn of 1990 and was appropriately named Hastings House, after the family who for more than six centuries were associated with Castle Donington and Donington Park (see *The history of Donington Hall*, pp. 116–54).

Donington Hall in 1982.

Impact of recession

As the second oil crisis gathered momentum during 1979, an economic slump spread rapidly around the world and the airline industry fell into its most depressed state for many years. The UK experienced a severe economic recession with interest rates up to 14 per cent, soaring inflation and staggering levels of unemployment.

One of the more famous casualties of the early 1980s was Laker Airways, the privately owned, independent British airline founded by Freddie Laker in 1966. His airline was originally a charter operation, flying passengers and cargo worldwide, but it made aviation history when Laker introduced the world's first long-haul low-cost scheduled Skytrain service from Gatwick to New York in September 1977. The company's business model was ahead of its time and did prosper for a while, but then faltered when its main competitors – Pan Am, British Airways and TWA – all dropped their fares in a cut-price war. It eventually went bankrupt in February 1982.

The Shorts 330 was a reliable 30-seater aircraft, ideally suited to British Midland's needs in the early 1980s when the UK was dealing with economic recession and an unprecedented slump in air traffic.

For British Midland the recession highlighted the vulnerable nature of its UK trunk routes. Merseyside and the north-east, crucial within the British Midland network, had for years been areas of economic decay. The downturn accelerated this process, with business traffic dropping alarmingly. By the autumn of 1980, the Heathrow to Liverpool route, previously a winner, had been cut to four times daily. Even in the East Midlands, BMA's hub and a comparatively prosperous region, the effects of recession were hard felt. In order to match capacity with the reduced demand the 80-seater Viscounts were reintroduced on most routes and two of the larger DC-9s were placed in storage at Teesside for the winter of 1980–1 pending an upturn in the market. To sustain the business urgent action was required: first, to limit the vulnerability of the airline's scheduled routes and, secondly, to maximize operational efficiency in those areas which were particularly at risk as markets changed. As a means of addressing reduced passenger numbers across the network and lowering running costs per mile, it was decided to introduce two smaller high-tech plane types into the fleet.

The first new aircraft to be introduced was the 30-seater Shorts 330, a two-crew commuter aircraft developed by the Shorts brothers in Belfast. G-BJFK was leased from new and began service on the Heathrow to East Midlands and Birmingham routes in 1981.[93] So popular was this type that a new model, the 36-seater Shorts 360, was soon identified as being the forerunner of a new generation of turbo-prop commuter aircraft. Some £18 million was assigned to purchase six of these modern well-equipped aircraft direct from the Irish manufacturer. The Shorts 360 offered low fuel consumption and the benefits of a high return on the initial investment. With a 600-mile (966 km) range the 360 was well suited to its purpose. However, it was a challenging aircraft to fly, being unpressurized and therefore flown below 10,000 ft (3,000 m) amongst the weather.[94] Tests showed that the amount of fuel needed to fly a Shorts 360 from East Midlands to Heathrow would only take a Viscount as far as the beginning of the take-off runway.

British Midland acquired a fleet of 11 Shorts 360s between 1981 and 1986. G-BMHY is seen here painted in the old BMA livery, which was phased out after 1986.

The second type, introduced in the early 1980s, was the pressurized 40-seater Fokker F-27 Friendship.[95] The effectiveness of the Fokker led to further acquisitions of models of a higher specification during 1983 and 1984. With the expansion of the F-27s and the Shorts 360s there followed a corresponding decline in the number of Viscounts operated by the airline. By 1984, only six Viscounts remained of the 27 acquired since 1967. The final BMA Viscount took off on a round trip from East Midlands Airport via Bournemouth on 20 February 1988.[96]

Having addressed the needs of the fleet, the BBW Partnership looked hard at various business opportunities and decided, once again, to re-enter the holiday and tour market, with a strictly

In 1982, BMA acquired a small fleet of Fokker F-27 Friendships. This 44-seater aircraft was frequently seen at Liverpool and in the Channel Islands.

limited operation. The company's under-utilized DC-9s would fly villa-owners and self-catering holiday-makers from East Midlands and Birmingham to Palma. These flights were sufficiently successful for British Midland to plan a return to the European IT market from the summer of 1982, its first such involvement for almost ten years. A programme of flights from both East Midlands and Birmingham to a total of ten Mediterranean destinations was announced. The airline would use two of their 707 aircraft, which were accordingly refurbished as 211-seaters, with new wide-body look interiors. By the holiday season of 1983, British Midland had three Boeing 707s flying capacity loads of holiday-makers to Tenerife, Corfu and Crete from East Midlands and Birmingham; and to Athens, Malaga, Palma, Rimini, Tenerife and across the Atlantic from Manchester.

Anneka Rice in front of British Midland's Boeing 737-300 (G-OBMB) at Suceava Airport in November 1990. The company flew about a hundred skilled volunteers and television crew to northern Romania to renovate a dilapidated orphanage in the nearby town of Siret. Some the BMA cabin crew insisted on remaining on the ground to help with the five-day challenge.

Another profitable source of revenue during these troubled years was one-off charter work. In 1984, the BBC chartered an aircraft to fly personnel and friends to and from the Ascension Islands for Christmas. In 1986, Freddie Mercury splashed out on a lavish 40th birthday party by flying guests on his celebrity A-list from Heathrow to Ibiza for the weekend. In November 1990, Mentor Films, on behalf of the BBC, were offered a free charter with crew for an Anneka Challenge. The BMA plane flew a team of 120 builders, craftsmen and caterers to Suceava in Romania to turn a dilapidated and rat-infested children's home, in the nearby town of Siret, into a clean, habitable, properly equipped orphanage. Once news of the achievement was released the authorities running the Siret Orphanage were inundated with donations. Other charter opportunities came from transporting football and rugby teams to away matches, as company incentives and treats for their customers and staff, and from winter visits to Father Christmas in Lapland.

Unfortunately, there were growing concerns about the environmental impact of the noisy, fuel-thirsty Boeing 707 fleet. By the late 1980s this long-serving jet had reached the end of its usefulness. The outdated 707 fleet was finally sold off in 1988, bringing all long-haul operations and charter work to a temporary halt.

The fight for domestic trunk routes

In 1979, Michael Bishop made an important decision. The small independent would challenge the national flag carrier's monopoly of the UK's domestic trunk routes. A successful outcome would not only address the present problems of low growth on British Midland's existing regional routes, but tackle the long-term agenda head on. After carefully preparing a detailed business plan, BMA applied to the Civil Aviation Authority (CAA) in 1981 for licences to fly the two most prestigious routes in the UK, Heathrow to Glasgow and Heathrow to Edinburgh. A victory would give BMA two important routes with consistent passenger demand and sustainable profits. The company would use their DC-9s to operate in direct competition with BA's existing no-frills Shuttle service.

BMA were making history as they campaigned with high-profile advertising for a fair deal for business travellers who to date were deprived of choice by the effects of outdated regulation. The proposal predictably met with hostility from British Airways, who had recently appointed Sir John King (later Lord King) as chairman with the mission of preparing the national flag carrier for privatization. Previously British Airways had been friendly to BMA, their largest interline partner, but competing for valuable trunk routes was another matter. British Airways, and to a lesser extent British Caledonian, were fearful of BMA's proven efficiency and claimed that their equivalent services were low volume and unprofitable, in their attempts to quash the fledgling airline's challenge.[97] After four months of deliberation the CAA rejected BMA's application, ruling that it was in no one's interest to have a third party vying for limited business. The refusal was anticipated so Michael Bishop simply lodged an appeal and began serious political lobbying. He eventually went over the heads of the CAA through the junior minister, Ian Sproat, to the secretary of state for trade and industry, Nicholas Ridley, and finally to the prime minister herself.

Graham Norman, commercial director, and Michael Bishop, managing director, photographed at the ticket desk at East Midland Airport, celebrating the winning of licences to operate scheduled services from Heathrow to Scotland in 1982. The book was filled with letters of support for this hard won battle.

The appeal was well timed for BMA's claim was for nothing more than the right to compete in a free domestic market, unimpeded by government restrictions or the vested interests of the incumbent airlines. This struck a particularly favourable chord with the Conservative administration of the day, which overturned the CAA's decision and awarded British Midland full rights on the two Scottish routes in question. After three and a half years of persuasion British Midland launched their Heathrow to Glasgow route on 25 October 1982. The operation flew seven return flights on weekdays and four at weekends for a return fare of £88. A British Midland ticket was £11 cheaper than BA's Shuttle and included an allocated seat, newspapers and sweets and a delicious hot meal,

British Midland were famous for their high-quality hot meals, a feature on all DC-9 services.

quite different from BA's ticket at the gate, no-food, grab-a-seat service. The route led to immediate savings for business travellers and within months the service had proved to be so popular that it was expanded to eight return flights a day.

The Heathrow to Edinburgh service was inaugurated on 7 March 1983 with a similar frequency. British Midland took 22 per cent of BA's Heathrow passengers from the outset because they simply offered a better product at a better price. In the long term the increased competition led to increased traffic for all concerned, as British Midland had predicted and the government had anticipated. By the end of the decade British Midland alone were carrying nearly half a million passengers a year.

Flushed with the success of the new Scottish scheduled services, British Midland applied to the CAA in early 1983 for a licence on the third most important high-volume domestic trunk route in the UK, Heathrow to Belfast. The Irish airport they requested was the new Belfast Harbour Airport, only two miles from the city centre. Following a hearing in June, the CAA acknowledged the desirability of competition and accepted British Midland's argument that passengers preferred its conventional advanced booking service to the walk-on Shuttle model provided by British Airways. This was proved by the remarkable success of British Midland's services between Heathrow and Edinburgh/Glasgow, which amounted to 28 per cent of all traffic on these routes in 1983. To pacify the national flag carrier for their objection to this decision, the CAA directed that the Belfast airport to be served by BM should be Aldergrove, not the Harbour Airport as requested. British Airways, still outraged, then requested a judicial review, claiming the reasons behind the original CAA decision were flawed. After a hearing in the High Court, where George Carman, the celebrated barrister, appeared for British Midland, the national flag carrier's case was rejected. The first British Midland flight from Heathrow to Belfast took off on 26 March 1984.[98]

The new inflight product included a delicious hot breakfast, or a traditional cream tea, and was a huge success with business and domestic travellers alike. At the time the new service began, Northern Ireland was deeply embroiled in political unrest and anti-government feeling. A high-profile awareness campaign of the BMA brand, as an alternative to the national flag carrier, was well received in Belfast. Within three months British Midlands Airways were claiming 45 per cent

British Midland's *Holidaymaker* magazine was the perfect way to choose a holiday to Jersey or Guernsey in the early 1980s.

of the market and as passenger numbers continued to grow, prices fell.

Feeling the pressure of the competition by BMA from Heathrow to Glasgow, Edinburgh and Belfast, British Airways launched their Super Shuttle, which went some way towards matching the quality in-flight service offered by the independent carrier. But it was British Midland who were setting the standards, and in recognition of their achievement they were voted Best Domestic Airline in 1983 by *Executive Travel* magazine, for the first of many times.[99]

By the mid-1980s, British Midland had broken British Airways' domestic monopoly out of Heathrow and were able to claim second place to the national carrier for UK flight movements to and from the London hub. Passengers

To express the prestige associated with winning the Scottish and Irish trunk routes a new uniform was commissioned in 1985 from Anushka Zbrowski, a young fashion graduate from Nottingham. She designed a smart Chanel inspired boxy edge-to-edge jacket with knee-length straight skirt, both in navy fabric. The suit was worn with a white, blue and navy floral-sprig print blouse, a small neck scarf and a neat navy upturned hat with blue trim and prominent BMA badge. The raincoat and tabard, for in-flight service, were co-ordinated with the basic outfit. The blouse fabric was also used for summer dresses. Accessories were all navy to enforce the impact of this stylish design. Within a year the blue trim had been updated to red, to tie in with the company's new corporate image. This uniform was short lived.

had options, but were loyal to the airline that offered a wide choice of return flights on all major trunk routes, the option of advanced booking and seat selection, the offer of quality in-flight meals and, as always, friendly service. With a new-found confidence BMA pressed the British Airports Authority to ensure that British Midland's check-in and ticket desks, now fully computerized, had a high-profile presence in the departure halls they served across the UK. The public at large could not fail to notice that British Midland were now an important carrier out of Heathrow Terminal 1. The summer timetable for 1985 showed that the independent airline were operating a schedule of UK services with eight destinations from Heathrow, four from East Midlands and two from Birmingham.[100] To support the extended domestic network, a DC-9-15 series aircraft was purchased outright from KLM in 1982, and in 1984 another two 105-seater DC-9-32 series were leased. In less than three years the independent carrier had lifted themselves from a position of precarious uncertainty to an airline on a solid footing with 40 additional take-off and landing slots at Heathrow each day.

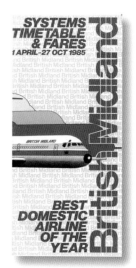

Heathrow was now the company's main operating base and a new dedicated passenger departure lounge was opened in Terminal 1 for the comfort of BMA's UK customers, who now topped 60,000 per month.[101] With record profits in hand, a decent marketing budget enabled the company to launch a nationwide advertising campaign to promote the BMA product and network of scheduled services to the travel trade and corporate customers.[102] From the beginning to the end of the 1980s the sales and marketing team had grown from being the efforts of just one man to a whole team of dedicated personnel.

A small deviation in the mid-1980s took BMA's aspirations back to the mid- and long-haul markets. They applied for licences, which were granted, to fly from Birmingham to New York via

British Midland occupied a central position with four check-in desks in Terminal 1 at Heathrow by 1989.

Belfast, and from Manchester to New York via Glasgow Abbotsinch. The national flag carrier and the BAA appealed to the government against the CAA decision, which resulted in the later licence being modified to Prestwick rather than Glasgow. Neither of these routes was ever operated for on this occasion the BBW Partnership decided to postpone the battle for the North Atlantic routes to another day, and instead to consolidate the domestic operation they had developed so successfully over the past 20 years.

In 1989, plans were in the air to take a similar slice of the action on the route from Heathrow to Dublin. The new service was launched on 28 April 1989 with an encouraging take-up. BMA were soon claiming more than 250,000 passengers on their Irish routes, outshining British Airways and Aer Lingus, the national airlines. The Irish flag carrier were so angered by the success of the independent that they took the unprecedented step of cancelling their interline agreement with BMA, causing difficulties to the travelling public who wished to make connections with the airline to other destinations. The European Commission ruled that such action was illegal and fined Aer Lingus 750,000 euros.

The Rt Hon Mrs Margaret Thatcher, prime minister, with staff at Donington Hall in 1986. Shortly before this visit Michael Bishop was awarded a CBE for his achievement in winning the battle for open skies over Britain.

A British Midland group of airlines

As the commercial airline industry was slowly recovering from the recession of the early 1980s, the directors of British Midland decided to withdraw from all loss-making routes and embrace a new UK regional strategy that would involve investment in business opportunities that required a lower cost base. They sought to create a group of local airlines, flying smaller aircraft, under the umbrella of the parent company. Each would operate largely autonomously, and with its own livery, as a subsidiary of the parent holding company.

Manx Airlines

The first opportunity presented itself in the spring of 1982 when Terry Liddiard, the company's handling services manager, brought to Michael Bishop's attention the case

for a small network based on the Isle of Man. BMA were already operating a handful of routes from the Isle of Man to England and Ireland, so they were familiar with the market. It had long

Terry Liddiard, managing director and driving force behind Manx Airlines, 1987–2002.

been apparent that the network of services from the island was inherently unprofitable with too many seats chasing too few passengers. It made perfect sense for British Midland and Air UK, another carrier serving the Isle of Man, to join forces. This was one of those rare occasions when competing carriers did not generate more business. The company name adopted for the new operation was Manx Airlines, an identity used after the Second World War, but one that had long ceased operations and had become that of an inactive company in the British & Commonwealth Shipping Group, who owned Air UK. The defunct company was bought for £250,000 by the two independent carriers with ownership of 75 per cent of the new airline held by British Midland, reflecting the split of passenger revenue. Terry Liddiard was appointed general manager of Manx Airlines (managing director in 1987) with Norman Brewitt as operational director.

The new airline with its high-frequency route structure was ready for operations within just three months, using a fleet of the cheapest aircraft available to them, a 73-seater Viscount 813 serving the London route and two 48-seater F-27 Friendships flying the Manchester, Liverpool and Belfast routes.[103] The livery of the aircraft, crucial to the image of the new airline, was a distinctive two-tone green on a white fuselage with green tail and red flash as a background for the Three Legs

The first new Manx passenger ticket.

In March 1984 two new Shorts 360s, G-LEGS and G-ISLE, joined the fleet at Ronaldsway.

independence emblem of the Isle of Man. A co-ordinated colour scheme was introduced for ground and cabin staff in the form of smart moss-green tailored suits with red-banded hats. The staff of the new Manx Airlines (pilots, cabin crew, ground staff and management) numbered 88.

In the first year (1983) Manx Airlines returned a loss in excess of £300,000 due to the high operating costs of their large aircraft. Being determined to improve the situation, they invested £4.5 million to replace the Fokker F-27 Friendships with two new 36-seater Shorts 360s (G-LEGS and G-ISLE), delivered in March 1984, which moved more people and cargo at lower costs (fuel, maintenance and landing fees). Traffic grew overnight, pushing the balance sheet into a healthy profit within just one year.[104] As new routes were added and the management team was strengthened, the enormous potential for the continued development of the reinstated airline from their base on the Isle of Man, a fast-growing financial centre, became clear.

One of the more exciting initiatives to be introduced in the early years was a half price, no frills, turn-up-and-fly service from the Isle of Man to Liverpool, known appropriately as Farecracker. In order to offer low fares, matching those of the boat journey across the Irish Sea to the mainland, Manx negotiated long and hard with the boards of the two airports to achieve an unprecedented no-landing-fee as an alternative to the usual passenger fee. Farecracker tickets revolutionized the public's travelling habits and were the forerunner of the budget airlines of the late 1990s. So successful was the impact of this novel format that the Steam Packet Company, already plagued by industrial disputes, ceased its sea passenger ferry service to and from Liverpool, leaving the way open

Airport bus advertising the Farecracker budget fares offered by Manx Airlines.

for Manx to capture even more passengers. The airline responded by increasing its schedule manyfold while adding new weekend services and removing the 24-hour booking restrictions. By 1986, Manx's low-cost service was moving in excess of 200,000 customers a year from the Isle of Man to Liverpool. Before Manx Airlines were set up in 1982, the same route attracted barely 25,000 passengers a year.[105]

Another productive business idea born out of the obvious was the utilization of the fleet around the clock. When the travelling public was asleep the seats of the Shorts 360s were temporarily removed to make way for early-morning newspapers, night-time mail and huge loads of freight, mainly kippers. To meet the needs of a 24-hour operation additional aircraft were leased, while staff numbers doubled year after year.[106] As routes and frequencies were refined, and an aggressive marketing policy was launched, even greater prosperity was achieved. During 1986, Manx Airlines carried nearly 400,000 passengers and made a net profit of £1.8 million. In July that year Manx's millionth passenger boarded a flight in Liverpool.

With passenger numbers growing annually the seat capacity of the Shorts 360s quickly became too small. Expansion continued with the delivery of the first two high-cost, high-technology jets. A new 85-seater 4-engined BAe 146 (G-OJET) arrived in December 1987 and a 68-seater twin-engined BAe ATP (G-UIET) flew in some months later. They proved to be popular and reliable although both aircraft types experienced teething problems during their introductory period. The ATP was a particularly

The first copy of the passenger magazine *Manx Tails* (1982) featured articles on the history of Ronaldsway, the airport serving the Isle of Man, and the Manx athletics team who would be competing in the Commonwealth Games in Brisbane later that year.

cost-effective model at a time of soaring fuel prices and high interest rates.[107] In anticipation of further growth a computerized system was introduced for passenger reservations and flight information, and a dedicated maintenance hanger was built at Ronaldsway, costing in excess of £1 million.

Continuing the impetus for expansion, the company now looked to widen their base beyond the Manx operations with a new hub on the mainland, from where they would be allowed to fly into Europe. Following an encouraging trial period of services out of Cardiff seven new routes were secured from the CAA, which began operating in March 1991 under the umbrella of a subsidiary company, Manx Airlines Europe.[108] Unfortunately, these exciting developments coincided with the

BAe 146-200 (G-MIMA) arrived in March 1993. This 96-seater aircraft took over the Isle of Man to Heathrow service.

first Gulf War (1990–1) and the ensuing economic recession that hit domestic air services so hard that more than twenty airlines went out of business worldwide. Manx, however, kept a tight rein on operating costs and still returned a healthy profit of £1.6 million as they moved into Europe.[109] To support a two-hub operation of this size the company now employed nearly 400 members of staff.

BAe Jetstream J31 (G-GLAM) over Ramsey, Isle of Man.

Between 1990 and 1992 additional mini-hubs had been established across the British Isles as the rate of expansion exceeded all expectations with more and more routes and ever increasing frequencies.[110] So successful was the Manx operation that by 1993 the airline had a fleet of 16 aircraft, was operating 70 different routes, including three daily pairs of slots in and out of Heathrow each week, and was carrying in excess of 1.2 million passengers a year.[111]

Manx Airlines Europe negotiated to become a British Airways franchise airline in early 1995.[112] Becoming a regional partner for the national carrier was a major coup for Manx, who now flew

ISLE OF MAN

25p   MANX AIRLINES BAe ATP

ISLE OF MAN

25p   MANX AIRLINES BAe 146 200

30 of their routes under the flight codes of the national flag carrier. Manx also painted their fleet in the livery of their new partner, wore their uniforms and took advantage of a worldwide sales and marketing team. As profits continued to soar more European routes were added and the first of 27 50-seater Embraer 145 jets joined the fleet.[113] In recognition of their remarkable climb to stardom *Air Transport World* magazine voted Manx Airlines/Manx Airlines Europe the accolade of Regional Airline of the Year in 1996.

With national and international success of this magnitude the name Manx Airlines Europe was no longer considered to be appropriate so, in 1996, it was changed to British Regional Air Lines (BRAL). Terry Liddiard and his co-directors now turned their thoughts to floating the company and raising cash to the tune of £90 million. With the advice and expertise of Grahame Elliott, the flotation happened in 1998. Within two months of signing the deal world recession threatened again in the wake of unrest in the Middle East and the new airline stock collapsed following uncertainty in the stock market about airline shares.[114] City confidence in the newly floated company plummeted and BRAL's own share price fell by nearly half. Over the next three years recovery was steady and surprisingly quick following moves to cut costs and enhance revenue. When plans were announced to expand with the purchase of another British Airways subsidiary, Brymon Airways, which operated out of Bristol with Embraer 145s, the national flag carrier responded by turning the tables and offering to purchase BRAL. Michael Bishop negotiated hard until a good offer was on the table.

Manx had become a victim of its own success. In 2002, this small regional carrier ceased to exist when British Airways bought out the holding company, BRAL Group, for £72 million.

Loganair

A further prospect for the parent company to take on an ailing business was waiting north of the border in Scotland. The airline in question was Loganair, a small regional car-

rier serving the Highlands and Islands which would tie in perfectly with BMA's existing trunk routes to Glasgow and Edinburgh.

Loganair were established in Scotland in 1962, as an air taxi service for the Logan Construction Company operating a single Piper Aztec from Edinburgh. The service gradually expanded into an airline but, as in the case of other independents, the national flag carrier excluded Loganair from all popular and profitable routes. Growth was spurred on after 1975 when British Airways withdrew from many of its thin Scottish services and Loganair, under the ownership of the Royal Bank of Scotland (1968–83), successfully took these on. In 1981, Loganair made a trading loss of £1 million but in the same year won the right to challenge the

BAe ATP in Loganair livery, 1989.

might of British Airways and compete on the important trunk route from Glasgow to Belfast Harbour. By moving their operation to the Belfast City Airport Loganair shrewdly managed to win the market share. There followed a marked expansion in the airline's route network and fleet, a success story that the management team was ill equipped to cope with. The bank began to doubt the viability of their investment, so when a substantial passenger contract was cancelled they decided it was time to sell out.

A majority shareholding in Loganair was sold to British Midland Airways in December 1983. The problems of the ailing airline were obvious, with aircraft committed to operating little-utilized routes to tiny airstrips on hillsides, small islands and even beach runways, as at Barra. Routes were difficult to operate economically because of the geography of the Highlands and then, to top it all, there was the obligation to continue the Scottish Air Ambulance service to the Western Isles, Orkney and the Shetland Islands, a commitment begun in 1933. Loganair were an even greater challenge than Manx, but with Scott Grier OBE as managing director and the introduction of a 36-seater Shorts 360 (G-GLBD), one of the quietest turbo-props in service, hefty losses turned to modest profits within the first year of business.

Loganair's route network in 1991.

Loganair at Glasgow Airport.

Riding a wave of success and optimism, two 90-seater BAe 146s were brought into the fleet by the parent company in 1988. These turbofan jets were an asset in expanding the growing scheduled services and charter network to the Channel Islands and mainland Europe. Loganair became the second busiest airline at Manchester, the dominant carrier at Belfast City airport, and a significant player in the development of scheduled services out of Southampton. With aircraft utilization a vital factor, Loganair secured contracts with the Post Office for the night movement of mail and datapost.

Despite a healthy level of success, the promising 1980s gave way to the turbulent 1990s and difficult business decisions had to be made. In 1994, Loganair's fleet and major business routes around the UK were transferred to the sister airline Manx Airlines Europe, while their loss-making routes were tactically taken over by the original Manx operation handled by Terry Liddiard and his team.[115] Loganair still managed their operations around the Highlands and Islands of Scotland, but the routes and services were trimmed and consolidated.

Loganair De Havilland Canada DHC-6 Twin Otters were ideally suited to operating in poor weather conditions.

Within months the re-created Loganair forged a significant relationship with British Airways when their core Scottish routes became a franchise operation. Henceforth Loganair's De Havilland DHC-6 20-seater Twin Otter (leased from Manx) would be flown in the livery of the national flag carrier but with the professionalism that typified the Loganair operation. Whilst still under the ownership of the British Midland holding company, a further transfer of Scottish services to Manx took place in 1996. The highly specialized inter-island services were all that remained of Loganair by 1997 and these were subsequently the focus of a management buy-out.

London City Airport

A further opportunity to extend British Midland's group of autonomous companies presented itself in 1987, when a rather specialist niche was identified. This was the prospect of being involved at the outset with London City Airport, a new single-runway airstrip being developed by the engineering company Mowlem to serve the financial districts of London on a former Docklands site. The runway, being only 1,000 metres long, was only intended for use by short take-off and landing (STOL) aircraft and there were stringent rules imposed regarding noise impact and times of operations.

Dash 7 (G-BNGF) in London City Airways' livery, 1989.

Having monitored the scheme with some initial optimism, the British Midland holding company set up London City Airways in 1986. To serve the new operation two De Havilland Canada 50-seater turbo-prop DHC-7s, popularly known as Dash 7s, were leased and three others ordered for delivery in 1988. This was the perfect low-noise aircraft and one of the few modern types capable of landing on the small Docklands airstrip. Scheduled services to Brussels and Paris began with great anticipation in October 1987, with Amsterdam added to the route network the following year.

A short-term suspension of the Paris service in early 1988 had a devastating financial effect on the viability of the company at the crucial stage of its launch. Passenger numbers never did meet expectations and unfortunately the propeller-driven Dash 7 was perceived as old-fashioned by the City business set, who aspired to the modernity of jets. If the new venture was to be a success the company would have to introduce a fleet of British Aerospace 146 jets at their earliest convenience, but for this to happen the runway needed extending. It was also known that ground transport links to the new airport needed addressing urgently, this being the responsibility of the local authority. London City Airways was very quickly recognized as a premature investment from which British Midland promptly withdrew, although more than 20 years later London City has finally become a thriving airport.

London City Airport.

Winning the route to Amsterdam

By 1986, BMA were poised to fight the next phase of competition – the deregulation of short-haul European routes and the development of the airline's Heathrow-based European network. The airline were determined to break the cartels and commercial agreements that existed between some European governments and their national flag carriers. Such monopolies protected the profits of the state airlines but thwarted true competition. They also damaged the business economy across Europe and openly hindered the growth of tourism by keeping ticket prices high.

As with the previous battle for deregulation of the UK trunk routes, British Midland led the way. Bishop persistently lobbied the European Commission (the executive branch of the European Union) until they accepted the notion of a liberalized market and agreed that aviation would be reformed as part of the wider drive to socio-economic unity throughout the Community. Despite a backlash from member states including France, Spain, Portugal and Italy, who feared the effects of rivalry with their national carriers, a 'Three Package' ten-year reform plan was defined by 1987.

The Heathrow to Amsterdam service began in 1986.

The first success, and another milestone for British Midland, was an agreement reached between the British and Netherlands governments in June 1986 which broke a 67-year monopoly by the flag carriers of the two countries. The door was open for BMA to apply to the CAA for a licence to fly from Heathrow to Amsterdam, Europe's second busiest air route. The objections were quick to follow, as expected, this time in the shape of misleading propaganda from the BAA, who claimed that Heathrow's two-runway airport was near to saturation, with 275,000 movements in 1986, and that the international terminal was already bursting, with too many passengers.[116]

The licence to Amsterdam might have been denied had British Midland not been able to show they were already an established European carrier from the London hub. Back in 1974, the company set a precedent when they flew daily scheduled flights from Heathrow to Strasburg. To the dismay of BMA's competitors, the airline had managed the previous year (1985) to get the wording of the Heathrow Traffic Distribution Rules of 1977 changed, from 'did not' operate to Europe to 'had not previously' operated to Europe, an alteration that

◼ LONDON SERVICES ◆

HEATHROW - AMSTERDAM

Frequency	Dep.	Arr.	Flight No.	Valid	Aircraft	
DAILY ex SU	0755	0955	BD101	29 Jun - 27 Sep	DC9	HB
DAILY	0755	0855	BD101	28 Sep - 26 Oct	DC9	HB
DAILY	1115	1315	BD103	29 Jun - 27 Sep	DC9	CM
DAILY	1115	1215	BD103	28 Sep - 26 Oct	DC9	CM
DAILY	1415	1615	BD105	29 Jun - 27 Sep	DC9	CM
DAILY	1415	1515	BD105	28 Sep - 26 Oct	DC9	CM
DAILY	1745	1945	BD107	29 Jun - 27 Sep	DC9	AT
DAILY	1745	1845	BD107	28 Sep - 26 Oct	DC9	AT
TH FR SU	2045	2245	BD109	29 Jun - 27 Sep	DC9	CM

AMSTERDAM - HEATHROW

DAILY ex SU	0725	0725	BD100	29 Jun - 27 Sep	DC9	CB
DAILY	0930	1030	BD102	28 Sep - 26 Oct	DC9	CB
DAILY	1030	1030	BD102	29 Jun - 27 Sep	DC9	CM
DAILY	1245	1345	BD104	28 Sep - 26 Oct	DC9	CM
DAILY	1345	1345	BD104	29 Jun - 27 Sep	DC9	CM
DAILY	1545	1645	BD106	28 Sep - 26 Oct	DC9	AT
DAILY	1645	1645	BD106	29 Jun - 27 Sep	DC9	AT
DAILY	1915	2015	BD108	28 Sep - 26 Oct	DC9	CM
TH FR SU	2015	2015	BD108	29 Jun - 27 Sep	DC9	CM

excluded many carriers from flying into Heathrow.[117] When the US carrier United Airlines purchased Pan Am's routes to Heathrow, after its collapse in 1991, they were denied access to Heathrow. The British government was so embarrassed that once again the Rules were changed to allow any carrier who had slots to fly into Heathrow. By 1993, slot trading had become an accepted practice, though then a legal grey area within the airline industry. Talks to create a regulated slot market continued for the next 15 years until, in May 2008, the European Commission accepted that slot trading was not illegal and acknowledged that the informal market between carriers, especially at London Heathrow, had stimulated competition and was in the best interests of passengers.[118]

Alex Grant began his career with British Midland in 1985 as marketing manager with responsibility for the launch of the Heathrow to Amsterdam service. Since that time he has been director of alliance and network strategy (1998–2001), managing director of bmi regional (2001–4) and today he is chief operations officer of bmi mainline.

The new route from Heathrow to Amsterdam began on 29 June 1986, with fares lower than the state-owned airlines and a product that included high-quality in-flight food and complimentary drinks in a one-class cabin. The new three-day executive fare brought savings of up to 25 per cent to business travellers. The press, travel trade and corporate customers looked up and took notice of British Midland's first international scheduled service from Heathrow. A new sales and marketing team was set up in the Netherlands by the company's sales executive, Max Hunt, to promote the British Midland brand to a Dutch audience. The service was so well received that British Midland were awarded the runner-up prize in the Anglo-Dutch Awards for Enterprise later that year. Within just two years BMA had stolen 28 per cent of the market from KLM.

The Heathrow to Amsterdam route was acknowledged throughout the airline industry as the forerunner of structural changes within the European short-haul sector. Over the next decade British Midland led a sustained campaign for the right to other scheduled international routes from their new primary hub at London Heathrow.

British Midland operated five daily return flights from London Heathrow to Amsterdam's Schiphol in 1986.

A new image with Diamond Service

In 1984, British Midland Airways were still fundamentally a little-known regional airline fondly called the 'friendly independent', with obvious issues of identification. In a world where image was considered paramount it was time for BMA to look at how they presented themselves to the public, and for this they turned to Ludlow Associates, a London-based design consultancy.[119] Between 1985 and 1986 the airline went through significant changes, both practical and cultural. The brand was rejuvenated, the aircraft livery was revamped and most excitingly a new product was created: that is the airline's entire service.[120]

The name 'Midland' had no link with Heathrow, but a complete change of name was considered inappropriate. The initials BMA had long been associated in the public mind with the British Medical Association, so the new trading name dropped the word 'Airways' in favour of simply British Midland, in line with the business name. For 20 years the airline's fleet had been wearing virtually the same outdated livery but

British Midland timetables and literature followed a strict colour palette, but a flexible design format, after 1986.

this would now be modernized with the introduction of a meaningful diamond motif that would be unique to British Midland. The airline's dominant colours would in future be based on the national flag, with a powerful blue dominating. The new image translated on to aircraft as the upper body in blue, with the airline's name in upper- and lower-case white lettering, and the lower section in grey

In 1988, an imaginative new uniform was introduced to mark the airline's 50th anniversary and to celebrate the new Diamond brand product. This uniform was a fully co-ordinated affair in grey and red, designed by The Gibson Line, a Nottingham-based firm who specialized in the manufacture of executive corporate wear. Women wore a single-breasted light-weight belted wool jacket with an inverted double-pleated skirt and a tall, boxy felt hat. To complement the basic uniform an eye-catching large red, white and grey diamond print fabric was produced for blouses, ties and summer dresses. Accessories included neck scarves, cardigans, tank-tops, waistcoats, trench coats and grey shoes in a choice of three heel heights. The Gibson Line uniform was contemporary and fun, and quite unlike other airline uniforms of its day.

separated by a subtle white dividing line. The powerful red BM logo, with its evocative diamond motif standing between the letters, sat comfortably on the tail fin and was repeated in front of the British Midland name on the upper fuselage. Ground vehicles were resprayed as befitted their shape. Printed literature that had previously boasted a wide palette of colours and various fonts would now display consistency across the board, with the same red, white and blue colours and a predominance of the diamond symbol.

While the new image was being developed, the product came under close scrutiny. British Midland had always prided themselves in providing a top-rate service, one of the reasons they had so many devoted customers, but now it was time to reward faithful customers and encourage loyalty. The new product was launched on the company's major UK trunk routes, from Heathrow to Glasgow, Edinburgh, Belfast and Teesside, in the summer of 1986, and was proudly called Diamond Service. This one-class service for all passengers offered complimentary drinks and delicious hot food, presented in style. Diamond Service was without doubt the equivalent service to business class on other carriers, but was associated with less expensive fares. The very first scheduled flight from Heathrow

After 21 years of service, British Midland's final Viscount flight took off for a round trip from Bournemouth to East Midlands and back on 20 February 1988.

to Amsterdam, in June 1986, took off in a freshly painted DC-9 with passengers enjoying the already much talked-about Diamond Service product, which went way beyond people's expectations of airline service.[121] Such was the popularity of Diamond Service that over the next three years it was introduced on other key trunk routes – from Heathrow to Leeds Bradford (1987), from East Midlands to Glasgow, Belfast, Paris and Amsterdam (1988), from Heathrow to Dublin and Liverpool, and from Birmingham to Brussels (1989).[122] The company's fleet of DC-9s was impressively renamed after ten of the world's most famous diamonds.[123]

To promote the repackaged airline, even greater emphasis was placed on marketing and sales.

DC-9 (G-PKBM) was officially named *The Tiffany Diamond* on 1 September 1987 to coincide with the launch of Diamond Club. Present at this, the first naming ceremony, was Rosamond Monckton of Tiffany's with Michael Bishop.

As profits continued to roll in from the new prestigious Heathrow trunk routes, further investment was made in promoting the brand. The travel trade were offered incentive schemes and corporate customers were wooed by targeted advertising to blue-chip companies.[124] At Heathrow, Colin Roberts was instrumental in securing the company the respect it deserved, together with a high-profile presence on island 'A' in Terminal 1, despite being thwarted at every turn by the BAA, who ran the business of the airport. His tenacity and forcefulness earned him the cheeky nickname of the Derby

The board and senior management team of British Midland taken at the company conference in Guernsey in 1989. Left to right back row: Colin Roberts (sales and marketing director), Captain David Court (operations director), Terry Soult (technical director), Graham Norman (commercial director), Terry Liddiard (Manx) and Scott Grier (Loganair). Left to right seated: Austin Reid (financial director), John Wolfe (director), Michael Bishop (chairman and managing director), Stuart Balmforth (director).

Strangler, though he certainly got things done and achieved a level playing field on which to compete with the national flag carrier. British Midland may have had an older fleet than British Airways, but they had secured an advantage. To bring together all aspects of customer service, a new post of service director was created, with Graham Norman in charge. The travel industry was quick to acknowledge British Midland's excellent brand and product, with a flood of awards (*Awards*, p. 155).

To complement BM's Diamond Service, in 1987, Diamond Club was launched to reward frequent flyers. Membership was free and offered numerous advantages, such as the use of an exclusive Diamond Club air-port lounge with comfortable facilities and free refreshments, discounts on car rental and quality gifts to appeal to the business traveller. As customer expectations grew so did the style and quality of the Diamond Club product. In 1990, the gifts were dropped in favour of an air-miles scheme that rewarded frequent flyers with free flights. Membership was divided into three categories (gold, silver and bronze) with attractive rewards for loyalty. In 1992 a new high-profile Diamond Club lounge was opened in Terminal 1 at Heathrow.

This British Midland DC-9 (G-BMAK), also known as *The Stewart Diamond*, joined the fleet in March 1984.

With the success of Diamond Service and Diamond Club new aircraft were needed to meet passenger demand on the short-haul commuter routes. To replace the remaining 70-seater Viscounts and supplement the 85- and 115-seater DC-9 jet fleet, a new type was introduced in 1988. The choice was limited but, in a never-to-be-repeated deal, British Midland became one of British Aerospace's first customers for the brand-new 72-seater Advanced Turbo Prop.[125] The ATP was a short-range (1,000 mile / 1,600 km), low-noise, fuel-efficient aircraft, which in addition to the obvious virtues boasted digital electronics (glass cockpit), good short-field performance and low seat-mile costs, and was no-ticeably quiet upon take-off. The new BAe ATPs were delivered in 1988 and went into service on the new twice daily Diamond Service from East Midlands to Amsterdam and the new six-times daily route from Heathrow to Birmingham.[126] Although reliable and economical to run, the BAe ATP had propellers and was never seen as a modern aircraft by customers or pilots, and never established itself as a winner with British Midland. Jet aircraft were the future, so before the ATP fleet had any chance of expansion it was abandoned.

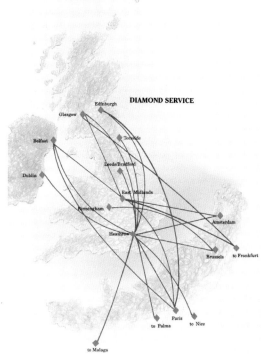

The Diamond Service network in 1991.

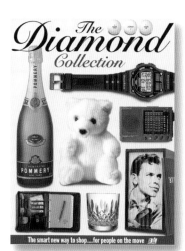

British Midland's exclusive collection of top-brand merchandise was available to Diamond Club members at tax-free prices, to order from the comfort of their homes.

British Midland introduced the 72-seater BAe ATP in 1988. This model was ideally suited to low-volume domestic travel.

Enter the Boeing 737

As British Midland continued the struggle for deregulation across Europe during the mid-1980s, the BBW partners decided to retire their Boeing 707 fleet. This celebrated aircraft had been pushed out of service due to fuel costs and noise issues. Until market conditions changed any new jets would have to be models that were not too large to accommodate anticipated passenger numbers on the busiest trunk routes. Various candidates were studied for their suitability and earning power until the decision was made, in 1987, to buy the 136-seater Boeing 737, a modern narrow-bodied, medium-range jet aircraft.

Boeing 737-300 (G-OBMA), flying over the mountains of Washington State en route for delivery to British Midland in November 1987.

The Boeing 737 was a reliable and effective addition to the British Midland fleet and an enormous step upwards for the company. This state-of-the-art jet cruised at a speed of 550 mph (885 kph) with a range of 1,750 miles (2,820 km) that would take it deep into Europe. The on-board flight-management system gave pilots automatic control and guidance in the very worst of weather conditions.[127] Pilot training was carried out initially in Seattle, but later with Orbit Flight Training at East Midlands Airport, and then in Dublin, where BM pilots had access to an Aer Lingus 737 simulator. Over a period of 20 years British Midland operated 45 new 737s (300s, 400s and 500s) in what became known as the 'classic' model, a series that proved to be the most ordered and produced commercial passenger jetliner of its time. According to 2006 statistics, a Boeing 737 departs or lands somewhere in the world every five seconds.

British Midland's first Boeing 737-300 (G-OBMA) took off from Heathrow to Edinburgh on 1 December 1987, positioning the airline as a serious player in the world of aviation. Within a month a second model (G-OBMB) had been delivered for service on the eight-times daily Belfast route.

The Boeing 737 was chosen by British Midland as their frontline aircraft during the fly-past to mark the 50th anniversary of Heathrow Airport in 1996.

The Flight Training Centre at Coalville, Leicestershire, was opened in 1991. The company closed the Whitwick facility in 1999, having moved this important operation to a larger purpose-built training school at Stockley Close near Heathrow in July that year.

The interior layout of the new 737s was a single aisle with blocks of three seats upholstered in luxurious two-tone blue leather and spaced to provide generous leg-room. With two larger 168-seat 737-400 jets scheduled for delivery in the autumn of 1988, and a third in early 1989, attention focused once again on a return to long-haul operations.

The Boeing 737 jet marked another milestone in the history of British Midland, though tragically, within the first two months of service, one of the new 737-400 series crashed onto the embankment of the M1 motorway near Kegworth in Leicestershire. The aircraft (G-OBME) was on a scheduled flight from Heathrow to Belfast on 8 January 1989 when a fan blade on the left engine suddenly ruptured. The pilot promptly disengaged the plane's autopilot and attempted to land at East Midlands Airport only a few minutes' flight away. It was impossible to identify from the cockpit the source of the pounding noise or the severe vibrations and smoke pouring into the cabin. The working right engine was inadvertently shut down instead of the malfunctioning left one. The passengers and cabin crew could see the sparks in the left engine but from the flight deck there was no such view. The pilot was unaware that his 400 series aircraft had been designed so the air-conditioning system fed both engines, and not just the right one, as in previous models. A sequence of technical manoeuvres followed but the aircraft was by now gliding too slowly to avoid crashing. Of the 126 passengers and crew on board, 47 people lost their lives that night and 79 were seriously injured. Michael Bishop was present at the accident site together with other senior executives of the airline within an hour to deal with the immediate consequences of the crash.

In the aftermath of the disaster the airline provided counselling and financial support to the injured and the families of those who died.[128] The inquest into the tragedy came to a conclusion of accidental death. The official report made 31 safety recommendations.

In 1991, British Midland opened an exemplary pilot training school at Coalville in Leicestershire, not far from Donington Hall and East Midlands Airport. The new facility had a one-cell Boeing 737-300 flight simulator and was built on the site of the recently abandoned Whitwick Colliery. The £10 million school was run by Ron Hardy, the flight training centre manager, with a small dedicated team of personnel.[129] It would serve the airline 24 hours a day for just seven years.

A partnership with SAS Scandinavian Airlines

As British Midland were coming to grips with their rapidly expanding business and vast financial commitments in a new aircraft fleet, it was realized that enhanced financial controls and systems would have to be put in place. It was decided to recruit externally for a financial executive with a proven track record. Austin Reid joined the company from Hertz in 1985 as the first non-partner director.[130]

The first task that Austin Reid set himself was the restructuring of external finances. The company's relationship with Chemical Bank, their most important source of capital loans to date, was unwound in favour of a more aggressive relationship with the City. He then looked at the day-to-day financial management of the business and secured new advantageous facilities. The next step was to bring together under one umbrella the principal company and its three airline subsidiaries. For this to happen a new air transport holding company was set up in the name of Airlines of Britain Holdings (1987). The new company owned British Midland, Loganair and London City Airways outright and 75 per cent of Manx Airlines. In 1988, Airlines of Britain announced record profits in excess of £11 million as business reached record levels and British Midland celebrated 50 years of service in the aviation business.

Austin Reid joined the board of British Midland in 1985 as the first non-partner director.

By 1988, financial issues had been addressed, so attention now turned to the capital that would be needed for expansion. With the demise of British Caledonian in 1987 British Midland's profile within the British airline industry had received a boost and, equally important, the gateway into Europe was now open wider. The original partnership of Bishop, Balmforth and Wolfe (BBW), who owned the airline outright, realized that the time was right to develop the business – either by floating the company, an idea eventually rejected, or by securing an industry partner.

With advice from Goldman Sachs, the investment bankers, a new financial partner was found in Scandinavian Airlines Systems (SAS), the national airline of Denmark, Norway and Sweden. Founded in 1946, SAS at the time were in an expansive mood to form global alliances and provide their own customers with a new seamless service for international travel. The Scandinavian airline, led by Jan Carlson, the chief executive officer, invested £25 million in British Midland in exchange for a 24.9 per cent shareholding which valued the entire company at £100 million. This not only opened the door to BMA for international growth

SAS and British Midland working together, 1989.

The BBW Partnership, by Andrew Festing RA, in 1995. From left to right: Stuart Balmforth (standing), John Wolfe and Sir Michael Bishop.

with worldwide alliances, but also provided an opportunity for the original working partners – Bishop, Balmforth and Wolfe – to take for the first time some personal financial reward from the business they had so successfully developed. British Midland were now positioned in an environment whereby they would survive long term.

By the terms of the deal, SAS had the option of becoming an outright purchaser of the independent airline in 1992 if both sides agreed. In the event, this option was not exercised though the Scandinavian airline took the opportunity to take a further 9.9 per cent of the company, increasing their shareholding to 35 per cent. This arrangement gave the BBW partners a second opportunity to dispose of shares. Two years later SAS increased their stake in British Midland by another 5 per cent, raising their total investment to 40 per cent. By the mid-1990s, two of the original partners, Stuart Balmforth (1994) and John Wolfe (1996), had retired from British Midland and a new management team had been established with Austin Reid as group managing director.

Open skies across Europe

Having so vocally campaigned for competition on the major UK trunk routes, British Midland were ready by the late 1980s to take the same hard-line campaign to Europe. The measures to guide member states towards free and open competition, introduced by the European Heads of Government in 1987, had begun unravelling slowly, but it was quite clear that many members were resisting the spirit of reform as they continued to regulate their airlines in accordance with their individual agendas.

British Midland were determined to use the freedoms of the First Package of reforms (December 1987) and in this spirit applied to the CAA in the summer of 1988 to add 11 prime international destinations to their network of scheduled services from Heathrow.[131] Slots were no issue at the London hub for British Midland held 13 per cent of these, but once again the National and European flag carriers intervened for fear of competition in what they saw as a limited market. The CAA approved the applications, leaving British Midland to introduce the new routes when the timing and the company's infrastructure were right to handle the increase in business.

The company were determined to maximize the opportunities offered by the European reforms and approvals of the CAA. They began by commissioning an authoritative research document looking at the significance of civil aviation to the economy and the technical problems of achieving more aircraft movements. *Heathrow – Handling the Demand* outlined simple measures to create 25 per cent more movements a day with the same two runways. By introducing shorter run-ins, two-way traffic and shorter lateral separation, movements could be increased from the 1990 level of 375,000 to 500,000 per year. The document created enormous public interest and was followed by another campaign known as *A Fair Deal?* which looked unemotionally at the top 20 European routes. The new report identified the inflated air fares of most national airlines, costing British business up to £236 million a year. The research illustrated how open skies would bring prices down by 30–40 per cent, generating enormous collective savings for the business community. The simplicity of

Hundreds of encouraging letters were received in response to British Midland's research document, *A Fair Deal?*

the report was startling and struck a chord that gathered its own momentum. Copies were sent to every member of the House of Commons and leaders of industry, stimulating a flood of positive responses. Only days after the launch of *A Fair Deal?*, on 29 May 1991, Michael Bishop was knighted in the Queen's Birthday Honours. With the European Parliament's Second and Third Package of reforms (1990 and 1993), the air routes to Europe were eventually approved. In less than five years the price of fares had dropped by 20 per cent and a huge number of new routes were opened by airlines across Europe, British Midland amongst them.

To match the demand of increased capacities on existing and new routes a new jet aircraft was introduced to the fleet in 1994 in the shape of the Fokker 100, a 100-seat, short-range, twin turbofan airliner. Over the next two years a further five new Fokker 100s and three Fokker 70s, both boasting low operating costs, joined the BMA fleet.[132] To safeguard their slot allocation and scheduling interests at Heathrow, BMA became a founder member of the new independent body known as Airport Coordination Limited (ACL), whose job it was to balance the supply and demand when airport capacity was scarce. Tim Walden, BMA's industry affairs manager, was invited onto the board of ACL.[133]

As predicted, deregulation proved beyond doubt that competition had a real effect in reducing fares. It also vastly improved the customer experience as facilities, both on the ground and in the air, were upgraded to keep abreast of the competition.[134] British Midland could confidently claim that they had been at the forefront and a catalyst for the changes. The practical outcome of the independent airline's unique contribution is best illustrated by the balance of the com-

Michael Bishop was knighted in June 1991 for his exceptional contribution to the airline industry.

pany's business revenue, which was completely transformed as a result of European liberalization. By 1997, British Midland were generating more than 60 per cent of their income from international operations while a decade earlier they had relied almost entirely on domestic traffic. The airline were firmly established as 'the serious alternative' to Europe's national flag-carrier airlines.

The actual date marking deregulation for European aviation is recorded as 1 April 1997. As important a landmark as this was, almost all major carriers in the meantime had adopted operational and marketing devices, such as code-sharing and alliances, to offer services beyond their existing route network and so eliminate the need to expand their route numbers. British Midland Airways was no exception.

Another of the more important consequences of deregulation in Europe was the emergence of the budget carriers. Originally created in 1971 in the United States by Southwest Airlines, the format was subsequently introduced into the UK by Ryanair[135] in 1985, followed later by easyJet in 1995. British Midland would introduce their own low-cost airline, bmibaby, in 2002.

British Midland's first Fokker 100 was delivered on 27 April 1994. It operated the Leeds Bradford to Heathrow route.

Code-sharing

During the 1990s, British Midland sought alternative ways to strengthen their presence and identity on the continent by turning to something more sophisticated than traditional interline partnerships with other airlines. They adopted a system known as code-sharing, a scheme that had been up and running to link regional feeder carriers to larger airlines since the beginning of the decade. Code-sharing (or common flight numbers) offered direct connections, a preference for most travellers and travel agents, while also allowing airlines to extend their reach into cities or routes beyond those they actually served.[136]

British Midland's first code-sharing agreement was forged with United Airlines in 1992. Henceforth, United's transatlantic passengers would travel on from London Heathow to multiple UK and key European destinations where British Midland had traffic rights, with the minimum of confusion or the need to rehandle baggage.[137] Even though the onward flight was not necessarily operated by British Midland's own aircraft, the airline gained exposure through the display of their flight numbers beside those of United Airlines on the arrival and departure boards in the passenger lounge. To handle the calculations and values of each sector of a passenger's journey British Midland updated their 14-year-old in-house IBM revenue accounting system with new tech-

Tim Walden (second from right) welcoming Cathay Pacific Airways, a new code-sharing partner, in July 1995. Tim Walden joined Derby Aviation in 1958. During his 39 years of service he primarily dealt with regulatory matters and Interline/code-sharing agreements with other airlines. In 1989, he became involved with slot allocations and in 1992 took up the post of chairman of the Heathrow Scheduling Committee, a role he held for 12 years. Following his official retirement from British Midland in 1997, Walden continued part-time until 2004.

nology known as CPATA, originally developed by Cathay Pacific. This advanced technology provided the management with instant access to crucial information about how, and from where, business was being generated.

Code-sharing earned the company enormous sums in additional revenue. Throughout the 1990s British Midland struck up many mutually beneficial transient code-sharing agreements with airlines worldwide: American Airlines (1993); Air Canada, Austrian Airlines, Alitalia and Malaysia Airlines (1994); Virgin Atlantic[138] and Cathay Pacific (1995);[139] Air New Zealand,[140] Air Lanka and Royal Brunei (1996); Gulf Air and Icelandair (1997). To allay any concerns over the operation of agreements British Midland were instrumental in introducing a code-sharing Code of Conduct. By the winter of 1997, British Midland were able to list 16 code-sharing partners and offer customers 118 flights per day to 25 European destinations from Heathrow. Code-sharing was a promiscuous business and, like all carriers, British Midland were happy to forge relationships with anyone who could forward their cause.

The airline for Europe

During the 1990s, British Midland's route network to Europe grew in stature and popularity with the addition of 18 new scheduled services from Heathrow to Bergen, Brussels, Budapest, Copenhagen, Frankfurt, Hanover, Malaga, Manchester, Nice, Oslo, Palma, Paris Charles de Gaulle, Paris Orly, Prague, Stuttgart, Stockholm, Warsaw and Zurich; and 8 from East Midlands to Aberdeen, Brussels, Dublin, Faro, Frankfurt, Malaga, Nice and Palma.[141] With each new route the profile of the British Midland brand was enhanced and the company's strategic presence within the airline industry grew. With volume passengers paying value fares, the increased revenue and profitability for the airline was much increased.

As the company grew, they continued to listen to customer needs. To their dismay, research revealed that what had begun as a crusade for cheaper business fares, with a one-class service through-out the plane, was no longer felt to be appropriate. Business travellers still wanted cheaper fares but they needed flexible ticketing and added comforts. The airline's answer was another original idea – Diamond EuroClass – a separate business cabin on European routes introduced in 1993. Business passengers could now enjoy priority check-in, the use of a relaxing business lounge before boarding and access to a more spacious and comfortable front cabin which was refitted with wider seats. A system of flexible fare options was now available with the opportunity of savings of up to 40 per cent when compared with business-class tickets from other carriers on the same route. For regular travellers bulk discounts

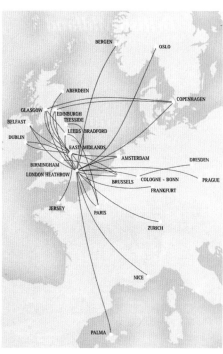

British Midland 'Airline for Europe' route map, 1996.

In advance of the company's 60th anniversary a new uniform was commissioned from Jaeger Corporate Wear in 1996. The design process was long but eventually emerged as a complete departure from uniforms that had gone before. The result was a sophisticated look in dark navy with co-ordinated skirts, jackets, trousers and coats. A new silky printed fabric was introduced, in navy with a small red and white diamond motif, for blouses and summer skirts. The boater-style hat had a flat narrow brim and wide band of red ribbon. Brevet (winged) lapel badges announced the name and title of the wearer. Members of staff were personally fitted for their uniforms, which cost in excess of £300 each. Jane Shilton handbags and Bally shoes completed the look that became known as the 'Airline for Europe' uniform.

were introduced with the Diamond EuroPass, a booklet of five return tickets for the price of four.[142] The first Diamond EuroClass lounge, with Internet facilities and capacity for 200 travellers, was opened at Heathrow's Terminal 1 in 1993.[143] Throughout the 1990s, British Midland's Diamond

By 1999, the European network included Brussels, Hanover and Zurich.

EuroClass product was regularly updated and improved. British Midland were amongst the first European carriers to offer all their customers a vegetarian meal option and introduce a no-smoking policy on all scheduled flights.[144]

Aware of the importance of Internet communication, British Midland became the first airline to introduce a booking system, known as CyberSeat, whereby customers could browse a website to choose products and then make a secure reservation by credit card payment or check last-minute availability online. In 1996, 80 per cent of British Midland's air tickets were still being sold through the travel trade and 20 per cent through the company's Reservation Centre at East Midlands Airport. By 2007, the figures showed an enormous shift in buying habits with 45 per cent sold on the Internet, 50 per cent through the travel trade and only 5 per cent via the Call Centre, now outsourced to Pune in India.

In 1996, British Midland confidently announced a new strap-line, 'The Airline for Europe', a label reflective of the many accolades that continued to be awarded to the airline year after year by the travel industry. Profits in that year exceeded £7 million, an increase of nearly 75 per cent on the previous 12 months. The number of passengers carried on all British Midland scheduled routes had risen to a new high of 5.6 million.

With passenger numbers and route expansion surpassing all expectations, the time was right to address the future needs of the short-haul fleet. In April 1997, the company made a momentous decision when they placed an order with Airbus Industrie for ten new A321-200 single-aisle aircraft with ten options. This choice amounted to the largest single order placed by any UK carrier with the European manufacturing consortium to date.

The A321 offered the best seat-mile costs of any single-aisle aircraft. Unlike the earlier Boeing 737 series, with its small flight deck and conventional flying controls, the Airbus had a spacious flight

One of British Midland's Airbus A321-200 aircraft under construction at the Daimler-Benz Aerospace factory in Hamburg, Germany.

deck fitted with complex computerized systems which allowed the aircraft to climb quickly to high altitudes, where greater comfort was assured and fuel consumption lower. With such sophisticated computer intervention (ECAM – electronic centralized aircraft monitoring), the aircraft operated within a flight-envelope that enhanced crew awareness and ultimately aided safety. The weight-saving advantages of a fully computerized aircraft

Airbus A321-200 (G-MIDA) is shown here in the British Midland Diamond livery in use until 2001, when the airline was rebranded and renamed.

British Midland's first Airbus A320 (G-MIDZ) was delivered in January 1999 and is seen here in the bmi interim livery.

were larger payloads and better economies all round. With this superb jet British Midland were poised to offer greater seating capacity for business and leisure passengers and utilize their existing slot portfolio at Heathrow with improved efficiency. The first 196-seater Airbus 321-200 (G-MIDA) was handed over to Sir Michael Bishop in a ceremony at Belfast International Airport on 3 April 1998.[145] By April 2000, a further nine Airbus 321-200s had been delivered for use on the company's established UK and European trunk routes.

To complement the needs of the business, it was decided to adjust the balance of the Airbus Industrie order to the smaller 150-seat A320-200 model. The first of these single-aisle jets (G-MIDZ) arrived in January 1999. The remainder of the order had been delivered by May 2002.

Embraer 145 (G-RJXA) in British Midland livery.

The momentum for expansion and providing added value for the customer experience continued unchecked as the millennium approached. A costly refurbishment programme of all Diamond Club lounges was begun across the network in 1997.[146] An order worth £120 million was placed with Embraer, the Brazilian aircraft manufacturer, for a new fleet of ten 50-seater regional jet aircraft.[147] The Embraer 145 was a low-wing turbofan with a range of 1,350 miles (2,170 km), and was ideally suited to the company's short-haul network, where small capacities were the norm. The first three were delivered for the summer season of 1999.

In August 2000, British Midland were granted approval to carry assistance dogs in the cabin on the Heathrow to Paris Charles de Gaulle route as part of the Pet Travel Scheme.

In 2000, British Midland introduced state-of-the-art technology with e-tickets to speed up passenger check-in, and joined the Pet Travel Scheme Network, which welcomed assistance dogs to travel in the passenger cabin and domestic pets in the cargo hold, if their owners had previously acquired an official pet passport. Within the first year of this scheme being introduced the airline carried more than 150 dogs and 80 cats in and out of Heathrow from Europe.[148]

The Star Alliance and a joint venture with Lufthansa

In 1997, British Midland's partner SAS became a founder member, together with the German national airline Lufthansa, of the Star Alliance, the world's first multilateral airline alliance.[149] The modern airline alliance system was simply an extension of bilateral code-sharing agreements, but this time the customer received even greater benefits. The rewards for passengers of belonging included access to members' airport lounges for business customers, flight schedules which offered almost

Lufthansa flags.

flawless travel on a single ticket, even with different carriers within the alliance, special fares and discounts and an integrated frequent flyer programme which meant that points towards free flights mounted even quicker.[150]

British Midland with its significant and established route network were quickly identified as a very attractive carrier for inclusion in one of the multilateral airline groups (Oneworld, SkyTeam and Star).[151] During 1997, the independent carrier were courted by some of Europe's biggest airlines as they clambered to get BMA on board and seek a stake in the company. At the outset British Midland were reluctant to commit to anyone, but after weighing up the financial and operational benefits of all their options a decision was made to sign up to the Star Alliance. The official date of joining would be 1 July 2000.

Before entrusting themselves to the Star Alliance, British Midland completed a significant deal with Lufthansa, the German national airline, in November 1999. Lufthansa had guaranteed to deliver British Midland to their Star partners and to facilitate this they agreed to take a stake in the independent carrier.[152] As a means of implementing the joint venture, SAS, one of Lufthansa's partners in the Star Alliance, diluted by half their 40 per cent holding in British Midland, retaining just 20 per cent. With an eye on British Midland's Heathrow slots, the German flag carrier paid SAS £91.4 million for the available 20 per cent stake. The announcement of the independent carrier's intention to join the Star Alliance, with immediate effect, positioned them for strong growth as a serious competitor in the global market place.[153] In March 2000, British Midland proudly unveiled their first aircraft in a Star Alliance livery.

Consequent to the shareholders' agreement, negotiated between the two carriers, a three-way European Joint Venture revenue and profit-sharing deal was set up with the approval of the European

Sir Michael Bishop (centre) shaking hands with Jürgen Weber, chairman and ceo of Deutsche Lufthansa AG (left), and Jan Stenberg, president and ceo of Scandinavian Airlines System (right), in 2000.

This early version of the Star Alliance livery was nicknamed the 'washing line'.

Commission. This placed British Midland in a more healthy position to utilize better their precious Heathrow slots that by the rules of the European Commission would be lost if not used. With the Joint Venture in place a new initiative was introduced for European travellers when British Midland and its two shareholders, SAS and Lufthansa, began three-way business activities that included co-ord-inated sales and marketing events, the joint use of lounges and airport facilities, a reciprocal frequent flyer programme and lastly, code-sharing on all routes from Heathrow and Manchester. This significant development once again en-hanced the company's presence throughout Europe with the travelling public, and en-forced the company's position within the aviation industry as a global player.[154] New destinations from Heathrow, introduced at this time, were to Barcelona, Rome, Milan and Madrid. Previous plans to expand the network into Germany and Scandinavia were

bmi and other members of the Star Alliance welcoming Swiss International Air Lines (SWISS) as a new partner in 2006.

halted and BM's very profitable London to Frankfurt route was dropped.[155] This massive upheaval of the European route network in one stroke was in the short term very costly.

By the terms of the eight-year European Joint Venture deal, shaped by Nigel Turner, BM's financial director, and Tim Bye, legal director and company secretary,[156] the three partners would henceforth pool their revenues and costs in their shared European network. On 31 December 2007, the European Joint Venture expired. The shareholders' agreement was in due course re-organised, but remained in place until 10 October 2008 when Sir Michael Bishop exercised an option whereby Lufthansa would purchase his personal holding in the company in early 2009.

Plans for a return to long-haul

In 1996, Sir Michael Bishop decided to revive his battle to smash the transatlantic airline monopolies. It had been 15 years since British Midland had flown to the US, though during this time Sir Michael had taken his fight to other arenas. Due to a handful of long outdated Bermuda II rules, British Midland were still excluded from operating the lucrative long-haul routes out of Heathrow. More than 17 million passengers were travelling between the London hub and the US each year but none in a British Midland aircraft. The US had already signed open-skies agreements with other EU member states, but not with the British government. To win the battle for these coveted routes, Sir Michael realized that he would have to plan ahead and prove British Midland's lasting commitment to long-haul operations from Heathrow. The company would need a fleet of long-haul aircraft and the facilities to maintain such an operation. John Prescott, secretary of state for the environment, transport and the regions, wrote to Sir Michael stressing these prerequisites before negotiating with the US for British Midland's entry to these routes.

The first decision to be made was which aircraft type: whether like Virgin Atlantic to operate high-capacity aircraft, possibly buying the Airbus 340, or learn from BA, who were rapidly slimming down to the Boeing 777 to concentrate on high-yield point-to-point markets. The short-list was narrowed down to two medium-size, wide-bodied, jets – the Boeing 767 and the Airbus A330. Both offered crucially needed additional capacity to meet predicted passenger growth, bearing in mind that extra space was needed to accommodate spacious seats and generous leg room in the premium cabin.[157] Either would suit the company's anticipated expansion into the long-haul market, but in the end it was the flexibility, technical sophistication and superb performance of the Airbus that won. British Midland were already committed to this aircraft family, having previously introduced two of the narrow-bodied models into their short-haul fleet. An order was soon in place to buy four Airbus A330-200s, a 244-seater wide-bodied aircraft that had the added attraction, over the smaller Airbus models, of an advanced data-link system (CPDLC) that generated messages by satellite between the pilot and Air Traffic Control to obtain flight-path clearances without the need for radio communications. The on-board communications addressing and reporting system (ACARS) used to obtain weather reports and obtain pre-departure Air Traffic Control clearances was an added attraction.

Long before British Midland's first Airbus A330 landed at Heathrow, in April 2001, it was decided to build a dedicated maintenance hangar at the London hub. The new building provided the company with a valuable asset in the shape of a first-rate engineering facility with office space

Cockpit of an Airbus A330-200.

attached. The hangar's huge 6,500 sq m (70,000 sq ft) size was also a desirable visual presence on the airport complex with the airline's brand name visible to all. The British Midland Hangar was built in 1992 on a prime site near the Eastern Perimeter Road leased from BAA. Once operational the new facility not only handled the BM fleet, but took on service contracts from other carriers who flew into Heathrow but had no such operation of their own.

Artist's impression of the new training centre at Stockley Close.

To support the Heathrow operation a new £15 million Airbus flight simulator and training centre was built to replace the old facility at Whitwick in Leicestershire.[158] At the outset, thoughts turned to the vacant plot next to the Hangar as a suitable position for the new state-of-the-art centre but, due to underground obstacles, a green-field site was chosen at Stockley Close, no more than a mile from the airport. The new 10,400 sq m (111,800 sq ft), four-storey building included four flight

The design team.

deck simulator cells, an atrium for three different cabin simulators, training rooms for pilots, cabin crew and engineers, and much more. New staff would be put through their paces with a four-week training programme that embraced trolley runs, first-aid techniques and passenger anger management. The company believed that formal education and training, as a means of nurturing their workforce, was paramount. Two hundred personnel would be passing through the new centre every 24 hours, many of them on their annual two-day refresher courses. The training centre at Stockley Close opened on 5 July 1999.

The reservation centre in the library at Donington Hall. The centre was moved to East Midland Airport in 1998.

Although some members of the senior management team voiced the opinion that it would be advantageous to move the administrative headquarters south to be nearer to everything aviation and reinforce the company's presence at Heathrow, this was eventually rejected as part of a hard-nosed business decision. The London operation functioned very efficiently with the existing crew and pilot facilities in The Queen's Building next to Terminal 1 at Heathrow while, with the advantages of modern technology, the administrative headquarters could remain exactly where it was in the Midlands.[159] The benefits of remaining at Donington Hall, the spiritual home of the company, far outweighed anything to be gained by moving south. The company's reservation centre was moved from the library in Donington Hall to a purpose-built facility at East Midlands Airport in 1998, and eventually outsourced to India in 2005.[160] The operations department, which dealt with obstacles as diverse as bomb scares, volcanic eruptions and industrial action, was moved to the library.

In addition to the all-important decisions regarding fleet and facilities, the company made two significant changes to its structure to safeguard trading interests and consolidate the business's well-being at this time. The first took place in October 1996, when the company was split into two divisions – British Midland the airline and BM Aviation Services, covering engineering and ground handling. A further reorganization separated engineering and ground services, leaving the door open, in April 2001, for the sale of the later operation when industrial and union issues affected the efficient running of this successful division of the company. Three enthusiastic bidders fought fiercely for BM Handling Services, which were eventually purchased by a firm already in the business, the Go-Ahead Aviation Group, later Aviance UK, who paid the market valuation of £60 million. As part of the 2001 deal, staff jobs were secured under a TUPE (Transfer of Undertakings and Protection of Employment) agreement, while a five-year service contract was signed to provide both parties with continuity.[161] The second step was the gradual de-merger of the company's regional airlines – Manx Airlines, British Regional Air Lines (previously Manx Airlines Europe), Loganair and British Midland Regional – which all went on to flourish as separate entities.[162]

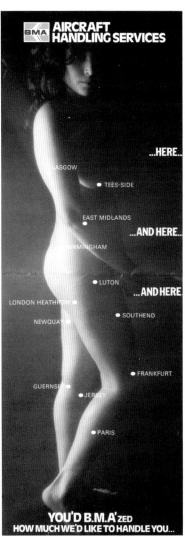

British Midland Handling Services attracted a great deal of business as a result of their efficient service and punchy advertising campaigns. The poster illustrated here dates from the late 1970s.

British Midland Regional

Following European deregulation BM identified another business opportunity with Business Air Ltd,[163] a tiny independent Scottish regional airline with obvious potential. The carrier, founded in Aberdeen in 1987, flew a package of scheduled services around Britain for the business commuter in their three 15-seater Embraer Bandeirantes turboprops. British Midland knew the operation well for they had been wet-leasing Business Air their 36-seater Saab 340 twin turboprop fleet when their own capacity at Heathrow was excessive.[164] To structure the deal the chief executive of Business Air, Ian Woodley, bought back shares from his investors and sold them on to British Midland. [165]

For two years after the official brand launch in March 1998, the new subsidiary, originally known as British Midland Commuter, operated under the umbrella of the parent company with decision-making directed from Donington Hall.[166] When, in 2000, British Midland began to tighten the purse strings as thoughts of returning to the long-haul market resurfaced, Austin Reid cut the Scottish-based operation adrift and left it to soar or crash with its own board of directors and fleet of 11 new Embraer 145 jets. The Brazillian 49-seater Embraers proved to be superb aircraft for a high-frequency operation with excellent passenger appeal, a range of 1,500 miles (2,400 km) and a cruise speed over 450 mph (720 kph). Probably the only disadvantage of this compact jet was the lack of overhead locker space. British Midland Commuter benefited greatly when BM began seriously focusing their attentions on operations out of Heathrow, and many of the more traditional business routes from the Midlands were handed over.

With their new-found independence, renamed British Midland Regional (February 2001) and led by Alex Grant, the first managing director, the airline began negotiating for services supplied by the parent company at a market rate. This turned losses into profits as the deals struck were very favourable. In time self-sufficiency stretched to all matters of training, recruitment, cabin services and maintenance, though the regional company were proud to wear the livery and uniforms of British Midland and reap the benefits of their sales division, marketing and advertising campaigns.

Under new management British Midland Regional created their own unique business model, which included a full complimentary in-flight service for all passengers and fast-track security and check-in for higher-paying corporate customers. The airline were proud of their high-frequency dependable morning and evening service on business routes across Britain and into Europe,

Crawford Rix was managing director of bmi regional from 2004 to 2006. He then took over as managing director of bmibaby.

an important pre-requisite for the modern business traveller. In the middle of the day, when regular customers were less likely to fly, new single daily rotations were tried. If the take-up was high enough, these routes were integrated into the flight timetable and grew to become full service operations. At weekends, when business customers were at leisure, the Embraer jets flew charters for premier league football clubs and for corporate sponsored events.

British Midland Regional gradually inherited all the mother company's UK routes except those networks out of Heathrow and East Midlands for which other plans took precedence. Within a very short space of time this small regional business became a prosperous arm of British Midland.

Resurrecting the transatlantic battle

By 1997, the A330 fleet was on order, the new Hangar at Heathrow was fully operational, the foundations of the simulator and training centre at Stockley Close had been dug and the first steps towards restructuring the business had been implemented. British Midland were now ready to return to the transatlantic market.

Completing the transport jigsaw (1997) identified aviation as the forgotten piece of the transport system.

In true fighting spirit Sir Michael Bishop began a lengthy campaign, kicking off with an attack in the House of Commons on the government's transport policy by means of a forceful report commissioned by British Midland. *Completing the transport jigsaw* (November 1997) spelt out how the British aviation industry was a success story recognized around the world, yet the forgotten piece of the transport jigsaw, a situation that needed urgently addressing. The report placed British Midland in the spotlight and was promptly followed with applications for route licences to operate scheduled services to ten key US cities from Heathrow (January 1998).[167] Sir Michael was privately optimistic about a positive outcome but once again the application went to appeal, leaving him with no alternative but to retaliate with a high-profile, hard-hitting national awareness campaign, targeted at audiences across the board. He lobbied fiercely with international speeches and a new research document, *Make the air fair* (September 1999), which was packed with facts, figures and convincing arguments.[168] In the late 1990s innocent customers were forced to pay higher fares than they should because the carriers flying the transatlantic routes from Heathrow were flouting competition law and fixing prices between themselves.[169] The figures were staggering – business class fares from the UK to the US were 172 per cent more expensive than comparative fares from other European cities to the US. To challenge such bad practice the press were briefed and responded accordingly with high-profile media coverage. The public at large were invited to sign a petition online.[170] In the ensuing debate the Tory front bench turned their back on traditional Conservative pro-competition policy, and it was the Labour government of the day, championed by John Prescott, the new deputy prime minister, who stood up for the interests of the British consumer and the UK plc by bravely supporting more competition on transatlantic routes from Heathrow. Sir Richard

Tim Bye joined the airline in 1998 as legal director and company secretary. Bye was promoted to the board in 2003 and became deputy chief executive officer the following year.

The new long-haul product offered business customers a choice of menu with food prepared and served by an on-board chef.

Branson, who had built his lucrative airline Virgin Atlantic on the back of the bilateral agreement, felt threatened by the potential of competition from British Midland and was quick to shout scorn on Prescott as the man killing off UK aviation. Eventually, after two hard years of delicate negotiations that involved securing a one-off deal with BM's Star Alliance partner United Airlines, giving British Midland connections into the US and the US carrier coveted links into Europe, the two governments were ready to sign a phased deal modifying the restrictive nature of Bermuda II. Sir Michael was quietly confident.

In January 2000, the US government representatives were making plans to come to Britain to sign the deal with their British counterparts. At the last minute, Bob Ayling, the chief executive of British Airways, lobbied prime minister Tony Blair that increased competition would damage BA at a time of slump in profits. BA claimed that concessions favouring bmi should not be made to the American negotiators until UK carriers had access to the US domestic market. The unions also lobbied against the reform of Bermuda II so at the last moment the Labour government put aside its free-market ethos and intervened to quash the agreement and force the US delegates, who had just arrived in London, to return home empty handed.[171]

With his usual strong-willed determination Sir Michael Bishop responded promptly to the failed negotiations, from which British Midland would have benefited, by applying

The comfortable business cabin seats, introduced in 2001, were eventually reutilized in the premium economy cabin when lie-flat beds were installed for business customers in 2007.

BERMUDA II

In 1991, Bermuda II was modified, replacing Pan Am and TWA with American Airlines and United Airlines as the US's favoured carriers. In exchange for allowing these airlines to operate to Heathrow, British Airways gained the right to code-share with a US airline and Virgin Atlantic were permitted to operate from Heathrow. Four airlines should have been enough to offer sufficient choice to passengers and real competition, but in reality the fares were identical. Following the revised legislation the two governments made a number of attempts at introducing a more liberalized regime but major policy disagreements

ensured that all efforts failed. In 1995, a further annex to Bermuda II was introduced, lifting certain route and fare restrictions on scheduled flights serving Heathrow and Gatwick. In 2003 the European Court of Justice decreed that Bermuda II and other EU member state agreements were illegal. The European Commission was granted a mandate to take over negotiations with the US on behalf of all member states. On 30 April 2007, a new Open-Skies Agreement was signed by the United States and the European Union (of which the UK is part), replacing Bermuda II. This came into effect on 30 March 2008.

for licences to fly from Manchester to Washington DC and Manchester to Chicago. With three of the large A330 Airbuses due for delivery within the year, an in-house development team was assigned the task of creating the new long-haul product: the passenger service would deliver the wow factor and on-board safety would offer medical technology never before delivered in flight.[172] Business customers, now known as guests, not passengers, would receive the ultimate in-flight experience. This would include an on-board chef for personal meal selection, state-of-the-art entertainment systems and ergonomically designed seats with 127 cm of leg room and a deep recline.

Marking the announcement that British Midland would be flying their new A330 Airbus fleet from Manchester International Airport. Left to right: Geoff Muirhead, managing director Manchester Airport, Sir Michael Bishop and Austin Reid.

Passengers travelling in the premium economy and economy cabins would also benefit from an enhanced product that would include complimentary magazines and newspapers, superior meals and generously adjustable seats with footrests – all in all, a product usually associated with business class on other airlines. The service would be luxuriously over-staffed with 11 hand-picked cabin-crew members looking after 244 passengers, a ratio of more than double that laid down by CAA guidelines.[173]

The first Airbus A330-200 (G-WWBM) was delivered to Manchester Airport on 27 April 2001 in readiness for its first commercial flight to Washington DC on 12 May. The second Airbus (G-WWBD) flew in on 9 May and made its inaugural scheduled service to Chicago on 8 June. The US operations began as a joint venture with United Airlines, each carrier sharing responsibility for seat sales and costs, but this limited agreement collapsed when United sought to reduce their costs after the tragic events of 11 September 2001. The third Airbus (G-WWBB) was handed over on 30 May 2001 but was immediately wet-leased with a British Midland crew to South African Airways for 18 months.[174] Through necesssity the fourth A330 was placed with Emirates who needed extra capacity.

This is to certify that

ALISON WEATHERLEY

flew on the historical bmi british midland ETOPS proving flight
on Thursday 10 May 2001 from
Manchester International Airport to
Washington Dulles International Airport
on board Airbus A330-200, registration G-WWBM,

Captain John Quick
A330 chief pilot

Captain Geoff Linaker
general manager flight operations

bmi

Rebranding an airline

Before trying once again to resurrect the transatlantic battle, which had been so cruelly snatched from his grasp, Sir Michael Bishop diverted his attention to practical matters. With a scheduled service network of 30 domestic and European destinations and the kudos of being a key member of the Star Alliance, British Midland would look to the challenges of the future.

British Midland needed to ensure that the business remained competitive and maintained momentum. With this in mind there began a major reorganization of the senior management team. Invitations were extended to key players from the world of industry to bring to the business their wealth of expertise.[175] James Hogan returned to BM as chief operating officer, after a short absence, bringing with him a boost to staff morale and a philosophy of risks and rewards as a means of growing the business.[176] The rising stars within the company were Tim Bye, and Nigel Turner who was promoted to chief financial officer in June 1999.[177]

Nigel Turner joined British Midland in 1987 with experience in financial reporting. In 1995, he became financial director and four years later chief financial officer. At the age of 46, in 2004, he became chief executive of bmi.

Developments in the management structure led to a brusque overhaul of strategy and some carefully considered long-term plans. All aspects of the business were carefully looked at, starting with the approach to communications. As the new millennium approached British Midland had outgrown the brand they had so successfully created and were not in good shape as the aviation landscape was becoming increasingly globalized. The public at large did not recognize British Midland as a carrier with a proven pedigree. New commercial challenges and a fresh impetus required an original look. To create the airline's new corporate identity and address future promotional needs a hard-hitting campaign was commissioned with James Hogan driving the project.[178] Many firms were invited to pitch for the work but in the event the talents of London-based advertising consultants Bartle, Bogle & Hegarty (BBH) and international branding consultancy Landor Associates were employed to respond to the brief.[179]

The first stage of rebranding the company as a formidable international player was the choice of a new name. 'British Midland' was too insular for an airline with transatlantic aspirations and a growing fleet of long-haul aircraft. Research showed that the public still perceived British Midland as

second fiddle to the national airline and not a completely different carrier. The first name chosen was British Blue, but this was considered too similar to JetBlue, a recently launched Californian low-cost carrier. The name settled upon was 'bmi', with lower-case letters leaving no doubt that this was nothing to do with the national flag carrier British Airways.

The first model in the Airbus A330-200 series (G-WWBM) was delivered on 27 April 2001, complete with the distinctive new bmi 'wave' livery.

Acronyms were very popular as company names but in this instance the letters had no meaning whatsoever. To some the spoken name did suggest British Midland International, but this was never intended. For two years the words 'British Midland' were kept as an appendage to bmi while the new identity was gently eased into public awareness. As human nature came into play the name was automatically shortened.

The next task was to create a new visual image to match the new name, keeping what was relevant of the old while addressing the future ambitions of the business. In the knowledge that there was too much similarity between the stern corporate colour palettes of BM and BA, the company's most fierce adversary, a fresher shade of 'sailing' blue was selected for the livery and used as a wave motif across the fuselage. This was tied in with a white undercarriage, the shadow of a Union Jack on the tail fin and small flashes of bright red used as functional indicators. The design as a whole communicated relaxation and Britishness in a subliminal way, and stood out boldly on the ground or up above the clouds when

Every aspect of the airline's visual image was addressed in the 2001 rebranding.

measured against other airline liveries worldwide.[180] All other aspects of the new identity highlighted the company's core values of 'can-do' and its reputation for warm and friendly customer service. Airport signage and all printed material boldly shouted the new name. On-board food and its presentation was stylishly modernized as part of the invigoration of the long-haul product. Uniforms were smartened up with a handful of small changes that included the loss of all traces of the diamond motif and the introduction of the new corporate palette of blue shades for blouses, ties and hat bands.

British Midland Regional were also brought in line with the new bmi rebranding with a new name, bmi regional, and revamped aircraft livery, signage, uniforms and advertising literature.[181]

The practical process of change evolved gradually. Rebranding planes is a costly business as it takes them out of service for at least a week. Change by its very nature can be hard to embrace, both for the public and the company's staff, so a pragmatic and cautious route was followed. The official unveiling took place on 1 February 2001, to great applause from the world's press, at the airline's Heathrow Hangar. With terrorist events in New York seven months later turning the airline industry upside-down, the new bmi brand never received the launch it deserved as budgets were pulled across the board.

The impact of 9/11

On the morning of 11 September 2001, 19 terrorists affiliated to al-Qaeda hijacked and crashed four commercial passenger jet airliners over the US, killing 2,973 innocent civilians. In the aftermath of this unspeakable atrocity the problems of an already struggling airline industry were further exacerbated as travel capacity worldwide reduced by more than 20 per cent overnight.

Shortly before this appalling act of violence took place the senior management at bmi had begun a strategy meeting on the future expansion of the business. Within moments of the news breaking all plans were deemed irrelevant and the course of action was changed to damage limitation mode.

The battering caused to the aviation industry by the fall-out from 9/11 was not the only matter for grave concern in the early years of the new millennium. In 2001, there was an outbreak of foot-and-mouth disease in the UK that caused serious consequences for tourism both in cities and the countryside. In 2003, there was the start of the Second Gulf War in Iraq, the emergence of the avian influenza A (H5N1) virus and fears of an al-Qaeda missile attack at Heathrow, each of which, in its own way, caused travellers to think twice before flying. To top it all, between November 2002 and July 2003 there was an outbreak of SARS, a respiratory disease that reached near pandemic proportions when 774 people died worldwide. This life-threatening disease originated in Guangdong Province in China and was spread unknowingly by human carriers flying to Asia, Canada and America.[182] As time would tell, the SARS virus affected worldwide aviation demand even more than the Iraq War.[183]

In common with other full-service airlines bmi struggled following 9/11, forfeiting an estimated £35 million in lost revenue. Business managers were now questioning the need for their employees to travel at all, and if they had to go they would go cheaply. Feeder passengers from the company's Star Alliance partners were no longer booking on connecting flights around the UK and into Europe.[184] bmi's fledgling transatlantic routes (2001) and more recent European routes acquired after the European Joint Venture (1999) were simply not well enough established for guaranteed survival. bmi reassessed their whole operation, an exercise that led to cost-cutting measures which came into immediate effect, and long-term strategies that were implemented over the coming months and years. Before the year was out the company began a raft of restructuring changes that included the grounding of aircraft surplus to needs, an overhaul of domestic fares to and from Heathrow, a reduction in seat capacity for the winter 2001 timetable and cuts in the workforce, achieved wherever possible through natural wastage.[185]

Despite every effort bmi slumped £19.6m into the red in 2002, with its first pre-tax losses for ten years, amidst the toughest trading environment the airline industry had ever seen.[186] The previous year the company recorded a pre-tax profit of £12.4m, but this included the exceptional gain from the sale of the ground-handling business in April 2001. Even when traffic began to recover, there had been a massive change imposed on the industry by the budget revolution engineered by a younger generation of airline entrepreneurs.[187] The new competition was prepared to get rid of seat allocations, in-flight meals and reclining seats and fly to out-of-the-way airports in an obsessive drive to keep costs to an absolute minimum. In its usual reaction to adversity bmi placed itself in the front line against the intruders and embraced a new business opportunity.

bmibaby

In January 2002, bmi announced the launch of bmibaby, its completely independent, no-frills operation from East Midlands Airport. The new low-cost airline was born out of bmi mainline, who handed over three Boeing 737s and the popular tourist destinations of Barcelona, Nice, Palma, Faro, Malaga, Alicante, Prague and Dublin. From bmi regional the new low-budget carrier was gifted the traditional trunk routes from East Midlands to Edinburgh, Glasgow, Paris and Brussels.[188] Following a high-profile advertising and marketing campaign, during which 16,000 free tickets were given away, bmibaby made a remarkable start with sales of nearly 50,000 seats in the first four days of Internet business. The public and press waited eagerly for first-hand reports on bmibaby's maiden flight, which took off from East Midlands Airport for Malaga on 20 March 2002.

Tony Davis, managing director of bmibaby from the launch in 2002–5.

Having followed the remarkable impact of Ryanair, easyJet and Go, bmi had begun debating the option of creating their own low-cost model back in the spring of 2001. Research had shown that there were more than 8 million people living within an hour's drive of East Midlands Airport, and to date they had no low-cost carrier to serve them. The business plan for a budget operation was on the table by the summer but, with the launch of bmi's transatlantic Airbus operation imminent (May 2001), followed shortly by 9/11, the moment to push ahead had not arrived. The impetus to act was the surprise announcement in December 2001 that Go, the low-cost airline created by British Airways, were planning to expand their own no-frills operation with a new hub at East Midlands Airport.[189]

In true bmi style the company responded quickly and, in less than three months from start to launch, a small in-house management team together with Landor, who had recently completed the new bmi branding, developed the strategy for a low-cost operation and fine-tuned the product.

As more and more Boeing 737-500s were taken over from the main-line operation to meet the needs of bmibaby, it was impossible to repaint every aircraft in the full livery in the short term. G-BVKD, seen here at East Midlands Airport in 2002, is wearing bmibaby titles on the blue fuselage of the old company livery.

The management team recognized from the outset that consumer demand would be driven by price and when operating within an unpredictable market it was crucial to remain aware of the competition and react quickly.[190] The no-frills market was all about volume and cost.

The 'baby' name, dreamt up by the advertising consultants, implied a young, agile and fun airline with personality. This was then visualized by the branding team as a witty fictional character known as 'Tiny', a Bart Simpson-like individual with attitude. The bmibaby fleet livery bore a distinctive relationship to the main airline – same blue, same red detail, same typeface, same underlying graphics – but instead of the blue wave which reflected quality and depth of experience, the 'Tiny' logo was emblazoned across a white fuselage, suggesting a no-frills product. The welcoming mood of the airline was further enforced with a casual uniform of red puffer jacket, chinos, T-shirts and loafers.

The fleet allocated to bmibaby was the 148-seater Boeing 737-300s, previously used on bmi's European business routes, as many of these were now standing idle due to the company's post-9/11 cutbacks. The 737 was ideally suited to the new venture, being a cost-effective jet aircraft perfect for carrying domestic passengers and holiday-makers on city breaks or to destinations around the Mediterranean. As with other bmi operations, the economic benefits of a single-type fleet were obvious. With their own Air Operator's Certificate in hand, the costs of running the new low-cost operation were controlled separately from the main airline, as appropriate to a business working in a different segment of the airline industry. In the anxious period following 9/11, many of the company's staff who lived in the Midlands were eager to be part of the new bmibaby operation.

Customers from the outset liked the fun-loving, low-cost brand, offering one-way tickets starting at £25. They welcomed seat allocation at check-in, which avoided the scrum experienced with other low-cost carriers. They felt confident travelling under the umbrella of a long-established airline whose reputation for friendly service was guaranteed. A high visual presence at East Midlands Airport, together with extensive advertising in the Midlands, has kept passenger numbers high and ever increasing. By sponsoring TV weather forecasts within the appropriate catchment areas, the bmibaby brand reaches a massive audience of potential customers.[191]

Within the first year of trading, bmibaby exceeded their sales forecast from East Midlands Airport by 100 per cent. They promptly began expanding, with the opening of a second UK base

Boeing 737-500 (G-BVKB), named *foxy baby*, wearing its very distinctive bmibaby livery.

at Cardiff International Airport, the first low-cost airline base for Wales. During 2002, bmibaby carried more than 700,000 passengers and achieved a nearly perfect punctuality record. In May 2003, Manchester became bmibaby's third base, followed by Birmingham in January 2005.[192] The success of the low-cost operation at Birmingham was exceptional and within just 18 months the budget operation was operating nine 737 jets across a route network of 21 holiday and business destinations, making it bmibaby's largest hub. With the enormous uptake in passengers using the no-frills option, bmibaby introduced a new initiative in 2007, whereby customers could choose from a range of optional services and extras (flexible ticketing, use of the executive lounges, on-line check-in) and pay only for the items they wanted.

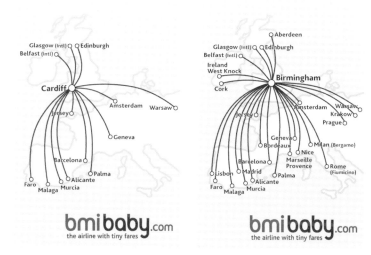

bmibaby route maps out of Cardiff and Birmingham in 2007. In addition bmibaby served 14 destinations from East Midlands and another 13 from Manchester.

Today, bmibaby is recognized as a significant player in the UK's low-budget market with a fleet flying to 30 destinations in nine European countries with 20 Boeing 737s.[193] It stands as yet another substantial division of the parent company, carrying almost 40 per cent of the group's 10.5 million passengers in 2007.

Boeing 737-500 (G-BVKD) freshly resprayed with a Welsh promotional livery for bmibaby, 2004.

Climbing back

With the new low-budget model under their belts the company turned to the business of long-term survival following the unprecedented downturn in world aviation. The senior management had been reshuffled and from this there followed a stand-alone recovery plan known as Project Blue Sky, led by Austin Reid, the group managing director. By promptly reassessing their whole operation, and setting enormous cost-saving targets of £100m over three years, the airline were convinced they could return to healthy sustainable profits. Even when taking into account soaring fuel bills and the increases in airport charges that had to be found to pay for new state-of-the-art security checks and the building of Terminal 5 at Heathrow,[194] bmi felt confident of a climb back to prosperity. They were smaller than British Airways and easyJet, which gave them the ability to adapt more quickly to the changes in the market place, an advantage they exploited in the relevant segments of the busi-

Austin Reid was group managing director from 1997 to 2004.

ness. They also realized that it was crucial to go beyond price alone, for the time would come when consumers would tire of very cheap travel and be prepared to pay a little more for creature comforts.

The company were brutally honest and frank with their staff about the cost base across the business and made the necessary cuts without mercy. The workforce of 4,850 would be reduced by 10 per cent by natural wastage and redundancies. Below-wing ground handling, ticket reservations and some aspects of information technology would all have to be outsourced.[195] The Reservations department was moved from its base at East Midlands Airport, initially to Rotherham (2002), then to Mumbai (2004) and finally to Pune (2006).The Engineering department would be streamlined and cabin crews would need to be slimmed down to more accpetable levels. Substantial marketing budgets were withdrawn and the decision was

made to stop paying travel agents commission, a long outdated practice. The valuable Airbus A320 and Boeing 737 simulators at Stockley Close were sold to GE Capital Aviation Training (GECAT), who already rented cell space there for their own A330 simulator model.[196] The existing CPATA Revenue Accounting System remained in house until 2006, when it was replaced by a new system known as REVERA, which was run from Mumbai and overseen by a small team at Donington Hall.[197]

An important aspect of the business, from which the management team took advantage in these difficult years, was its regional strength. The short-haul operation (bmi regional) was quick off the mark with a handful of new routes that were promptly evaluated for their uptake. If they

bmi's A330 Manchester to Chicago service began in 2001.

were popular with passengers, they were worthy of remaining in the timetable (Manchester to Toulouse and Aberdeen to Groningen), but if they failed to meet expectations they were promptly dropped (Glasgow to Knock, Manchester to Norwich). The transatlantic operation from Manchester was obviously ripe for expansion, with many untapped destinations in its sights. The Chicago service had been very successful since its introduction in 2001, attracting a loyal clientele who welcomed a non-stop flight to the US without travelling first to Heathrow. Passengers were rightly impressed with the exceptional long-haul product which in its second year of operation (2003), won Best Airline Serving the US in *Holiday Which?*, toppling Virgin Atlantic from their coveted slot.[198] In 2004, four new long-haul routes were introduced from Manchester to the popular holiday destinations of Las Vegas, Antigua, St Lucia and Barbados.[199]

Disappointingly, the service to Washington DC never really flourished. This was due in part to the awkward arrival slot, late in the day, which meant that passengers were unable to make comfortable onward connections across the US. When demand temporarily dropped in the winter of 2003–4, the company sought lucrative charter opportunities to keep their Airbus flying. For four months the A330-200 was wet-leased to the Ministry of Defence and flew military personnel to and from Brize Norton, Ascension Island and the Falklands in a Star Alliance livery. Similar opportunities were grabbed when SAS and South African Airways required extra capacity. After a hopeful relaunch of the Manchester to Washington route, in the spring of 2005 passenger numbers sadly languished again so the A330, allocated to this route, was temporarily pulled for another long-haul scheduled operation in need of greater capacity. The Washington route was handed a Boeing 757,

A bmi Airbus A320 taxies to the stand at Manchester International Airport, July 2003.

a smaller, less sophisticated jet which proved to be unpopular with passengers. The service lost credibility and folded.[200]

Charter flights continued to be important revenue earners in the early years of the new millennium. In July 2005, the British government chartered a bmi aircraft to transport visiting heads of state from Heathrow to Prestwick for the G8 summit. In the summer of 2006, Madonna used the services of bmi to move her entourage of 200 dancers, musicians and tech-

The inaugural services from Manchester to Barbados and Antigua took off on 26 and 27 November and to St Lucia on 13 December 2004. Sir Michael Bishop and Nigel Turner were warmly welcomed in true Caribbean style.

nicians around Europe for six weeks on the second leg of her Confessions Concert Tour.[201]

The aggressive cost-cutting measures had an immediate effect on the company's profitability with trading losses in 2003 half those of the previous year.[202] Customers responded positively to a new low fare structure for all domestic and international destinations from its regional hubs, and the scrapping of its full-service fares in favour of a simpler, less expensive pricing structure for both domestic and European passengers travelling from Heathrow. The loss of hot meals and over-generous baggage allowances was a small price to pay for bmi's new attractive fares, always friendly service and punctual flights.[203] The demise of the old bmi business prototype in the wake of aggressive competition was sad but necessary.[204] Passenger numbers said it all – a record-breaking 9.4 million flew with bmi in 2003, a 20 per cent increase on the previous year. In 2004, bmi was still the UK's second largest full-service scheduled airline, measured by passenger numbers, operating 40 routes to 29 destinations throughout the UK, continental Europe and North America.[205]

The Falkland contract for the MOD operated from January to April 2004. The A330 assigned to this task was reconfigued with a double business-class cabin to meet the needs of the army.

REORGANIZING THE BUSINESS

By 2003, bmi's recovery was well in hand but by no means completely secure. Sir Michael Bishop decided it was time to tidy up the share structure of the company and think towards the future. In anticipation of change, the tiny shareholdings which had been given as incentives to members of the senior management team over the years were repatriated, leaving the original partners with their 60 per cent stake once again. Lufthansa subsequently increased their 20 per cent holding by acquiring a further stake of 10 per cent minus one share, leaving the three original partners (the BBW Partnership) with

50 per cent plus one share. With an opportunity in place, Stuart Balmforth and John Wolfe decided it was time to retire completely from the company they had already stepped back from on a day-to-day basis, leaving the door open for Sir Michael Bishop to buy their respective shareholdings. On 20 May 2006, the 28-year-old partnership ended, leaving Sir Michael Bishop as the sole owner of a new investment company and a personal stake in British Midland plc (bmi) of 50 per cent plus one share. On 10 October 2008, Sir Michael exercised an option which required Lufthansa to purchase his controlling stake in bmi.

The New Business Model

By 2004, bmi had moved back into the black with a modest pre-tax profit of £2.1 million. With confidence re-established Nigel Turner was promoted to chief executive officer, following the retirement of Austin Reid, and Tim Bye to deputy ceo. The time was right to begin a complete overhaul of the company's domestic and European network out of Heathrow with a New Business Model. As a precursor to the airline's make-over Turner stamped his mark on the culture of the company by introducing a 'business casual' no-ties dress code in the office as a symbol of modern Britain and to mark the beginning of an era of change for the organization.

Since 9/11 attitudes had changed towards travelling short haul in the more expensive front cabin. The market was conscious of saving unnecessary expenditure and it 'looked better' to travel in the back of the plane in a smaller seat. Apart from the key business destinations (Edinburgh, Glasgow, Belfast, Dublin and Brussels), all routes now came under the umbrella of a single-class service, and to shorten time spent at the airport customers were encouraged to use the check-in on-line service from the comfort of their homes or offices and use the self-service machines on arrival in the terminal.[206] There was no reprieve for routes, even long-established ones, that did not pay their way. The unprofitable ones, where there was vastly too much capacity and not enough demand, were swiftly suspended (Heathrow to Milan, Madrid and Paris).[207] Every detail of the business came under close scrutiny. Pre-tax profits in 2005 topped £10 million, showing the airline was clearly back on course.

Not all activity was focused on cutting back. There were also excellent opportunities to expand the airline's European route network by picking up routes from Heathrow to Venice and Alicante (March 2003), to Aberdeen, Inverness and Naples (March 2004), to Lyons for the winter ski season

Between February 2002 and March 2008, bmi took delivery of 11 Airbus A319s.

(December 2005) and to Jersey (January 2007) after a break of six years. To meet the needs of reduced capacities on existing services out of Heathrow, the smaller 144-seater Airbus 319 was introduced as a replacement for the larger Airbus models, the A321s and A320s, as their leases expired.

The New Business Model was a remarkable success in dealing with the airline's survival, but as with so many hard-hitting exercises there was a price to pay for cutbacks that affected the passenger experience. Market research unleashed powerful emotions amongst bmi customers. They were confused about the overlap of the various products (bmi, bmibaby and bmi regional) and fare structures, and many were disgruntled, having never warmed to buying on-board meals. To address these potentially serious issues the bmi brand was refreshed with a new campaign known as 'bmi time', launched in 2007. To reward regular customers complimentary food and drink was reintroduced for higher-level Diamond Club cardholders and, to please everyone, more attractive ways of winning free flights were initiated.[208] Since the days of Derby Airways and British Midland the business has been built upon loyalty, and loyalty deserves reward.

bmi regional

In the wake of 9/11, bmi regional, a separate and independent branch of the mainline operation, also acted with financial prudence to ensure survival. Under the guidance of Alex Grant, managing director (2001–4), and then Crawford Rix (2004–6), it too recorded climbing passenger numbers and a return to profitability within just a couple of years. By 2006, Stewart Adams was at the helm and the time was deemed right for the serious expansion of bmi regional's route network. In an unprecedented move, 94 low-fare scheduled flights were introduced in one fair swoop to the popular destinations of Amsterdam, Paris and Belfast from the airline's four British hubs (Aberdeen, East Midlands, Manchester and Leeds Bradford). This was just the beginning of year-by-year growth for the all-jet operation that clearly had the edge over its regional competitors.[209] The regional operation remained very focused so when a new service failed to meet anticipated passenger demand, at either end of the route, it was immediately terminated – Leeds–Lille was axed after just four months.

Stewart Adams has been the managing director of bmi regional since 2006. He began his career with Business Air, rising to become general manager in 1987. When British Midland acquired that company in 1997 Adams was absorbed into the new subsidiary, as general manager of operations.

In 2007, extra frequencies were added to all flights out of Aberdeen, East Midlands, Manchester and Leeds Bradford, while passengers looking for reliable, non-stop, full-service flights to international destinations had even more choice.[210] The Scottish transport minister Tavish Scott praised the airline's initiative, which brought a boost to business and tourism in the north-east and Scotland. In 2007, the CAA proudly announced that once again bmi regional were the most punctual scheduled airline operating in the UK.[211]

bmi regional continue to prosper on high-yield business customers and remains another successful division of the parent company, with a modern fleet of 17 Embraer 145 and 135 jets serving 15 destinations across the UK and into Europe from six regional airports. The operation has its own maintenance hangar at Aberdeen, with a staff of four hundred. Not everyone wants to move through Heathrow.

During the 2007–8 football season, bmi regional transported Arsenal around the UK to away fixtures in the Premiership League in their Embraer fleet. A similar charter contract has been signed for 2008–9, plus another with their rivals, Chelsea.

Mid- and long-haul out of Heathrow

Having failed to unblock the restrictive Bermuda II legislation, due to the political clout of the national flag carrier (2000), bmi simply regrouped and came out fighting again. The travelling public deserved greater choice and competitive fares and bmi was going to win this fight on their behalf.

Over the next seven years the debate was fraught and confrontational with many highs and lows. British Airways and Virgin Atlantic, the two UK airlines who enjoyed the lucrative transatlantic market, continued to bring pressure to bear on the government, leaving encouraging talks between the UK and US shattered (2002).[212] When the European Court of Justice came to the decision that the bilateral protective agreement was unlawful, Sir Michael was rightly optimistic (2003). When Stansted was made the preferred choice for a new runway ahead of Heathrow (2003), Sir Michael reacted fiercely, for he had campaigned hard for years for a Heathrow expansion strategy as a tool for competition. When Cathay Pacific won the right to fly from Heathrow to America, Sir Michael objected strongly,

Robert Palmer joined bmi as chief financial officer in October 2007. Since then Palmer has addressed hedging policies, to reflect the changing fuel price environment, and developed cost reduction programmes to ensure bmi remains financially sound during the present difficult economic climate.

having fought unsuccessfully for this right on behalf of bmi for many years.[213] When Rod Eddington, of British Airways, and Sir Richard Branson, of Virgin Atlantic, suddenly called for

From 2005 to 2008 bmi operated 24 mainline check-in desks at Terminal 1 at Heathrow, with 8 additional long-haul desks for flights to Saudi Arabia. A major programme of refurbishment began at Terminal 1 in March 2008 and in the short term reduced bmi's check-in desks to just 15.

Brussels to take over the open skies talks on behalf of member states, Sir Michael was initially interested, but quickly became suspicious of delaying tactics. When promising transport talks took place between the European Union and the United States in Brussels, Sir Michael was quietly delighted (2006), but when they stalled he once again saw the answer to the protracted problem slipping away (2006). Would long-haul air passengers flying out of Heathrow never have a serious alternative? Angry, but never completely worn down by such injustice, Sir Michael continued lobbying the Labour government of the day. He believed that in principle, the US and the European Commission (who now represented all member states, including the UK) were committed to liberalization and open skies and that one day his determination would succeed. The real sticking points seemed to come from the US Congress, who focused on ownership and control of airlines, and on access to domestic markets.

Meanwhile, as a means of addressing the shrinking European market, the management of bmi, led by Tony Whitby, the director of network planning, developed a new Heathrow strategy aimed at pushing the airline towards greater involvement in the mid- and long-haul markets. bmi aspired to become a network carrier rather than simply a point-to-point operator.

The first real opportunity came in October 2004. Agreement was reached between the UK and Indian governments to allow more flights to and from the sub-continent, one of the most lucrative routes in aviation. India needed more capacity as their holiday and business markets were galloping ahead. bmi were encouraged and applied immediately for licences to fly to Mumbai and Bangalore, knowing they would offer passengers better value fares than those previously available. Even though British Airways had earned very high profits on its routes to India in 2003, the CAA awarded the majority of the additional frequencies to the national flag carrier with bmi receiving just four and Virgin seven. bmi began their first ever long-haul service out of Heathrow, to Mumbai, on 14 May 2005. As fate would have it, after more than a year of encouraging passenger uptake and an

Nigel Turner, with ambassadors Ally Thompson and Carlos Sequeira, being greeted by Abdallah Al-Mouallimi, the head of the Jeddah Chamber of Commerce. The inaugural flight from Heathrow to Jeddah landed on 18 May 2006.

increase to daily frequencies, the Airbus serving the Indian route developed stress fractures in the undercarriage that were discovered on a daily inspection, and had to be suspended. By the time the problem was cured three months later, Virgin Atlantic, BA and India's own carriers Jet Airways and Air India had stepped in and taken the market share. In this instance seat capacity was saturated and further competition was simply not viable. The Mumbai service was suspended in October 2006.

During the summer of 2005, bmi established a firmer foothold in the long-haul market from Heathrow when BA suspended their services to Saudi Arabia, after incurring unacceptable losses, and bmi stepped in with their own operation to the Kingdom. bmi carefully evaluated all aspects of crew safety before confidently committing to these challenging routes. In preparation for the exciting new destinations, bmi ground and cabin crews were trained in cultural awareness and the

bmi's operation from Heathrow to Saudi Arabia began with three weekly services to both Jeddah and Riyadh (2005–6). With the agreement of both governments more frequencies have recently been permitted which should lead to more services on all routes to the Kingdom in 2009.

wearing of an abaya, the traditional over-garment worn by women in many countries of the Arabian peninsula, whilst staying in Saudi Arabia. The Heathrow to Riyadh route began on 1 September 2005 with a healthy passenger take-up from the outset. This was followed by the Heathrow to Jeddah operation which was also well received. Unfortunately its launch, on 18 May 2006, was shortly before a new security protocol was introduced at Heathrow, following revelations of an al-Qaeda transatlantic aircraft plot, causing frustration and confusion for all passengers at

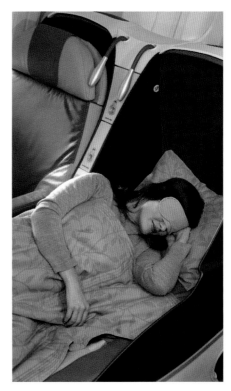

In 2007, Italian designer lie-flat beds were installed in the business cabin of bmi's A330 fleet.

the London hub. As always bmi staff handled anxious passengers with friendly efficiency and the service suffered no problems. The Airbus A330 assigned to these important new long-haul routes had a two-cabin configuration with 42 business seats. All passengers enjoyed the updated version of the superior long-haul product developed originally for the transatlantic routes out of Manchester. Saudi customers responded enthusiastically to bmi's superior service, which echoed their own cultural hospitality. In March 2008, a further destination was added to the timetable, this time to Damman, one of the largest seaports on the Persian Gulf. Increased frequencies are expected on all routes to the Kingdom in 2009.

In March 2006, a bilateral air service agreement was finally ratified after five years of fragile negotiations between the governments of the UK and the Russian Federation. With a commercial code-share partnership in place between bmi and Transaero, the British independent won the right to fly to Moscow, its first mid-haul route out of Heathrow. A daily scheduled service began on 29 October 2006 in a 2-cabin Airbus A320. The success of this route justified an increase in frequency to twice daily from October 2008. When Chelsea played Manchester United in the European Cup Final at the Luzhniki stadium in Moscow on 21 May 2008, three extra charter flights were laid on for football supporters fortunate enough to acquire tickets for the match.[214]

Nigel Turner and Alexander Krinichansky, executive director of Transaero, celebrating bmi's new route to Moscow.

As 2007 came and went, some of the company's longer-serving top personnel left, leaving the senior management team in need of refreshing. Talented individuals from within the world of aviation were brought into the company, people who offered a new approach to the business.[215]

Never choosing to stand still for a moment, bmi refitted all three of their wide-bodied A330s in the summer of 2007 to keep abreast of passenger expectations. The business cabins now boasted luxurious two-tone beige leather seats that converted into 1.8 m long beds, and which stored 15-inch in-flight entertainment TV screens. Premium economy customers, travelling from Manchester to Chicago and the Caribbean, would now travel in unprecedented comfort in the reutilized 49-inch pitch business class seats. The new configuration was 18 business flat beds, 30 business premium seats and 170 economy seats.

The training centre at Stockley Close is an important asset to the company. Two hundred personnel attend training programmes and refresher courses here every day, covering all aspects of safety and service on the ground and in the air.

In March 2007, the EU and the US reached a landmark decision when they signed the first stage of an air transport agreement to remove all restrictions on routes, fares and frequencies between Europe and the US. The new freedom, known as 'open skies', would mark a prelude to global liberalization of air transport and would bring with it genuine competition and overwhelming benefits to travellers. The CAA estimated that UK travellers alone would save up to £250m a year. This long overdue open-skies deal liberated bmi to grab some of the lucrative transatlantic routes out of Heathrow that for so long had been beyond their grasp. The independent carrier could at last exploit their valuable landing and take-off slots.

In the event another more exciting opportunity took immediate precedence and slowed the impetus to take early advantage of the open-skies deal when it came into effect

The personalized in-flight entertainment system in the business cabin offers an extensive choice of films for viewing on 15-inch screens.

on 29 March 2008. bmi's European and American competitors could fight unhindered for a share of the transatlantic market from Heathrow. Several new carriers from both sides of the Atlantic jumped in, offering attractively priced business class travel, but rapidly crashed as profit margins dropped when fuel prices escalated beyond all reasonable expectations.

Flying to the rescue of BMed

In February 2007, bmi temporarily set aside transatlantic plans and fast-tracked their expansion into the mid-haul market from Heathrow with the acquisition of BMed, a franchise operator for British Airways.

With one clean stroke bmi moved from holding a single mid-range route to Moscow to adding 17 new destinations in 16 countries throughout Africa, the Middle East and Central Asia (the Commonwealth of Independent States).[216] These were niche markets for bmi with untapped opportunities for growth. Some were in countries with mature economies, such as Jordan and Turkey, and others lay in territories that would involve more challenging diplomacy – such as Azerbaijan, an oil and natural gas rich country, and Kazakhstan, a country with vast mineral resources and enormous economic potential covering a territory equivalent in size to the whole of western Europe. The

The new BMed routes included destinations as diverse as Aleppo, Almaty and Tehran.

acquisition of BMed, formerly British Mediterranean, led from the front by Nigel Turner and Tim Bye, was the perfect fit for bmi. The struggling franchisee had a fleet of eight Airbus aircraft, just like bmi's own, and operated out of Heathrow, the company's principal hub.[217]

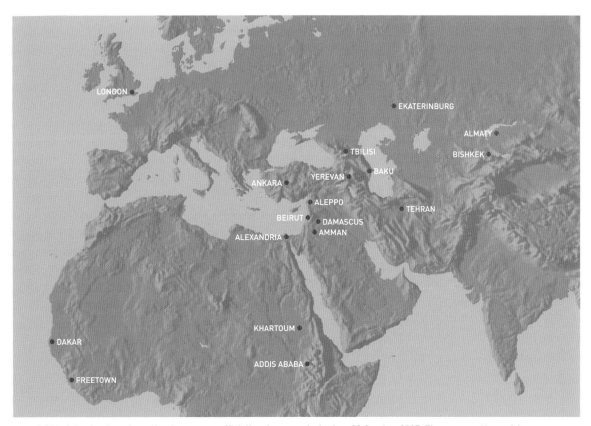

The 17 BMed destinations from Heathrow were officially taken over by bmi on 28 October 2007. The route to Alexandria was never added to the timetable as the company favoured and secured the licence to fly to Cairo instead.

Geoff Linaker is bmi's director of operations. He began his career with the company in 1979 as a Midlands Viscount pilot, rising steadily through the ranks to become chief pilot. He flew the airline's maiden Airbus A330 flight from Manchester to Washington DC on 10 May 2001. In 1990, Linaker moved into the management of the flight operation.

The story of BMed prior to the bmi takeover was typical of an independent airline struggling against world events and the might of its competitors. The airline was founded in 1994, by a group of private investors, and had flown under British Airways colours as a franchisee since 1997. Although at first glance it was secure, the carrier had been brought to the brink of collapse by soaring oil prices and the suspension of one of its most successful routes (Heathrow to Beirut) during the war in Lebanon (2006). Unfortunately BMed, who flew to some of the most unusual destinations on the planet, were never really big enough to uphold their extensive route network, so when the Syrian-born financier Wafic Said, whose family owned 49 per cent of the shares, withdrew his support, it was imperative to find a purchaser. Sir Michael Bishop stepped in with a rescue plan.[218] In true bmi spirit the airline would meet adversity by bringing top quality service and affordable prices to routes previously denied such treatment.

The bmi Hangar at Heathrow boasts 6,500 sq m of workshop space. It is seen here in May 2008 with Airbus A321-200 (G-MEDF) in for a routine check. This model, acquired from BMed in October 2007, wears a temporary bmi livery.

Nigel Turner with members of the crew on arrival at Cairo from Heathrow. The new code-share agreement between bmi and Egyptair was signed in November 2007.

During the summer of 2007 plans were speedily developed for the new mid-haul product while a dedicated project management team led by Tim Bye focused on integrating the BMed business into bmi's mainline operation with the minimum of fuss. Harmonizing all aspects of the operating procedures – IT systems, sales and marketing, facilities, engineering – and incorporating the ex-BMed workforce into one seamless community with the existing bmi staff, was a complicated matter. Nevertheless, it was handled with the utmost efficiency, on schedule and within budget.[219] The new product, developed for a new market, offered quality meals and drinks to the standards expected from bmi, with a touch of luxury for business customers, who would be served plated meals from a trolley. Passengers awaiting take-off to the exciting new destinations from Heathrow would enjoy the usual comforts associated with bmi's dedicated lounges.

Even before the first ex-BMed Airbus A321 (G-MEDL) had taken off for Baku in Azerbaijan on 28 October 2007, an understanding was signed with EgyptAir that led to another new route from Heathrow. The service was to Cairo, the Egyptian capital, a move that hastened the decision to abandon Heathrow–Alexandria, an ex-BMed route that never found its way into the bmi timetable. bmi's Heathrow to Cairo service was soon generating attractive competition and invigorated this previously limited market as customers now had choice. The other 16 ex-BMed routes out of Heathrow were positively welcomed by the travelling public, so much so that while five further Airbus A330s were sought, in a very tight supply market, two Boeing 757s were leased in the short term to increase capacity. In the spring of 2009 bmi will cease their transatlantic operation out of Manchester, releasing two A330 aircraft which will then operate from Heathrow to Cairo and Amman. Momentum for mid-haul growth out of the London hub remains paramount.

In September 2007 a further opportunity to fly to the Middle East was seized when an agreement was signed with the Israeli government to relax air travel controls between the two countries. Despite protests from the established carriers, bmi began their scheduled service to Tel Aviv on 14 March 2008. The airline offered fares to this popular holiday and business destination at lower prices than the competition. Within two months of introducing the new route passenger numbers had exceeded all expectations.

The launch of the Heathrow to Tel Aviv route on 14 March 2008 marked bmi's 19th medium-haul service out of the London hub.

To support network growth two Boeing 757-200s were introduced in the summer of 2008 on wet-leases from Astraeus Airlines. The interior space was reconfigured for bmi required 50 fewer seats with more generous leg room and superior business seats than the plane's previous operator. G-STRY is seen here wearing a temporary bmi livery introduced when BMed was acquired.

Artist's impression of bmi's 18 new check-in desks in Zone B of Heathrow's refurbished Terminal 1. This phased building work was completed in November 2008. A further eight premium desks will be operational by March 2009. The redesigned departure concourse will give bmi an even greater presence at one of the world's busiest airports.

The year 2007 marked another milestone in the history of bmi when for the first time total revenues exceeded £1 billion and the group carried just under ten million passengers. More than half of bmi's destinations from Heathrow belonged to the mid- and long-haul markets, a complete contrast from just ten years earlier when the whole of the airlines operation focused on short-haul domestic and European routes. A fresh advertising campaign in the autumn of 2008 will target the small but growing market place for bmi's wide and distinctive network of destinations in the long- and mid-haul market out of Heathrow.

Footnote

On 20 May 2008 the bmi group celebrated 70 years in the business of aviation, having grown to become a major player in every aspect of UK aviation with a scheduled network of 48 services to four continents and operating 11.3 per cent of take-off and landing slots at Heathrow. The airline had survived, while others had fallen by the way, having carved a niche in a fiercely competitive industry dominated by one of the most powerful flag carriers in the world. This remarkable success was due to the sheer determination of Sir Michael Bishop, together with his partners and colleagues, who for 25 years fought for open skies to give passengers choice. As oil prices continued to soar during the summer of 2008, pushing more and more carriers to the brink, bmi remained resilient.

On 29 October 2008, Lufthansa, partners of bmi since 1999, announced that they would be increasing their shareholding in the company to 80 per cent in early 2009. The future shape and direction of the bmi group lies in the capable hands of Lufthansa.

An artist's impression of the new T2 (working title Heathrow East), the first phase of which is scheduled to open in late 2013. bmi will operate its domestic and short-haul operation from the main terminal, T2A, and its mid- and long-haul flights from T2B. The new terminal will handle 20 million passengers per year and will be home to all STAR Alliance carriers operating out of Heathrow.

Air Schools Limited

1 Burnaston airfield was not large enough for use as a bomber airfield.
2 Captain Roy Harben was awarded the DFC for his services on the Western Front.
3 By the Treaty of Versailles (peace treaty signed in 1918 after the First World War) Germany was banned from military aviation.
4 Air displays at Hendon were discontinued in January 1938 as the airfield was too small for modern aircraft.
5 On 10 April 1940, the flying unit at Burnaston was renumbered and renamed as 16 Elementary Flying Training School (EFTS) under the control of 51 Group, Flying Training Command (Northern England). The word 'Reserve' was dropped in line with other flying schools. At this time Tiger Moths were phased out in favour of Miles Magisters.
6 When the Air Ministry decided to standardize training on the Miles Magister, the Tiger Moths were reallocated to 22 EFTS at Cambridge. By 1940, there were 50 Magisters at Burnaston. This number soon swelled to 108.
7 Burnaston House was built for Ashton Mosley. By 1881, the mansion had passed to his son Ashton Nicholas Every Mosley, who was a county magistrate and colonel with the 1st Derby Militia. During the First World War Burnaston House was used as a boarding school.
8 Burnaston Airport was officially opened by Sir Kingsley Wood MP, secretary of state for air, on Saturday 17 June 1939.
9 Information from the Air Schools Ltd Minute Book (Donington Hall archive).
10 To reflect the 'large strides' made by the company, Harben's salary increased to £5,000 in 1939 with an incentive bonus of £1,000.
11 A new company was set up in 1941 known as Wolverhampton Flying Schools Ltd (28 EFTS). Ron Paine was chief engineer.
12 N Roy Harben, *The Complete Flying Course: a Handbook for Instructors and Pupils*, 1939.
13 In 1947, the in-house fleet of Air Schools Ltd consisted of a three-seater Miles Monarch and four ex-airforce Austers. The Monarch was valued at £1,850 and the four Austers at £2,400.
14 The Korean War began on 25 June 1950 and ended with a stalemate and cease-fire on 27 July 1953. It was a war fought in Korea with large-scale participation by other countries including the UK. The war began with the invasion of capitalist South Korea by forces from communist North Korea.
15 In 1954, the company merged Derby Aviation and Wolverhampton Aviation into a single entity based at Burnaston bearing the Derby name.
16 Elstree Aerodrome offered a fleet of Chipmunks for *ab initio* instruction, full Link and classroom tuition, radio and signals training, messing facilities and conversion courses.

Derby Aviation

17 Burnaston Engineering handled the heavy engineering contracts and Midland Packaging dealt with the military equipment work.
18 C A B Wilcock OBE had previously been chairman of the Civil Aviation's Committee on Licensing, Recruitment and Training, and Labour MP for Derby North (1945–62).
19 Alan Roxburgh was the former commanding officer at Wolverhampton.

Commercial passengers

20 G-AILL was built in 1946 and acquired by Air Schools Ltd in 1947.
21 G-AJZJ was built in 1947 and acquired in 1948 for £2,830.
22 G-AIUK was purchased for £16,000, secured by an overdraft from Westminster Bank.
23 For the 1954 summer season a total of 4 Rapides were in service.

Scheduled services with DC-3s and Marathons

24 In 1957, Derby Aero Surveys acquired Photo Flight Ltd, an aerial photography business with contracts in Europe, West Africa and Britain.
25 G-AOGZ, formerly RAF KN628. This DC-3 was given the name *Darley Dale*.
26 By 1959, the company owned five DC-3s and three Marathons. Derby Aviation was the only UK-based airline to operate the Marathon.
27 The Rolls-Royce contract was for eight years with slowly diminishing passenger numbers.
28 These assignments both flew into Blackbushe Airport in Hampshire.

Derby Airways

29 Routes offered in 1959 were Birmingham, Bristol, Cambridge, Cardiff, Derby, Glasgow, Gloucester, Guernsey, Isle of Man, Jersey, Luton, Northampton, Ostend, Oxford and Swansea. New routes that began in 1960 were Belfast, Carlisle, Enniskillen, Gatwick, Manchester and Newcastle.
30 Minutes of Air Schools Ltd, 12 January 1960, held at 78 Buckingham Gate, London.
31 Air Schools Ltd assigned the lease of Burnaston Aerodrome to British Midland Airways in 1971.
32 Wing Commander Alan Roxburgh was promoted to become chairman of Derby Airways in January 1962.
33 With the grass surface at Burnaston rapidly deteriorating, the closely spaced wheels of the Marathons made them dangerous and technically unfit for purpose.
34 IATA was formed in April 1945 in Havana, Cuba.

Argonauts and a banking partner

35 The Canadair Argonaut was a pressurized DC-4 powered by Rolls-Royce Merlin engines.
36 Three Argonauts went into service (G-ALHY, G-ALHS, G-ALHG) and two were dismantled for spares (G-ALHN, G-ALHP).
37 The original geographical boundaries for the sales team were too loose. They were redefined in 1964 to ensure efficiency.
38 The advertising budget for 1964 was £9,500.
39 From Birmingham, Derby, Luton, Manchester, Cardiff and Bristol to destinations including Alicante, Barcelona, Genoa, Klagenfurt, Luxemburg, Nice, Palma, Perpignan, Tarbes and Venice.

Plans to leave Burnaston

40 The first section of the M1 motorway (Watford to Rugby) opened in 1959. The continuation from junction 18 towards Yorkshire was carried out in a series of extensions between 1965 and 1968.
41 Castle Donington Airport was built in 1942 as a bomber Operational Training Unit. The badly deteriorated airport was acquired in 1963, for £37,500. Planning permission for the new airport was granted in February 1964.
42 By 1968, passenger numbers at the new airport reached 250,000. In 1969, four years after opening, the runway at East Midlands Airport was extended to 7,480 feet to meet the needs and demands of increased freight traffic.
43 A turbo-prop engine has a gas turbine engine to drive the propeller.
44 The Herald failed to attract significant sales and contributed to the decline of Handley Page, which collapsed in late 1969.
45 In 1964 Derby Airways' scheduled services included: Derby to Belfast, Birmingham, the Channel Islands, Dublin, Glasgow via Leeds, the Isle of Man, Luxemburg, Newcastle and Ostend via Birmingham. They also flew from Cambridge, Luton and Staverton to the Channel Islands.

New name, new hub

46 An interim livery was used from October 1964 until such time as the whole fleet could be repainted.

47 The final aircraft to leave Burnaston was a Chipmunk (G-AOTX), flown by Tony Topps, on 20 July 1965. In 1989, the site of Burnaston Airport was redeveloped as a Toyota car assembly plant.

48 Although far superior to its predecessor, the new East Midlands Airport was by world standards technically poor. Financially the venue was not an instant success, so in less than a decade further investment was made to improve the facilities, accommodate a new generation of jet aircraft and meet the phenomenal growth in passenger numbers flying to and from the new East Midlands hub. In 1973 Cargo Terminal 2 was opened at East Midlands Airport. A second runway extension and terminal upgrade took place in the late 1970s.

The Vickers Viscount

49 The third Viscount (G-APNE) was another Series 831.

50 Vickers-Armstrong customized their Viscounts for the original purchaser.

51 Pilots were trained on one of two fleets made up of sub-types that were completely different. Fleet 1 included Viscount 833/831 variants and 760s. Fleet 2 comprised 815/814s, 785/755s and 702s. This ensured widespread knowledge of operating procedures and the position of switches on various models.

52 Memories of the Vickers Viscount from Geoff Linaker who joined the company as a pilot in 1979, eventually becoming director of operations.

53 In February 1969, a 700 Series Viscount (G-AODG) suffered a landing accident at Castle Donington, and in March that year an 800 Series (G-AVJA) over-ran the runway at Manchester whilst on a training flight. An additional four second-hand Viscounts were delivered in time for the summer season, bringing the total fleet to 11. The last DC-3 was sold to Air Envoy in March 1969.

Minster Assets on board

54 Frank Marshall, technical manager, was appointed to the board as joint managing director in 1975. He joined the company in 1940 as an apprentice engineer.

55 Invicta was a non-scheduled operator based at Manston in East Kent. They operated two passenger Viscount 755s and three Douglas Skymaster cargo planes.

56 British Aircraft Corporation and Eastlease Ltd.

57 Pan American World Airways, commonly known as Pan Am, was the principal international airline of the United States from the 1930s until its collapse in 1991. The collapse was due to a combination of corporate mismanagement and government indifference to protect its prime carrier following the 1988 bombing of Pan Am flight 103 above Lockerbie in Scotland.

58 British Midland Airways secured its CAB permit from President Nixon on 2 June 1970.

First routes from Heathrow

59 The original airfield on the site of Heathrow Airport was built for the military during the First World War. By the 1930s it was known as the Great Western Aerodrome and was privately owned by Fairey Aviation and used for aircraft assembly and testing. In 1943 the aerodrome came under the control of the Ministry of Air to be developed as a Royal Air Force transfer base. Construction of runways began in 1944 on land that was originally acquired from the vicar of Harmondsworth. The new airport was named after the hamlet Heath Row that was demolished to make way for the airport.

60 Autair reinvented themselves as a package holiday company called Court Line. They eventually collapsed in 1974.

61 The other unwanted route licences claimed by BMA were from Teesside to Jersey and the Isle of Man.

62 By 1978, the service operated four times daily during the week and twice on Saturdays and Sundays.

Moving into the jet age

63 The second and third BAC One-Elevens (G-AXLM and G-AXLN) were delivered in March 1970.

64 BMA's advertising copy on taking delivery of the first BAC One-Eleven.

65 With the arrival of the One-Eleven jets the outdated short-bodied 700-Series Viscounts were sold.

66 Tony Topps, chief engineer, worked for the company from 1949 to 1993.

67 The 1973 oil crisis began in October when members of the Organization of Arab Petroleum Exporting Countries announced that, as a result of the ongoing Yom Kippur War, they would no longer ship oil to nations (the US, its allies in Western Europe, and Japan) that had supported Israel in its conflict with Syria and Egypt.

68 The InterCity 125 was named for its speed of 125 mph (200 kph) between cities in the UK. By the summer of 1977 a full service was up and running and had replaced locomotive-hauled trains. By the early 1980s the 125 had caught the public's imagination as a means of fast travel.

69 The 1981–2 miners' strike was a defining moment in British industrial relations, and significantly weakened the British trades union movement.

70 In 1973, two of the One-Elevens went to TransBrasil (G-AXLL and G-AXLN) and the third went to Court Line (G-AXLM).

Instant Airlines

71 BMA's first experience of 'wet-leasing' was in 1968 with Viscounts for Ghana Airways and Nigeria Airways.

72 British planes had to comply with British standards even when away from home.

73 The Boeing 707-321s were powered by JT4A turbo-jets.

74 Boeings 707-373C (N370WA), 707-338C (G-BFLD and G-BFLE) and 707-324C (GAZJM) all had JT3D turbofans. In 1978, two modern ex-Qantas Series 338C fan-engined 707s replaced two of the older series 321 aircraft.

75 Boeing 707-321C (G-BMAZ).

76 Ron Hardy joined Derby Airways in 1958 as a captain's assistant. With a few short breaks he served the company until his retirement in 1997. Hardy progressed from chief pilot to manager of the Flight Training Centre at Whitwick. By his retirement he had flown in excess of 21,000 miles.

77 Terry Liddiard was manager of handling services and route facilities during this unprecedented operation.

78 Between 1974 and 1982, BMA's Boeing 707s and crews flew in the colours and on behalf of Air Algeria, Air Inter (France), Bangladesh Biman, Cyprus Airways, DETA Mozambique Airways, East African Airways, El Al, Gulf Air, Iraqi Airways, Kenya Airways, Kuwait Airways, Libyan Arab, Malaysian Airways, Nigerian Airways, Pakistan International (PIA), Somali Airways, Sudan Airways, Syrian Arab Airlines, Tunis Air and Zambian Airways.

Arrival of the DC-9

79 The company's pilots later had access to their own DC-9 simulator at High Wycombe. It was disposed of in 1998 with the demise of the DC-9 fleet.

80 UK certification of the DC-9s was undertaken by KLM at Amsterdam.

81 The last Douglas DC-9 jet in the BMA fleet made its final flight from East Midlands Airport on 10 April 1996.

A management buy-out

82 The first British credit card, Barclaycard, was introduced in 1966.

83 Stuart Balmforth joined the company in 1960, when it was still Derby Airways, as assistant to the chief accountant, Alan Felts. Balmforth was promoted to chief accountant when Felts left in 1964. John Wolfe joined BMA in 1965 from BOAC as charter manager. The company named the BBW Partnership Ltd was registered in 1987.

84 Dr Beauchamp raised the loan to Bishop, Balmforth and Wolfe (the BBW Partnership) from Lloyds Bank International. BMA secured an overdraft facility with Lloyds Manchester for £1m.

85 In the short term Dr Beauchamp's freight 707 was leased to Maverick Transport, a Canadian company, but when this faltered the aircraft was refitted with passenger seating and joined the BMA fleet.

86 For the BBW Partnership, Michael Bishop held 51 per cent; while Stuart Balmforth and John Wolfe held 24.5 per cent each.

Route swapping

87 In 1979, the Shah of Iran fled his country. Although the new regime under Ayatollah Khomeini resumed oil exports they were inconsistent and at a lower volume, forcing world oil prices to rise.

88 In 1978, BMA operated eight Boeing 707s, including two turbofan models (G-BFLD and G-BFLE).

89 In 1978, the company introduced a second-hand IBM375 computer to handle the 300,000 paper transactions each month that had become a logistical nightmare. Frank Cooper has been the manager of revenue accounting since 1975.

90 In 1972, BOAC and BEA were combined under the newly formed British Airways Board. The separate airlines came together as British Airways in 1974.

91 In 1982, British Midland took back the Birmingham–Brussels route when the national carrier abandoned it. Flights were flown twice daily with Fokker F27 turbo-prop aircraft.

92 The Heathrow–Leeds Bradford route was cause for particular satisfaction as passenger numbers showed marked increases.

Impact of recession

93 Shorts 330 (G-BJFK) was returned in April 1984. Between 1983 and 1986, nine new Shorts 360s were acquired outright and two others leased. Many were employed on the Manx and Loganair operations.

94 Pilot training on the Shorts 360 was air-borne.

95 G-BMAE and G-BMAS. These were the first two of a fleet of ten Dutch-built Fokker F-27s leased by British Midland.

96 BMA's last Vickers Viscount was sold to BAe in 1988.

The fight for domestic trunk routes

97 British Caledonian came into being in November 1970 when the Scottish charter airline Caledonian Airways took over British United Airways (BUA). With the takeover Caledonian were transformed into a major scheduled airline. A series of setbacks during the early 1980s led to increasing financial difficulties. The airline looked for a merger partner to improve their competitive position. British Airways emerged victorious in the ensuing bidding war and gained control of their competitor in December 1987.

98 British Midland's Gatwick to Belfast route, which had begun on 1 November 1974, ceased at the end of January 1984.

99 Over the next 13 years, British Midland won this award eight times (1983, 1984, 1986, 1989, 1990, 1993, 1994, 1997).

100 The routes out of Heathrow were Belfast, Birmingham, East Midlands, Edinburgh, Glasgow, Leeds/Bradford, Liverpool and Teesside. The East Midlands routes were Belfast, Glasgow, Guernsey and Jersey. The three continental destinations were Paris, Brussels and Amsterdam, flown from Belfast, Glasgow, East Midlands and Birmingham.

101 The Heathrow lounge opened in 1984. Further dedicated BMA lounges were opened at Glasgow, Edinburgh and Belfast airports in 1985.

102 Led by Max Hunt, sales executive, who in 1989 handled the promotion of the new route from Heathrow to Dublin.

Manx Airlines

103 The Viscount came from British Midland, the F-27s from Air UK.

104 The leases for the F-27s were transferred to Loganair at the end of 1982.

105 A similar Farecracker service was introduced between Liverpool and Belfast in 1987.

106 The fourth and final Viscount, an 836, arrived in November 1985. In 1986 a fourth Shorts 360 was delivered (G-WACK).

107 By 1991 the fleet consisted of one BAe 146, three ATPs and three Shorts 360s.

108 The new routes were to Paris, Brussels, Düsseldorf, Belfast, Dublin, Glasgow and Jersey.

109 Two new 16-seater Jetstream J31s turbo-props were added to the fleet to service the Cardiff network. The first 29-seater Jetstream J41 was introduced in 1993.

110 The new hubs were Glasgow, Belfast City, Liverpool, Manchester and East Midlands.

111 From 1993 to 1995, Manx operated British Midland's route from East Midlands to Belfast.

112 British Midland's partners, SAS and Lufthansa, withdrew from any involvement in Manx as a prerequisite for the BA franchise.

113 Net profits were recorded as £3 million in 1997.

114 In 1999, British Airways announced profits down by 50 per cent.

Loganair

115 When Manx absorbed the Loganair routes and fleet, significant cost savings were achieved by the amalgamation of resources at the airports they both served.

Winning the route to Amsterdam

116 The British Airports Authority was established in 1965 by a Labour government who sought Parliamentary control over airports. In 1966, the British Airports Authority assumed ownership and responsibility for Heathrow, Gatwick, Stansted and Prestwick airports. Between 1971 and 1975, they acquired Edinburgh, Aberdeen and Glasgow airports. In 1986, the Airports Act was passed, the Authority was dissolved and all its property, rights and liabilities were passed to a new company, BAA. In 1987, BAA was floated on the stock market with capital of £1,225 million.

117 British Caledonian (taken over by BA in 1987) was one of those hit by the new wording of the Traffic Distribution Rules in 1985.

118 A report by the European Commission (2004) suggested that airlines should be allowed to buy and sell their runway slots as they pleased like other assets, and show them in their balance sheets.

A new image with Diamond Service

119 Chris Ludlow was the partner responsible for the campaign.

120 Alex Grant was brought in to work alongside Colin Roberts, director of sales and marketing, a post he took over in 1982.

121 Before 1986 cabin crew were selected from the 21–35-year-old age group. The new Age Discrimination Act (October 2006) made it illegal to have an upper or lower age limit for job applicants.

122 The Heathrow to Liverpool route was taken over by British Midland from Manx Airlines in 1988.

123 G-BMAA was renamed *The Shah Diamond*, G-BMAH became *The Florentine Diamond*, G-BMAB became *The Great Mogul Diamond*, G-BMAG became *The Nassak Diamond*, G-BMAI became *The Star of Este Diamond*, G-BMAK became *The Stewart Diamond*, G-BMAM became *The Cullinan Diamond*, G-BMWD became *The Orloff Diamond* and G-PKBM became *The Tiffany Diamond*.

124 The National Accounts Team signed up important corporate customers including British Telecom, IBM, United Distillers, Marks & Spencer, American Express and Thomas Cook.

125 BAe were keen for a launch customer and offered British Midland a bargain price which included taking their remaining Viscounts in part exchange.

126 The ATP took 70 minutes to travel from Heathrow to Teesside compared with 55 minutes by DC-9 on the same route (British Midland timetable, March to October 1988).

Enter the Boeing 737

127 By 1988, virtually the whole of British Midland's fleet was cleared to Cat 11, meaning that it had autopilot flight systems and therefore had clearance to land in most bad weather. The Boeing 737 equipment was in line with Cat 111A, implying clearance to operate in conditions as severe as blinding fog.

128 Colin Roberts played a leading and effective role in co-ordinating the support.

129 Ron Hardy, chief pilot, was instrumental in getting the Whitwick Training Centre built.

A partnership with SAS Scandinavian Airlines

130 Austin Reid had previously worked for the Hertz Corporation as European vice president of finance. In 1990, he became managing director of Airlines of Britain Holdings and managing director of BMA. When Austin Reid joined the company, Stuart Balmforth relinquished all financial responsibilities in favour of corporate issues.

Open skies across Europe

131 The routes requested from Heathrow in 1988 were Brussels, Düsseldorf, Frankfurt, Geneva, Milan, Malaga, Nice, Paris, Rome, Zurich and Palma.

132 The first new 100-seater Fokker 100 jet (G-BVJA) was introduced in 1994. Over the next two years, another five Fokker 100s (range of 1,300 miles / 2.090 km) and three 79-seater Fokker 70s were acquired.

133 Before ACL was established, British Airways had control of slot handling at all major UK airports. ACL was set up to address this unsatisfactory arrangement.

134 In 1993, there were 490 inter-European routes. By 1997, this number had only risen to 520. Of these only 6 per cent were operated by three or more carriers.

135 Ryanair was founded in 1985 by Cathal and Declan Ryan, Tony Ryan, their father (who was the founder of Guinness Peat Aviation), and Liam Lonergan, an Irish businessman. The airline began with a 14-seater Embraer turbo-prop aircraft flying between Waterford and Gatwick with hopes of breaking the duopoly on London–Ireland flights held by British Airways and Aer Lingus. Today, Ryanair operates over 500 routes to 26 countries. easyJet was begun with two Boeing 737-200 aircraft, wet-leased from Independent Aviation Group Ltd. The airline was floated on the London Stock Exchange in October 2000.

Code-sharing

136 The term 'code' refers to the identifier used in flight schedules, generally the two-character IATA airline designator code and flight number. British Midland/bmi uses BD. Most major airlines today have code-sharing partnerships with other airlines, and code-sharing is a key feature of the major airline alliances.

137 Under a code-sharing agreement, the airline that actually operates the flight (the one providing the plane, the crew and the ground handling services) is called the operating carrier. The company or companies that sell tickets for that flight but do not actually operate it are called marketing carriers.

138 On flights operating between the UK and New York, San Francisco, Los Angeles and Tokyo.

139 On flights to Hong Kong.

140 On flights from Heathrow to Auckland and Sydney.

The airline for Europe

141 Heathrow to Nice was introduced in 1991; Heathrow to Bergen and Paris Orly, East Midlands to Brussels, and Glasgow to Copenhagen in 1994; Heathrow to Prague and Zurich, East Midlands to Malaga, Nice and Palma, and Edinburgh to Copenhagen in 1995; Leeds Bradford to Paris Orly, and East Midlands to Dublin and Aberdeen in 1996; Heathrow to Warsaw, East Midlands to Faro, and Leeds Bradford to Jersey in 1998; and Heathrow to Hanover, Stuttgart and Budapest, Edinburgh to Frankfurt, and East Midlands to Frankfurt in 1999.

142 The Diamond Pass ticket book, valid for domestic air travel, was introduced in 1994.

143 The second dedicated Diamond EuroClass lounge was opened at East Midlands Airport in 1995.

144 British Midland was the first airline to offer a vegetarian menu option on domestic services within the UK in 1992. The no-smoking policy was introduced in 1993.

145 The first Airbus service began on 6 April 1998 on the Belfast to Heathrow route. A second began on 26 April 1998 on the Dublin to Heathrow route.

146 In 1997, Sir John Egan, chief executive of the British Airports Authority, opened a new international Diamond Club lounge at Heathrow Terminal 1 and the first Diamond EuroClub lounge overseas was unveiled at Amsterdam airport. In 1998, a Diamond EuroClub lounge was opened at Manchester International Airport.

147 The first route served by the new Embraer was the Leeds Bradford to Paris Charles de Gaulle that began operating in June 1999.

148 The Pet Travel Scheme began in 2000 from Heathrow to Paris and Amsterdam for assistance dogs. Destinations for domestic pet travel later included Madrid, Brussels, Milan Linate, Palma, Alicante and Nice.

The Star Alliance and joint venture with Lufthansa

149 The founder members of the Star Alliance, formed in May 1997, were United Airlines, Lufthansa, Air Canada, Scandinavian Airlines and Thai International. Additional members have joined since then: All Nippon Airways and Air New Zealand in 1999, Singapore Airlines, bmi, Mexicana (ended 2004), and the Austrian Airlines group in 2000, Asiana Airlines, LOT Polish Airlines, and Spanair in 2001, US Airways in 2004, TAP Portugal in 2005, Swiss International Air Lines and South African Airways in 2006, Air China and Shanghai Airlines in 2007, Turkish Airlines and EgyptAir in 2008; Air India and Continental are scheduled to join in 2009.

150 The creation of the Star Alliance was a milestone in airline history and sparked the formation of rivals, notably SkyTeam and Oneworld.

151 BA, American Airlines and Cathay Pacific belonged to Oneworld. Air France and Delta Air Lines belonged to SkyTeam. Lufthansa, SAS, United Airlines, Air Canada and Thai International belonged to Star.

152 In November 1999 British Midland was unofficially valued at £457m.

153 Nigel Turner, Alex Grant and Tony Whitby were instrumental in dealing with the complex commercial decisions regarding BMA joining the Star Alliance. Tim Bye handled all the legal negotiations of both the shareholders agreement and the Joint Venture with Lufthansa and SAS.

154 In 2000, British Midland launched new services from London Heathrow to Rome, Madrid, Milan Malpensa and Barcelona. In 2001 Heathrow to Milan Linate was added.

155 British Midland began an East Midlands to Frankfurt route in November 1999.

156 Tim Bye joined British Midland from TNT Express Worldwide of The Netherlands in 1998.

Plans for a return to long-haul

157 British Midland was the first UK airline to choose the Trent 772B engine that was manufactured at the Rolls-Royce Derby plant.

158 The Boeing 737 flight simulator base at Whitwick was closed on 12 October 1998. The 737 simulator together with a new Airbus A320 model was installed in the new 4-cell training centre at Stockley Close. The simulators were made available to other airlines that had no such facility of their own.

159 The construction of a new building, T2, will replace Terminal 2 and The Queen's Building by 2013.

160 The new £4 million British Midland Centre, for reservations, reservations training and the administration of Diamond Club, was opened on 4 September 1998.

161 Aviance continues to handle the company's below-the-wing baggage handling. Menzies handles all the company's cargo loading, unloading and related security requirements.

162 As part of the de-merger, Lufthansa and SAS agreed to dispose of their interests in the Regional Airline Group.

British Midland Regional

163 Business Air's UK bases included Aberdeen, Edinburgh, Glasgow, Leeds, Manchester and East Midlands.

164 Wet-leases included not just the plane but the complete crew, maintenance support and insurance.

165 Previous shareholders in Business Air Ltd included Lufthansa and Crossair.

166 Services of British Midland Commuter in 1998 were East Midlands to Aberdeen, Belfast, Brussels and Dublin; Leeds Bradford to Glasgow; Manchester to Glasgow, Edinburgh, Dundee and Aberdeen; and Aberdeen to Esbjerg.

Resurrecting the transatlantic battle

167 The routes requested from Heathrow in 1998 were New York, Boston, Washington DC, Miami, Atlanta, Denver, Chicago, Houston, Seattle and Los Angeles.

168 The *Make the Air Fair* campaign was launched at the Labour party conference in Bournemouth.

169 In 1991, the return business fare from Heathrow to New York by British Airways, Virgin Atlantic, American Airlines and United Airlines was identical, at £3,244.

170 The reports and campaigns were produced by Ray Eglington of Four Communications Group.

171 Bob Ayling was appointed chief executive of British Airways in 1996, during a period of turbulence when increased competition, high oil prices and a strong GBP had badly damaged BA's profits. Bob Ayling was removed from office in March 2000.

172 In April 2002, Tempus 2000 in-flight tele-medicine technology was installed on all long-haul Airbuses. bmi made aviation history when a passenger had an electrocardiogram (heart trace) recorded in flight and transmitted by satellite to physicians in the US. The doctor on the ground gave instant advice to the cabin crew, who administered treatment. The passenger made a full recovery and travels with bmi to this day (2008).

173 The pre-2007 configuration on the Airbus A330 was 24 business seats, 48 business premium seats and 172 economy seats.

174 SAA used their wet-leased Airbus on routes from Johannesburg to Milan and Paris. The plane flew in SAA livery.

Rebranding an airline

175 John Morgan joined from BA as director of marketing, sales and reservations in July 1999. Tony Davis was promoted to director of industry and government affairs in November 1999.

176 James Hogan joined BM from Hertz as service director in 1997. He left due to personal reasons but returned in 1999 as chief operating officer for another two years.

177 Nigel Turner joined British Midland in 1987. He served on the board of the National Air Traffic Services (NATS) from 2001 to 2004 and rejoined the NATS board in 2008.

178 With the rebranding achieved James Hogan left in July 2001.

179 Landor Associates were a San Francisco-based consultancy. The creative director handling the British Midland account from London was Peter Knapp.

180 In 1997, Bob Ayling decided to drop BA's traditional Union Flag tail-fin livery in favour of Utopia World art tail-fins in an effort to change its image from a strictly British and aloof carrier to a more cosmopolitan airline. By 1999, about 170 aircraft had been repainted. The move was not a success and the process was halted.

181 Alex Grant was the managing director of bmi regional when these changes took place.

The impact of 9/11

182 SARS is believed to originate in bats and is then passed to humans either directly or indirectly through civet cats.

183 In 2003, services to and from China fell by 45 per cent, and from Hong Kong to Western Europe and the US by 36 per cent and 69 per cent respectively. Flights to and from the Middle East were down by only 1 per cent.

184 bmi's scheduled services to Washington DC and Chicago were suspended for four days from 11 September 2001.

185 In October 2001, bmi announced that 600 jobs would be lost across the company's entire network from a workforce of 5,500.

186 The cost of grounding four planes after 9/11, and for paying redundancy money to staff surplus to the company's immediate needs, represented £8.5m (43%) of this figure.

187 One of the more talented visionaries of the so-called no-frills operation was Michael O'Leary, chief executive of Ryanair from 1994.

bmibaby

188 The East Midlands to Brussels service was handed back to bmi regional in 2003.

189 By November 2000, Rod Eddington had decided that Go (who operated out of Stansted and Bristol) had become a liability for BA as they were draining the airline's core business. In June 2001 Go were the subject of a management buy-out. In May 2002, easyJet agreed to buy Go for £374 million to expand their own operations. By April 2003, the airlines operated as one under the easyJet brand.

190 Tony Davis was the first managing director of bmibaby. When he left the company the position was taken over by David Bryon (2002–5) and then Crawford Rix (since 2006).

191 In 2007, bmibaby sponsored TV weather with Central, Granada, HTV Wales, Ulster and Jersey.

192 Two other bases, Teesside (2004–6) and Gatwick (2004–5), were tried but were not successful and promptly suspended.

193 In 2008, the bmibaby fleet consisted of 15 148-seat Boeing 737-300s and 5 131-seat Boeing 737-500s.

Climbing back

194 The increased airport charges imposed by the BAA came into effect in February 2003.

195 Below-wing activity was out-sourced to Aviance. Above-wing services were still operated by bmi uniformed staff under Andy Cookson, the director of ground services.

196 The value of the two simulators was £14 million.

197 The REVERA system was provided by Kale Consultants of Mumbai. In 2006, it was operated by 100 staff in India and 35 at Castle Donington.

198 The bmi long-haul service won 3rd place in the category *Best Inflight Video Programming* by the World Airline Entertainment Association in 2003, ahead of British Airways.

199 Manchester to Las Vegas was a year-round thrice-weekly service. The inaugural flight from Manchester to Las Vegas was on 31 October 2004. Weekly flights from Manchester to Antigua began on 27 November 2004. Twice-weekly flights from Manchester to Barbados began on 26 November 2004. The St Lucia service was not popular and folded after 6 months.

200 When the Heathrow to Mumbai route commenced in May 2005 it was allocated the A330 previously serving the Manchester to Washington route. A Boeing 757 was leased from Icelandic Air to service the Washington operation. The Manchester to Washington DC service was suspended on 30 October 2005.

201 In 2007, the turnover of bmi's charter operation exceeded £50 million.

202 Pre-tax loses in 2003 were £9.8m.

203 With stricter excess baggage controls, bmi increased its revenue from £30,000 to £100,000 per month.

204 'Food to go' was introduced for business and economy passengers on domestic and European flights from Heathrow in December 2002.

205 In 2000, bmi carried 6.7 million passengers. In 2002, they carried 7.5 million.

The New Business Model

206 By 2004, bmi offered self-service check-in machines at Heathrow, Edinburgh, Glasgow, Manchester, Belfast City and Leeds Bradford. By 2008, 65 per cent of customers were checking in on-line or at the self-serve machines at the airport, leaving just 35 per cent who still preferred to go to the check-in desk.

207 Heathrow to Milan and Madrid in March 2006, Heathrow to Paris in 2007.

208 Henceforth Gold, Silver and Blue-plus cardholders received free food once again.

bmi regional

209 Aberdeen–Norwich and East Midlands–Brussels (2003), Manchester–Norwich, Aberdeen–Groningen and Leeds Bradford–London City Airport (2004), Aberdeen–Amsterdam and Southampton–Amsterdam (2006).

210 In 2007, bmi regional added to its network of scheduled services Aberdeen–Brussels, Edinburgh–Brussels and Zurich, Leeds Bradford–Copenhagen and Lille, Manchester–Lyons and Aberdeen– Kristiansand (Norwegian centre for oil and gas engineering).

211 The parent airline bmi also kept its crown as the UK's most punctual airline out of Heathrow, 15 places ahead of its rival British Airways and 23 places ahead of Virgin Atlantic (2007).

Mid- and long-haul out of Heathrow

212 It took the European Commission three years before an agreement on open skies was made in May 2007.

213 This licence was granted as part of an agreement (2003) with the Hong Kong authorities to allow Virgin Atlantic the right to fly to Australia.

214 One extra flight from Gatwick to Moscow on 19 May and two from Manchester on the day of the match. Manchester United beat Chelsea in the penalty shoot-out.

215 Dominic Paul joined as director of airport services previously from Go, and Peter Spencer as managing director of bmi mainline from Qatar Airways. Robert Palmer joined as chief financial officer from easyJet.

Flying to the rescue of BMed

216 BMed's routes from Heathrow were to Khartoum in Sudan, to Dakar in Senegal, Freetown in Sierra Leone, Amman in Jordan, Damascus and Aleppo in Syria, Beirut in Lebanon, Ankara in Turkey, Baku in Azerbaijan, Tehran in Iran, Tbilisi in Georgia, Bishkek in Kyrgystan, Yerevan in Armenia, Addis Ababa in Ethiopia, Alexandria in Egypt, Ekaterinburg in the Russian Federation and Almaty in Kazakhstan.

217 BMed owned three A320s and five A321s when they were taken over by bmi in 2007. The BA franchisee were committed to the purchase of five further A321s with an option for five more. As part of the deal bmi took over BMed's order book.

218 Most of BMed's 770 employees were absorbed by bmi.

219 The integration met all CAA requirements and was completed by 28 October 2007, as planned.

Introduction

The fine country seats of our ancient families are important examples of England's heritage. There are country houses more palatial than Donington Hall and parklands more extensive and formal, but nowhere is there a more idyllic setting.

Donington Hall stands in Donington Park, in a verdant landscaped clearing at the point where three small valleys converge. To the west is a surviving thicket of the ancient deer forest and beyond is Donington Cliff, a densely wooded escarpment overhanging the banks of the River Trent. Upstream, a short distance towards the north, are the rustic remains of the medieval water-wheels of Kings Mills and Donington Cliff, a wild and romantic place with its projecting crag and hanging woods. To the east gently undulating hills rise and fall, and beyond is the village of Castle Donington. To the south stretch open expanses of lawns where cattle and deer wander freely amidst a scattering of aged oaks. Between the expanses of grass is the avenue drive from the Coppice Lodge entrance, which is now part of the Donington Park race-track.

For virtually four hundred years the Donington Park Estate, with its three manorial houses all built on the site of the present Donington Hall, has been the symbolic heart of the Hastings family. Today Donington Hall is the pride of bmi.

Early days

The origins of the park will probably always remain obscure though evidence suggests that there were deer roaming freely hereabouts in Roman times. In 1086, the beautiful domain of Donington (Dunitone) Park was mentioned in the Doomsday Book as a wood, twelve furlongs long and eight broad. During the Middle Ages the park was still thickly forested. Ancient documents reveal that it was a source of brushwood for fuel, a place to hunt wild game and a home for farmed animals such as cattle and pigs. The whole estate was enclosed by a hedge and maintained by a park-keeper who was responsible for the welfare of the stock and the laying in of winter feed.

From the 11th century onwards, the ownership of Donington Park passed by marriage from the Barons of Haulton to the Dukes of Lancaster and then to the Earls of Kent. By the 15th century, it had reverted to the Crown and was extended by the enclosure of Shortwode, an area of common grazing. By the later part of the following century the Donington Park Estate had been gifted by Elizabeth I to Robert Devereux, 2nd Earl of Essex, the military hero and royal favourite. With little need of more property the Earl of Essex decided in 1595 to sell Donington Park, together with its mills and fishery, to George Hastings, 4th Earl of Huntingdon, whose family were well established in Leicestershire, having owned extensive estates there for many generations. Four years later Essex was executed for defying his Queen and leading a disastrous campaign against Irish rebels in the Nine Years' War.

William Hastings, 1st Baron Hastings of Ashby de la Zouch (1431–1483)

Sir William Hastings was one of the great powers of the English realm during the mid-15th century when his second cousin, Edward IV, held the throne. In 1461, Sir William was appointed Lord Chamberlain and granted the stewardship of the Manor of Castle Donington, amongst other extensive lands in the Midlands, as a reward for his bravery on the battlefield. When Edward IV died in 1483,

Lord Hastings was arrested by the fearful late King's brother, Richard, Duke of Gloucester, and executed on Tower Hill on a trumped-up charge of treason. Lord Hastings' Leicestershire estates were automatically confiscated, though at a later date they were reinstated to his heirs.

By the mid-16th century, the Hastings' landed estates and titles had passed to George Hastings, 3rd Baron Hastings, 5th Baron Hungerford, 6th Baron Botreaux and 4th Baron de Moleyns (d. 1544). George Hastings was married to Anne Stafford, a descendant of the house of Plantagenet, but to her husband's great displeasure she had an affair with King Henry VIII in 1510. Hastings was so enraged that he banished his unfaithful wife to a convent. In 1529, however, George Hastings had no misgivings on graciously accepting an earldom from his monarch to add to his inherited credentials, a gesture of compensation for the indiscretion.

Henry Hastings, 3rd Earl of Huntingdon (1535–95), is remembered as a model Renaissance gentleman.

Francis Hastings (1514–61) was the eldest son and heir of the 1st Earl of Huntingdon. He was born and grew up at Ashby de la Zouch, and was married to Catherine Pole, daughter of Henry Pole, 1st Baron Montague, who bore him 11 children. At the coronation of Edward VI, in 1547, Francis Hastings, 2nd Earl of Huntingdon, took a prominent part in the jousting competition staged in celebration of the event. In 1553, Francis Hastings' eldest son, Henry Hastings, married Catherine Dudley, daughter of John Dudley, 1st Duke of Northumberland. Francis and Catherine Hastings had no issue.

Henry Hastings, 3rd Earl of Huntingdon (1535–95), was a younger brother of the 2nd Earl and is remembered as a model Renaissance gentleman. He was custodian of Mary, Queen of Scots, and also served as President of the Council of the North. He was politically competent and rose steadily through the ranks though unfortunately Queen Elizabeth mistrusted him, so some honours remained beyond his grasp. The 3rd Earl of Huntingdon neglected his inherited Leicestershire estates and died on the brink of bankruptcy. Being childless, he was succeeded by his brother, George Hastings, who considered himself to be 'the poorest Earl that her majesty hath in her kingdom'.

George Hastings, 4th Earl of Huntingdon (1540–1604)

George Hastings, 4th Earl of Huntingdon, was married to Dorothy Port and fathered five children. Like his father before him George Hastings served his county as representative for Derbyshire and Leicestershire in the House of Commons, and as Lord-Lieutenant of Rutland and Leicestershire. On inheriting the earldom and the mortgaged family estates in the Midlands, George Hastings, 4th Earl of Huntingdon, began immediately to deal with his reduced circumstances by rashly acquiring property. When Robert Devereux, 2nd Earl of Essex (1566–1601), decided to sell his Donington Park Estate in 1595, the 4th Earl of Huntingdon seized the opportunity with an offer of £3,000. This delightful 400-acre rural property lay westwards of the village of Castle Donington, a manor held by the Hastings family since 1461.

The 4th Earl of Huntingdon built the first Donington Park Manor House in the mid-1460s. It was built as a home for his widowed daughter-in-law, Lady Sarah Hastings née Harrington, and her four surviving sons. The tranquillity of Donington with its rolling hills and magnificent oaks was a welcome refuge for the 4th Earl's grandsons, who had tragically lost their father, Lord Francis Hastings (1571–95). The new Manor House was a substantial stone building constructed with materials from the remains of the old castle that overlooked the village of Castle Donington. The dwelling was a comfortable, well-lit Tudor-style residence with a profusion of steeply pitched roofs and numerous tall banks of chimneys. The building of this substantial house marked the transformation from medieval deer park to a working estate with a noble family in full-time residence.

George Hastings, 4th Earl Huntingdon (1540–1604) with his son Francis, 1565. The 4th Earl struggled with debt and was forced to forfeit many of his inherited properties. A magnificent stained glass window from the Hastings Chapel at Stoke Poges, an estate the 4th Earl was forced to sell in 1598, was saved and brought to Donington Hall two centuries later.

Henry Hastings (1586–1643), nobleman and literary patron, was the grandson and heir of the 4th Earl of Huntingdon. In 1601, Henry Hastings was married to Lady Elizabeth Stanley (1588–1633), the third and youngest daughter of Ferdinando Stanley, 5th Earl of Derby, and Lady Alice Spencer, his wife, who at one time was third in line to succeed to the throne of England. The union was judged by contemporaries to be a love-match and brought rejoicing at Donington Park. The young couple had only just begun their family when Henry Hastings succeeded to the title as 5th Earl of Huntingdon, and they had to move to the family seat at Ashby de la Zouch Castle. Their household there would have supported at least 50 individuals with little privacy for the family, which soon amounted to five children. Countess Elizabeth is known to have entertained elaborately at Ashby Castle with enormous feasts and masques, extravagant 17th-century entertainments. Whenever social etiquette allowed, Henry Hastings, 5th Earl of Huntingdon, returned to Donington Park, his childhood home. In 1610, Countess Elizabeth wrote to her husband from Ashby Castle:

Deare Sweet Hearte, ... I return to Don[ington] tomorrow or next day with companey and the need to suplye the rooms. ... As soon as I have supte, God willing I will to bed; and wishe you ther, and in my owne bed agayne, with as much ease as I use to walke betweene my little cabin and yours.

Ferdinando Hastings, 6th Earl of Huntingdon (1608–1655)

Ferdinando Hastings was the eldest son of the 5th Earl and Countess Elizabeth. He is remembered as a less than amicable child and a precocious youth who grew up to be a coward in the face of adversity, a characteristic quite alien to the Hastings family. In 1623, at the age of 15, Ferdinando Hastings was married to Lucy, daughter and sole heiress of Sir John Davies. The couple, on account of their youth, were separated for a few years until a suitable household had been set up for them at Donington Park.

In 1643, Ferdinando Hastings succeeded to the title as 6th Earl of Huntingdon, and as tradition demanded he returned with Countess Lucy and their family to live at Ashby Castle. During the English Civil War, Ferdinando Hastings claimed neutrality when the hostilities reached the Midlands, despite the fact that the Hastings family were known to be staunch Royalists. His late father, the 5th Earl of Huntingdon, had supported King Charles until his dying breath. In 1642, his brother, Lord Henry Hastings (1610–66), had fought at the battle of Edgehill and three years later had courageously taken the King to Ashby Castle after the disastrous battle of Naseby. This led to Lord Henry Hastings' banishment from the kingdom by Oliver Cromwell. Despite proclaiming impartiality, Ferdinando Hastings, 6th Earl of Huntingdon, had his Irish estates confiscated by Parliament after the downfall of Charles I. Ashby Castle, the Hastings family home for generations, was attacked and irretrievably damaged, and finally surrendered to Cromwell's forces. The 6th Earl of Huntingdon was forced to retreat to Donington Park Manor House, the home that promptly became the official residence of the Hastings family in the mid-17th century.

Henry Hastings, 5th Earl of Huntingdon (1586–1643), by Wenceslaus Hollar. The 5th Earl inherited the title from his grandfather in 1604 following the premature death of his father, Francis Hastings, in 1595.

The late 1640s were a sad time at Donington Park as one by one nearly all of Earl Ferdinando and Countess Lucy's children died. Lord Henry Hastings, the eldest son and heir, fell victim to smallpox at the age of 19 on the eve of his wedding. His intended future father-in-law, the eminent physician Sir Theodore de Mayerne (1573–1655), did all he could to save the young man, but in vain. The untimely death of this talented nobleman, already known for his sweet disposition, polished manners and proficiency in literature, caused great sorrow.

In 1650, a new heir, Theophilus Hastings, was born to the 6th Earl of Huntingdon and Countess Lucy. However, as family life was just beginning to re-establish itself at Donington Park Manor House, the economic stability of the Hastings family was once again shattered when, as the result of crippling debts, Earl Ferdinando was forced to exchange his spacious house and wooded park for the company of criminals and debtors in the Fleet prison. An Act of Parliament (1653) provided the means by which he managed to pay off his debts and secure his freedom, but the harrowing experience pushed Ferdinando Hastings to an early grave. He died shortly after returning to Donington Park, at the age of 47, in 1655. His only surviving son, the 4-year-old Theophilus Hastings, inherited the earldom of Huntingdon and what remained of the family estates.

Theophilus Hastings, 7th Earl of Huntingdon (1650–1701)

Theophilus Hastings, 7th Earl of Huntingdon, grew up at Donington Park and chose the path of a politician. He was summoned to Parliament during the reign of Charles II, to whom he had little loyalty, and continued his political career under James II, to whom he was fervently committed, an allegiance that later cost him a short spell in the Tower. Earl Theophilus was married twice, firstly

Theophilus Hastings, 7th Earl of Huntingdon (1650–1701), mezzotint of a portrait by Kneller. The 7th Earl of Huntingdon was rewarded generously for his support of King James II, the last Roman Catholic monarch of Great Britain.

in 1671 to Elizabeth Lewis and secondly in 1690 to Mary Fowler. He fathered 15 children, mostly daughters, several of whom earned themselves a permanent place in English history.

Elizabeth Hastings (1682–1739), Earl Theophilus' second daughter by his first wife, is particularly remembered. Her beauty, youth, grace and benevolence were celebrated by William Congreve (1637–1708), English playwright and poet, who referred to her as the divine Aspasia. She never married, and devoted her life to philanthropic deeds and religion. Her half-sisters, the Ladies Anne, Frances and Margaret Hastings, daughters of the 7th Earl's second wife, are also remembered for their religious humility and good deeds. The four sisters lived together at Ledstone Hall near Pontefract, the Fowler ancestral home.

George Hastings, son of Countess Elizabeth, inherited the earldom from his father in 1701. The 8th Earl of Huntingdon lived long enough to carry the sceptre at the coronation of Queen Anne but died in 1704 at the age of 9. The title and family lands passed to his half-brother, Theophilus Hastings, the son of Countess Mary, the 7th Earl's second wife.

Theophilus Hastings, 9th Earl of Huntingdon (1696–1746)

Theophilus Hastings inherited the title of 9th Earl of Huntingdon from his half-brother, Earl George, when he was 8 years of age. Theophilus played one small role in public life when he was invited to carry the Sword of State at the coronation of King George II in 1727.

In 1728, Earl Theophilus Hastings was married to Selina, second daughter of Washington, 2nd Earl Ferres, of Staunton Harold near Ashby de la Zouch. Within eight years, Countess Selina had given birth to seven children. Sadly four of these died in childhood and a fifth, a daughter named after her mother, died at the age of 26. Lady Elizabeth Hastings (1731–1808) was the only child to outlive her parents. Apart from a tendency to breed excessively, or probably because of it, Countess Selina was a very religious woman. When her husband's illustrious half-sister, Lady Elizabeth

Hastings, died in 1739, the Countess was delighted when he invited her companions, his full sisters the Ladies Anne, Frances and Margaret Hastings, to live with them at Donington Park Manor House. All four women were devout Methodists, involving themselves in personal holiness and religious devotion. Their behaviour was somewhat incompatible with the family's social standing.

Theophilus Hastings, 9th Earl of Huntingdon, was a private man, often aloof but known for his politeness and courtesy. Unlike other members of the Hastings family, he was reluctant to take part in national affairs, preferring to spend time with his family at Donington Park. He was never robust

and died of apoplexy at the age of 50 in 1746. Years later Countess Selina recalled a nightmare he had only weeks before his demise when death in the form of a skeleton appeared at the foot of the bed, crept under the bedclothes and lay motionless between him and his lady – a chilling premonition.

The 9th Earl of Huntingdon's widow, Countess Selina, is remembered as a leading Methodist. She had a more exacting and lofty concept of duty than her husband and a vigorous determination in everything she did. For the remainder of her life Countess Selina devoted her time and fortune to promoting what she proclaimed as the new light in religion. She was the patroness of impoverished Methodist ministers and invested thousands of pounds in the foundation of the Countess of Huntingdon's Connection. Her commitment and fervent beliefs led her to sell most of the family jewels to build chapels throughout the country. John Wesley (1703–91), George Whitefield (1714–70) and other Methodist leaders were frequent visitors to Donington Park Manor House, which became not only a family home but also a meeting place for religious dissenters who did not conform to the established church.

Francis Hastings (1729–89) inherited his father's title and became 10th Earl of Huntingdon at the age of 17. His failure to produce a legitimate heir left the question of the title unresolved. During the later years of her life Countess Selina, distressed at the thought of the peerage passing out of the immediate family line, commissioned a local solicitor to look into the matter. His efforts traced the line back to the Lutterworth branch of the family, descended from Sir Edward Hastings, a younger son of the 2nd Earl of Huntingdon. Through descent the line had passed to a young man called Colonel George Hastings, who had grown up at Donington Park Manor House with his distant cousins.

As a young adult Colonel George had fallen in love with his childhood sweetheart Selina Hastings, a younger daughter of Earl Theophilus and Countess Selina. The proposed marriage would have

Theophilus Hastings, 9th Earl of Huntingdon, unfinished mezzotint by John Faber, after a portrait by Sir Godfrey Kneller, 1735.

The 9th Earl of Huntingdon and Countess Selina with their children Henry and Selina, early 1740s. Portrait by the Italian painter Andrea Soldi, who came to England in 1735.

secured the Huntingdon peerage and kept the Hastings family estates intact, but tragically the bride collapsed and died on the eve of her wedding in May 1763. Colonel George Hastings left Donington Park heart-broken. A lapse of six years softened the shock, and he cultivated another relationship and married. His legal claim to the title of Earl of Huntingdon was abandoned for lack of money.

Francis Hastings, 10th Earl of Huntingdon (1729–1789)

Francis Hastings, 10th Earl of Huntingdon, was born and grew up at Donington Park Manor House. In keeping with his social standing his education was rounded off with a Grand Tour to the continent, where he fathered a son by a Parisian girl in 1747. On his return to England the 10th Earl of Huntingdon followed a successful career in politics and was even appointed Master of the Horse to the Royal Household, in 1760. The following year, Earl Francis was a Bearer of the Sword at the coronation of George III and took up the prestigious post of Lord of the Bedchamber, an honour he retained for nine years. In 1762, the 10th Earl made a terrible blunder when he incorrectly announced to the King that his first-born child (Prince George) was a girl.

One of the more pressing domestic tasks the 10th Earl of Huntingdon set himself was to refurbish his family home. By the 1750s, the home in which he had grown up was in such a dilapidated state that, according to a contemporary story, two maids in the house were nibbled in their sleep by rats. In the Age of Enlightenment he wanted to shake off medievalism and create a home of greater personal comfort with handsome formal rooms for entertaining, where privacy was respected and servants were invisible. Although it would have been desirable to rebuild from scratch, the choice was made to extend the original house. Builders and craftsmen were employed to construct two formal new classical-style Georgian wings to the north and south of the existing property and a detached kitchen to keep smells away from the main house. A bowling green and large walled kitchen garden would complete the mid-18th-century improvements at Donington Park Manor House.

The works were well underway before the 10th Earl of Huntingdon departed on one of his prolonged European sojourns. Strict instructions were finalized regarding the style of improvements, but with the master away his forceful mother, Countess Selina, became involved. On his return Earl Francis was devastated at the Gothic changes she had made to his classical

Francis Hastings, 10th Earl of Huntingdon (1729–89) by Sir Joshua Reynolds. He amused himself with women but never married. His affair with Louise Lany, a leading dancer at the Paris Opera, produced a son, Charles, born in 1752. The 10th Earl later acknowledged his illegitimate son and secured him a position but cruelly neglected his mistress.

design and the excessive bills she had run up. He wrote in distress to his sister, Lady Elizabeth Hastings, who had recently married John Rawdon, 1st Earl of Moira, that he would pay another £500 to have the house back to what it had been before the building works had begun. The extensions left a large rambling mansion in an eclectic mix of styles with a casual juxtaposition of shapes and an untidy roofscape.

Francis Hastings, 10th Earl of Huntingdon, led a full and productive life but with his wandering spirit he was not suited to a long-term commitment to marriage. With no legitimate heir to inherit his vast Hastings estates across the Midlands he chose his nephew and namesake, Francis Rawdon, the son of his sister Countess Elizabeth, as his heir. The 10th Earl of Huntingdon died suddenly while eating his dinner, at the age of 61. With his death the earldom of Huntingdon fell dormant while his wealth passed, as planned, to his nephew Francis Rawdon.

The Dowager Countess Selina (1707–91) by John Russell RA. Countess Selina was widowed at the age of 39 and to the displeasure of her family dedicated the remainder of her life to the promotion of Methodism. Countess Selina left her property and wealth to the 64 chapels she had established during her lifetime.

The Huntingdon earldom

The predicament of the dormant Huntingdon earldom lay unresolved for 30 years. In October 1816, a fresh search into the claim for the title was instigated when Captain Hans Francis Hastings, an army storekeeper, asked his young lawyer friend, Henry Nugent Bell, to look into the matter. Bell re-established the legality of the declaration made by Theophilus Hastings, 9th Earl of Huntingdon,

whereby in default of his issue the line of Sir Edward Hastings of Lutterworth, the younger son of the 2nd Earl of Huntingdon, inherited the earldom. Since the mid-16th century the line had passed down the generations, arriving by the early 19th century at the Rev. Theophilus Henry Hastings. When he died, without issue, his nephew Captain Hans Francis Hastings would inherit. The young Captain was the son of the late Colonel George Hastings, the man who gave up his claim due to lack of funds back in 1763.

Hans Francis Hastings claimed the earldom of Huntingdon in 1816, nearly 30 years after the death of Francis, the 10th Earl, who died without a legitimate heir in 1789. As the 11th Earl of Huntingdon, Hans Francis Hastings took up his seat in the House of Lords in 1819. He served as Governor of Jamaica from 1822 to 1824. The title has passed from father to son ever since. Francis John Clarence Plantagenet Hastings, 16th Earl of Huntingdon (1901–90) was an artist, academic and Labour politician. He died without male issue and was succeeded by the present holder, his distant cousin, William Edward Robin Hood Hastings Bass (b.1948) who took the additional name of Bass from his father-in-law, the racehorse owner Sir William Bass.

The succession of a poor tradesman to one of the ancient peerages in the kingdom was cause for great excitement and celebration at Castle Donington. When Captain Hans Francis Hastings visited Leicestershire, cheering crowds and peals of bells met the newly created 11th Earl of Huntingdon. A cavalcade of more than a hundred men followed his carriage on horseback. The new Earl's fourth son, born at the height of the excitement, was christened Edward Plantagenet Robin Hood Hastings.

DONINGTON PARK HALL.

Donington Park Manor House shortly before its demolition in 1790: 'A seat of nobility that merited no encomium.'

Despite having successfully claimed the title, the 11th Earl of Huntingdon was unable to recover the Hastings family estates or settle in the ancestral seat at Donington Park. Once the euphoria had died down the bond of mutual obligation which existed between the people of Castle Donington and Francis Rawdon-Hastings (by then created the 1st Marquis of Hastings) was reassessed. Donington Hall was his home and for economic as well as personal reasons his tenants would never desert him.

Francis Rawdon-Hastings, 2nd Earl of Moira and 1st Marquis of Hastings (1754–1826)

Francis Rawdon was the eldest son of Countess Elizabeth and her Irish husband, John Rawdon, 1st Earl of Moira, and the grandson of Theophilus Hastings, 9th Earl of Huntingdon. The young heir was a good-tempered young man and expert shot, taking after his mother, Countess Elizabeth, a noble lady with a well-cultivated mind, and his grandmother, the formidable Countess Selina.

Francis Rawdon spent his childhood in Ireland with frequent summer visits to his uncle Francis Hastings, 10th Earl of Huntingdon, at Donington Park in Leicestershire. He was educated at Harrow and Oxford, though never completed his degree, to the disappointment of his family. In 1771, at the age of 17, he joined the army as a lieutenant in the 5th Foot and shortly afterwards set sail with his regiment across the Atlantic to fight in the American War of Independence. Lieutenant Rawdon saw action at the battles of Bunker Hill, Brooklyn and White Plains, and took part in attacks on Fort Washington, Clinton and Charlestown. His engagement with the enemy was fearless and he returned home without injury and 'no more than two bullets through his cap'.

On his return to England Francis Rawdon was elected to Parliament and soon made a name for himself by quarrelling with Prime Minister William Pitt the Younger, joining the opposition and frequently speaking against the government. Like a true Irishman he was not averse to a good fight. He acted as second to the Duke of York in a duel with Lieutenant Colonel Lennox on Wimbledon Common in 1789.

Francis Rawdon became master of the Donington Park Estate in 1789, following the death of his uncle, Francis Hastings, 10th Earl of Huntingdon. Out of respect for his benefactor he immediately changed his name to Francis Rawdon-Hastings. From his father, John Rawdon, 1st Earl of Moira (1720–93), Francis Rawdon-Hastings inherited an Irish title but few desirable personal qualities.

Rebuilding Donington Park Manor House as Donington Hall

In 1790, a traveller named Throsby visited Donington Park Manor House and wrote enthusiastically about the many treasures hanging on the walls and decorating the mantelpieces. In the dining room were portraits of the Earl of Pembroke; Francis Hastings, 2nd Earl of Huntingdon; Henry Hastings, 3rd Earl of Huntingdon; Lady Dudley; George Hastings, 4th Earl of Huntingdon by Kneller; Lord Cornwallis by Gainsborough; and Theophilus Hastings, 9th Earl of Huntingdon, often compared to the ghost of Hamlet. The hall was a low room, formerly a chapel, and in it was a marble bust of Cromwell by Wittan and another of Peter the Great, thought to be a good likeness. In the library were two Dutch battle pieces of some merit, a small seascape and some religious figures on wainscot panels taken from Ashby de la Zouch castle. The most impressive picture in the Library was *King Solomon and the Queen of Sheba*. In the gallery hung a portrait of Theophilus Hastings, 7th Earl of

Huntingdon, and another of Lord Rawdon by Gainsborough, who was married to Elizabeth Hastings, the 10th Earl of Huntingdon's sister. In the butler's room were to be found some fine old miniature paintings preserved in a small chest.

Soon after Throsby's departure Francis Rawdon-Hastings inherited his late father's title and wealth. Even before this expected legacy he had decided to rebuild Donington Park Manor House in memory of his uncle, his foremost benefactor. The new mansion would be 'on a large and liberal scale' reflecting Rawdon-Hastings' social standing and personal architectural taste. In the spring of 1790, Humphrey Repton, the renowned landscape gardener, was invited to Donington Park. It was

agreed that he would produce ideas for a revised layout to the park and liaise with established local architects who would produce plans for the new mansion. The first set of drawings were considered inappropriate, so on Repton's rec-ommendation William Wilkins, then a virtually unknown architect with just one mausoleum to his name, was asked to prepare alternative de-signs. Wilkins was paid £21, the appropriate sum for full architectural drawings, on 25 July 1790.

In September that year Repton visited Donington Park again and provided Francis Rawdon-Hastings with two moveable views, that is before-and-after images of the old Manor House and new Hall, with flaps that could be folded back to reveal his and Wilkins' proposals. These beautiful watercolours, in Repton's own hand, show an imposing symmetrical house, even larger than the one that was actually built, sitting comfortably within an irregular land-scape. It was not unusual for Repton's exces-sively lavish and costly proposals not to be built as originally conceived. Francis Rawdon-Hastings, 2nd Earl of Moira, settled for a 'residence con-venient for either a large or small family ... fitting to the scenery of the place'.

Humphrey Repton's 'movable view' of the old Donington Park Manor House, viewed from the south-east, 1790.

Humphrey Repton's 'movable view' of the proposed new mansion in Donington Park, viewed from the south-east, 1790.

In 1791, Donington Park Manor House was finally pulled down after 200 years of history and many structural changes. Within just two years the new Donington Hall had risen from the rubble. Formal landscaping was restricted to the distant slopes, leaving the immediate surroundings as wide sweeping lawns with scattered trees looking as natural as it possibly could.

William Wilkins' Donington Hall was a rectangular house, two storeys high, built around a small gravelled courtyard. The south-facing front was divided into 13 bays by thin buttresses with crenellated

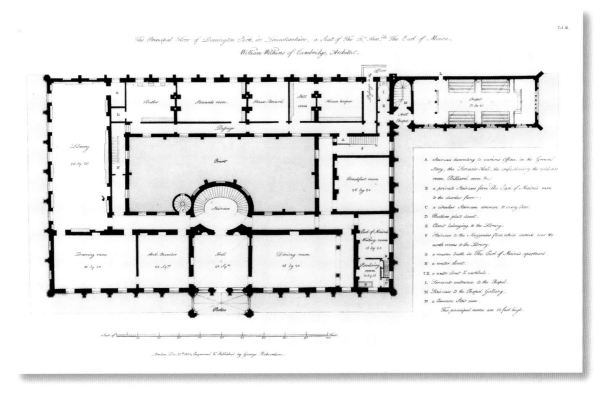

George Richardson's engraved plan *The Principal Floor of Donington Hall in Leicestershire, the seat of Francis Rawdon-Hastings, 2nd Earl of Moira, 1804.*

tops. There were large sash windows with hood-moulds and panelling below, and a parapet with pierced quatrefoils. An imposing tower, set forward to create a porte-cochère (an entrance designed for carriages), dominated the whole façade. This dramatic entrance with its double-height vaulted arch, enhanced with stone coats of arms, was topped with a glazed belvedere that originally housed the billiard room. The Gothic pointed entrance door was flanked by a pair of even taller Gothic windows with small round leaded lights and tracery stone decoration. Above was an inscription dedicating the building to Francis Hastings, 10th Earl of Huntingdon, with the date 1793, and a huge fanlight, filled with hand-painted heraldic glass. Richard Hand, the Warwickshire-born artist who developed the technique, created these beautiful glass panels, each of the nine dedicated to Francis Rawdon-Hastings' ancestors. The latter was particularly proud of his descent from George (Plantagenet), Duke of Clarence (1449–78), brother of kings Edward IV and Richard III, whose arms appear in the central panel.

Once through the front door the visitor stepped into a spacious double-height rib-vaulted entrance hall enhanced by an imposing Gothic fireplace, wooden Gothic doors with linen-fold decoration and canopied niches flanking the door to the oval staircase. Left of the hall was the ante-room, which in turn opened into the drawing room and on into the library along the west side of the house. A second drawing room on

Traceried fanlight window placed over the front entrance to Donington Hall.

the first floor, situated above the dining room, provided a retreat for feminine activities such as piano playing, singing, petit point and cards. The library was of enormous proportions, measuring 72 x 26 feet. It was fitted with bookcases to house the Earl's vast collection of books, while a mirrored end wall doubled the room's apparent length. With its westerly aspect the library was bathed in afternoon sun from full-height windows that overlooked the rolling hills and woodlands of the ancient deer park. To the right of the entrance hall was the 48 x 24 foot dining room, one of the most handsomely decorated rooms in the house. It had a shallow segmented coffered ceiling and a white marble chimney-piece with a classical frieze, a feature echoed by a similar frieze under the cornice. At the far end of the dining room were two oxblood scagliola (polished imitation marble) columns and two Ionic pilasters against the wall, marking an area for musicians or other entertainers. The breakfast room

Donington Hall soon after its completion in the early 19th century. The shadow of Hastings Chapel (1800) can be seen on the right edge of this delightful watercolour.

was on the east side of the house to capture the early morning sun. Adjoining the breakfast room was a small suite that included a writing room and the powdering room. This was a private space where the master could open his correspondence, contemplate his next military campaign or relax in a hot bath. Earl Francis slept in the large bedroom directly above the breakfast room. Linking the rooms on the east side of the house to the library was a long narrow gallery hung with family portraits. This gallery was broken by the stairway hall with its beautiful oval cantilevered staircase and Roman-style cast-iron balustrade. Across the back (north side) of the house was another lengthy corridor off which were small private sitting rooms for the butler, steward and housekeeper.

The bedrooms and dressing rooms were on the first floor, each leading off a communicating corridor around the central court. An additional oval bedroom suite was tucked away on the top

A painted glass 'sacred conversation' commissioned by Sir Edward Hastings in the late 16th century for his family Chapel at Stoke Poges. Two hundred years later this handsome window was brought to Donington Park to adorn the new Hastings Chapel that was built in 1800 as an addition to Donington Hall.

floor, though this was used for less salubrious activities during the occupancy of a later owner. The servants' hall, confectionary (for fruit preserving and jam making) and archive store were hidden away in the basement. The kitchen could have been situated here too but, in keeping with the fashion of the day, it was placed in a separate detached building at the back of the house. The kitchen was a large, three-bay, double-height structure with timbered ceiling and traditional fittings. Near the kitchen, to the north and north-east of the house, were the laundry, an octagonal game-larder, the ice-house, a stable block and ancillary offices. Donington Hall was one of the earliest English country seats to boast two bathrooms and six water closets. As well as the master's bathroom suite on the ground floor, a similar suite was installed above for the mistress of the house.

As an afterthought to the grand mansion, William Wilkins was invited to design a chapel for Donington Hall. The extension, completed in 1800, was an imposing Gothic structure stretching eastwards from the back north-east corner of the house to screen the stable block, kitchens and other service buildings behind. It featured wooden pews with inset carved panels, poppy-head finials in cast iron and an imposing hammer-beam vaulted ceiling. The gallery and stall canopies were in fibrous plaster by John Sutton, a celebrated local sculptor. At the east end of the Chapel was a stained-glass window depicting Sir Edward Hastings, the third son of the 1st Earl of Huntingdon (1304–54), kneeling before the Virgin and Child. This magnificent 'sacred conversation' dates from the 16th century and was brought from the Hastings Chapel at Stoke Poges to adorn the new Hastings Chapel at Castle Donington. The tall decorative wrought-iron communion rails, created by Robert Bakewell, were saved from the old Donington Park Manor House.

By 1801, William Wilkins' contract with Francis Rawdon-Hastings, now 2nd Earl of Moira, was finally coming to an end:

*From the forwardness of your house and the little
there now remains to finish, I feel conscious that my
services are but of little use. As few visits are necessary,
it is but right my salary should be reduced to half pay
and if you think proper, totally discontinued.*

Excessive patronage, growing debts and a military career

By the summer of 1795, the building of Donington Hall was virtually finished. Before the Chapel was commissioned, Francis Rawdon-Hastings, now 2nd Earl of Moira, accepted a new military command that necessitated his immediate departure for France, which was in the clutches of social unrest and revolution. His task was to aid the Royalist resistance movement in the north. Unfortunately the British forces were out-manoeuvred and the expedition turned out to be a complete fiasco, leaving hundreds massacred on the beaches of Brittany. Earl Francis had no alternative but to retreat to Britain with what remained of his army.

On his return to Donington Hall Earl Francis extended a warm invitation to the exiled Bourbon family, who were in desperate need of refuge abroad to escape almost certain death at the hands of the Parisian mob. His hospitality to the French royal visitors was so lavish that it included an open chequebook from Coutts Bank laid discreetly on each bedroom dressing table, with a short note suggesting that it be used for any personal needs. For years afterwards a portrait of the Comte d'Artois, brother of Louise XVI and later Charles X, looked down upon the owners of Donington Hall from the walls of the library, reminding them of their heritage of unrestrained generosity.

Francis Rawdon-Hastings, 2nd Earl of Moira, enjoyed his position as host and patron. Regrettably, one of his greatest friends and confidants, and a regular visitor to Donington Hall, was the Prince of Wales, son of George III, a man whose life was 'all fiddling and flowers, feasting and flattery, and frivolous folly'. The Prince Regent's extravagant tastes and lust for Mrs Fitzherbert not only drained Lord Francis' purse but also involved him in actively spying on Queen Caroline to procure evidence for a royal divorce. This unchivalrous behaviour by a man so highly admired was never completely forgotten by the Royal

Francis Rawdon-Hastings (1754–1826), 2nd Earl of Moira, had a long and successful career with the British army before moving into politics and eventually accepting the post of Governor General of India in the later years of his life.

Family. Earl Francis is remembered for his good and inspiring qualities. He was a great supporter of literature and scholarship, and was pleased to sponsor any seemingly worthwhile cause that came to his attention. A local boy, John Shakespeare, who showed a talent for languages received a thorough education courtesy of Earl Francis. One of Earl Francis' best-known protégés was Tom Moore, the Irish poet, who described his first impression of Donington Hall, in 1799, as 'exceedingly fine and grand but most uncomfortable'. Almost thirty years later Moore recalled another visit when he wrote ballads, chatted with fellow guests and had the freedom to browse through the thousands of volumes on the library shelves. Moore admired the wonderful collection of portraits, particularly 'the thoughtful portrait of Galileo, the pretty face of Nell Gwynne and the brawny figure of Venus professing to be a Titian'. Like all guests who visited Donington Hall, the poet took walks around the pond 'whose water continued to escape, like the 2nd Earl of Moira's own wealth, leaving it dry'. As a tribute of gratitude to his friend and patron, Moore dedicated his *Collection of Odes and Epistles* of 1806 to the 2nd Earl of Moira:

> *... I never feel a bliss so Pure and still,*
> *So heavenly calm, as when a Stream or hill*
> *Or veteran oak, like those Remembered well,*
> *Or breeze or echo, or some Wild-flower's smell*
> *Reminds my heart of many a Sylvan dream*
> *I once indulged by Trent's Inspiring stream;*
> *Of all my sunny morns and Moonlight nights*
> *On Donington's green lawns And breezy heights!*

The excessive patronage and lavish life-style at Donington Hall in the early years of the 19th century eventually began to take its toll. Like his ancestors Earl Francis was very soon plagued with financial problems. His inheritance of mortgaged estates generated little income. His collieries and iron foundries provided a modest amount, but in the short term he needed to rekindle his influential political and military career by leaving the peace and tranquillity of Donington Park.

In 1803, Earl Francis took the position of Commander-in-Chief of the army and was posted to Scotland. It was here that the 50-year-old Earl fell in love with a wealthy young Scottish heiress, Lady Flora Muir Campbell, Countess of Loudoun (1780–1840), a hereditary peeress in her own right.

The new mansion house in Donington Park was sometimes recorded as Donington Castle.

They were married the following year in London, bringing together two distinguished and illustrious ancient families. The Prince of Wales (later George IV), a close friend of the couple, gave away the bride. At last Donington Hall had the mistress it deserved and with her dowry some much needed money in the coffers.

Earl Francis and Countess Flora were soon the proud parents of five healthy children and Donington Hall was filled with the laughter of young voices. The Earl and his wife were generous patrons of local charities and every year invited their tenants and the local tradespeople to the Hall for a splendid party. Local newspapers reported with pride the military achievements of Earl Francis and were keen to announce when the family was in residence at Donington Hall. Behind the reports, however, the Earl and Countess were living far beyond their means with debts reaching staggering proportions.

To secure some income the Earl Francis turned to a political career. In 1806, he accepted the post of Master-General of the Ordnance in 'The Ministry of all the Talents' under the short-serving Whig Prime Minister William Grenville (1759–1834). Following the assassination, in 1812, of the next Prime Minister, Spencer Perceval, he was asked by the Prince Regent to form a Whig government. Once again Earl Francis eagerly accepted, but all attempts failed and the Tories returned to power under the Earl of Liverpool. By 1812, Britain was celebrating the end of the Napoleonic Wars, but at Donington Park Earl Francis was rejoicing in the fact that he had received the post he really desired. Within the year his luggage was packed and he had departed for Calcutta as Governor General of India and Commander-in-Chief of the British forces in India – another timely escape from his creditors. Countess Flora continued with the business of raising her young family and juggling the administration of their Leicestershire estates. She divided her time between the noble oaks and

Francis Rawdon-Hastings, 2nd Earl of Moira, received the additional title of 1st Marquis of Hastings in 1818. Seen here seated in his library at Donington Hall, he is remembered for having opened the famous Moira coal mines and medicinal springs. He invested in the development of Ashby de la Zouch and financed sand and rough-stone quarries throughout Leicestershire.

wandering deer of Donington Park and the newly refurbished family castle at Loudoun in Ayrshire. She is known to have made the occasional hazardous journey to India to visit her husband.

For the next 11 years Earl Francis served his country on the sub-continent. He had a remarkable capacity for rule and was as skilled as a public administrator as he was at soldiering. In 1818, he reached the summit of his career and was created Viscount Loudoun and Marquis of Hastings in recognition of his handling of the military operation in Nepal (1814–16), which won the allegiance of the Ghurkhas to the British Raj. A year later Earl Francis Rawdon-Hastings, 1st Marquis of Hastings, negotiated the purchase of the island of Singapore for Britain. His tenure in India ended in 1823 under a cloud of financial scandal, after which he returned to England and Castle Donington, to the relief of his family and tenants. The streets were bedecked with flowers and enthusiastic admirers unharnessed his carriage and pulled it the last stage of its journey up to Donington Hall.

During the final three years of his life, Francis Rawdon-Hastings, 1st Marquis of Hastings, divided his time between London and the House of Lords, Donington Park with his family, and Malta as the new Governor and Commander-in-Chief, a post he was appointed to in 1824. He would have preferred to retire from public life sooner, but he continued to live beyond his means and needed the income. The 1st Marquis of Hastings died at sea off the coast of Naples in 1826, leaving enormous debts. As a gesture of good will the East India Company, for whom he had secured extensive territories on the sub-continent, gave his widow, the Countess of Loudoun, £20,000.

Despite their many years of separation the 1st Marquis of Hastings and the Countess of Loudoun were a devoted couple. In a letter found after his death were instructions that his right hand should be cut off and preserved, and eventually placed in the coffin of his dear wife. He was buried with great ceremony in Malta, much against his private wishes. Francis Rawdon-Hastings, 2nd Earl of Moira and 1st Marquis of Hastings, was succeeded by his only surviving son, George Augustus Francis Rawdon-Hastings.

George Augustus Francis Rawdon-Hastings, 2nd Marquis of Hastings (1808–1844)

George Augustus Francis Rawdon-Hastings was a disappointment to the people of Castle Donington for he inherited none of the political ambition or war-like instincts of his father. He grew up amidst the open spaces of Donington Park surrounded by four adoring sisters and an over-protective mother,

but with little paternal guidance. At the age of 13, George Rawdon-Hastings was sent to Harrow, his father's old school, but he hated the place and after 18 months returned to Donington, where his studies were taken up by a series of tutors who found he had no interest in knowledge or learning. What he really enjoyed was foxhunting and, fortunately for him, Donington Park was in the heart of foxhunting country. The Quorn, the most famous hunt of them all, met frequently in front of his home.

As a young man George Rawdon-Hastings attended Court, having inherited his father's post as Lord of the Bedchamber to King George IV. Whilst engaged in the social life of the metropolis, this sensitive, immature, young man fell in love with the enchanting and irresponsible Barbara, Baroness Grey de Ruthyn (1810–58), a descendant of the old Hastings line. They were married in the summer of 1831 for George Rawdon-Hastings would never have contemplated marriage and a honeymoon during the hunting season.

It was an attraction of opposites though by no means an unsuccessful union. George, now the 2nd Marquis of

George Augustus Rawdon-Hastings, 2nd Marquis of Hastings, by Count D'Orsay, amateur French artist, 1841.

Hastings, and his wife, the Baroness Barbara, filled the Hall with children but lived separate lives. Barbara was nicknamed 'the jolly fast Marchioness' and lived for excitement, gambling and foreign travel. The 2nd Marquis of Hastings favoured a quieter, less ostentatious life. The Census Return of 1841 records that the 2nd Marquis of Hastings was living at Donington with his children, Reginald, Edith, Bertha, Victoria and Henry, but no wife. The household consisted of 36 servants, including a governess, a huntsman, two dog feeders and a pair of architects. A fashionable glass and wrought-iron conservatory was constructed on the west side of the house leading from the drawing room at this time.

The only upset in the otherwise tranquil life of the 2nd Marquis of Hastings was the scandalous treatment of his sister Lady Flora Rawdon-Hastings (1806–39), known as the 'white flower of the Hastings line'. Lady Flora was a Lady of the Bedchamber to the young Queen Victoria but, being an outspoken woman, openly expressed a dislike for some of her monarch's closest friends. In 1839, Lady Flora began suffering from stomach pains and grew fat. The royal physician, James Clark, incorrectly diagnosed the swelling as pregnancy and before long malicious rumours were spreading, for there were many at Court who still remembered her father's unchivalrous behaviour towards Queen Caroline. The insensitive accusations caused great distress

Barbara, Baroness Grey de Ruthyn (d.1858), wife of George, 2nd Marquis of Hastings. Her love of gambling and frequent visits to the continent were cause for scandal and gossip.

and aggravated her condition, which was liver cancer, from which she died at Buckingham Palace in the summer that year. This shameful business aroused bitterness against the Queen and her adviser Lord Melbourne, not only from Lady Flora's brother, the 2nd Marquis of Hastings, but the public at large. Some contemporaries felt that the thunder might have been louder and that the 2nd Marquis of Hastings should have at least fought a duel, but the duplicity of life at court was something with which he did not wish to be involved.

In common with most of his contemporaries, George Augustus Rawdon-Hastings, 2nd Marquis of Hastings, ate too much, drank too much and only took physical exercise in the saddle. His lifestyle took him to an early death in 1844 at just 35 years of age. He was genuinely mourned by the local community, who had grown to respect him for his direct dealings with them. The shops and businesses of Castle Donington and the Hastings' coal mines at nearby Moira closed on the day of his funeral. His death left five young children fatherless and Marchioness Flora expecting a sixth child, which was a daughter. Widowhood did not suit the 'jolly Marchioness' and she married Admiral Sir Hastings Reginald Yelverton within the year. Her six Rawdon-Hastings children spent their childhood at Donington Hall, being brought up by a succession of nurses, governesses and tutors.

Paulyn Reginald Serio, 3rd Marquis of Hastings, was expected to live up to the family name and follow a career in the army. Sadly, however, he drowned at the age of 18 in the hazardous waters of Liverpool Bay while out on manoeuvres with his Irish regiment. He was succeeded by his only brother, Henry Charles Plantagenet, 4th Marquis of Hastings (1842–68), a child of just 9 years. The Donington Park Estate had to face another long minority.

Short lease available on Donington Hall

By 1855, the household at Donington Hall was greatly depleted. The Ladies Edith and Bertha Rawdon-Hastings, the daughter of the 2nd Marquis and the 'jolly Marchioness', were married now to two of the younger sons of Thomas Clifton of Lytham St Anne's. Henry (Harry), the young heir, was boarding at Eton College. It made economic sense to find a tenant for Donington Hall, certainly until Harry Hastings had finished university, sown a few wild oats in London and was ready to take up his responsibilities as the 4th Marquis of Hastings when he reached his majority.

Between 1856 and 1860, Colonel Daniell leased Donington Park Estate and lived at Donington Hall. He was a competent sportsman with a passion for cricket and foxhunting, both of which he enjoyed at Donington. In the true tradition of the Hall, Colonel Daniell hosted a splendid farewell ball for the local community and was described by the press as universally respected by all classes. He later claimed that his four years at Donington Hall were amongst the happiest in his life.

Donington Hall, showing the conservatory leading out from the library, to the west of the house. This addition was built in 1842 and was used to celebrate the marriage of Lady Flora Abney-Hastings to Henry Fitzalan-Howard, 15th Duke of Norfolk, in 1877. By the turn of the 20th century the conservatory had been demolished.

With the tenant gone and the 'jolly Marchioness' now dead Donington Hall lay neglected and isolated for the next 18 months. The deer still roamed freely but the dust settled on the library shelves and the game-larder was empty. Only a skeleton staff remained. Occasionally, in the holidays, the young master and his friends from Oxford would return to Harry's ancestral home. The dust-sheets were pulled back, the stumps and bails were taken out of their box and ale was brought in from the village. The 4th Marquis of Hastings enjoyed his role as country squire and was an amiable host. The most extravagant patronage and festivities at the Hall were yet to come.

Henry (Harry) Charles Plantagenet, 4th Marquis of Hastings (1842–1868)

The 4th Marquis of Hastings, known as Harry Hastings, planned a splendid and extravagant celebration for his coming of age, on 22 July 1863. Ample funds had accumulated during his minority and were waiting to be spent. A full team of staff was employed to clean the stonework, repair the windows, decorate the rooms and refurbish just about everything that could be modernized. A new bell and speaking tube communicating system was installed between the principal rooms and a luxuriously tiled plunge pool was laid beneath the floor in Harry's private bathroom. In preparation for the visitors, who would soon be arriving en masse, an enormous temporary kitchen was constructed together with makeshift stables for 100 horses. The forthcoming celebration would be a lavish affair lasting the whole week of his birthday.

Harry Hastings on his 21st birthday, 22 July 1863.

The event began with a party in a marquee in front of the Hall for 200 school children, their teachers and the young master's tenants. The climax was a private banquet and fancy-dress ball for 300 personal acquaintances and society guests. The last guests called for their carriages well after dawn the following morning. Harry Hastings was in his element, the centre of attraction and the recipient of endless compliments. The local newspaper described what they saw in detail for their fascinated readers:

… The library was festooned with garlands of flowers linking the bookcases and lit by hundreds of flickering candles that glittered in the mirrored recesses. The whole room echoed to the sounds of Nicholson's quadrille and against this fairy-tale background turbaned Turks, hooded monks and rollicking cavaliers supported on their arms exquisitely gowned Indian princesses, Spanish dancers and dainty shepherdesses. The central character was Harry Hastings himself, dressed as King Charles II, in a costume of blue and scarlet velvet with silver lace, richly studded with brilliants and carrying a diamond-hilted sword…

But birthdays pass and Harry Hastings, who had no interest in country pursuits, was soon bored with life at Donington Hall. With excessive money at his disposal Harry journeyed south to London to enjoy cock-fighting dens and the pleasures of the brothel, to attend fashionable dinner parties and the opera, and in the season to visit Ascot, Henley and Cowes.

Harry Hastings had a passion for horse racing and gambling that began gently but all too quickly gathered momentum and became an obsession. He acquired his first horse in 1863, and was elected to the Jockey Club the same year. He built a fine gallop in Donington Park for his horses, which ran from the Coppice Lodge entrance along the wooded slopes above the Trent and dropped down through the Lime Grove beyond the Hall to Park Road. He maintained a large racing establishment and rarely had fewer than fifty animals in training. He is said to have paid £13,500 for Kangaroo in 1865, one of the largest sums paid for a race-

Bidding against his rival Harry Hastings, Henry Chaplin paid one thousand guineas for Hermit, this small dark chestnut colt. In 1867, Hermit joined a field of 30 runners on a miserable day at Epsom, and after ten false starts and against all the odds won the Derby by a neck with John Daley as his jockey. Harry Hastings lost thousands, having bet heavily against Hermit. Henry Chaplin had settled his old score. Hermit never recaptured his racing form but was a great success at stud.

horse at the time. He won more than £70,000 in bets when his colt Lecturer won the Cesarewitch and lost more than £140,000 when he bet against Hermit, entered by his arch-rival Henry Chaplin in the 1867 Derby. By the spring of 1868 Harry Hastings was broke.

The Pocket Venus

Henry Chaplin, 1st Viscount Chaplin (1840–1923), had been Harry Hastings' closest friend but events intervened and they ended up fierce adversaries. Hastings wooed and stole the affections of Chaplin's fiancée, who subsequently pushed the young heir to the brink on the racecourse.

The young lady was the beautiful society hostess Lady Florence Paget (1842–1907), known as the Pocket Venus, daughter of Sir Henry Paget, 2nd Marquis of Anglesey. Chaplin was the more dependable of the two, Hastings the more generous and exciting. Whatever their respective merits, Chaplin was the first to propose and Lady Florence accepted. A few days before the society wedding of the 1864 season Lady Florence departed alone to seek out some last-minute items for her trousseau. The driver dropped her at the fashionable London store of Marshall & Snelgrove in Oxford Street at about 10 o'clock. After some hurried purchases she left by the side entrance, stepped into a cab and was driven down Bond Street to St George's Church in Hanover Square. By noon on 15 July 1864 she was Harry Hastings' wife and had been elevated to Marchioness of Hastings. There was no honeymoon for the racing season was still in full swing. The bridal couple travelled north to Leicestershire by train from King's Cross, the London hub of the Great Northern Railway, a terminus opened in 1852. The staff at Donington Hall were fortunately expecting him as it was nearly his birthday and he always returned home for that, but they were astonished when the 22-year-old master turned up with a bride.

Florence, Marchioness of Hastings, lived to regret her rash behaviour. Harry Hastings soon tired of the bridal chamber and neglected his wife miserably. In spirit he was married to the turf. She was

Harry Hastings, 4th Marquis of Hastings (1842–68). He squandered a fortune on the race-track and dishonoured the family name. With his untimely death in 1868 his titles Earl of Moira and Marquis of Hastings became extinct. The earldom of Loudoun passed to his sister, Edith Maud Rawdon-Hastings. Harry's wife, Florence Hastings, was known by contemporaries as 'the rage of the park, the ballroom, the opera and the croquet lawn'.

unable to save him from overindulgences that eventually ruined his health and from overspending which completely depleted his finances. Donington Hall gave the unhappy couple little pleasure. To Florence it was the home she dreaded going to. To Harry it was little more than a spacious house where he could accommodate his boisterous friends and stage illegal cockfights. Perhaps the only serious emotion Donington Hall aroused in Harry was a sense of apprehension. There was a legend whereby if the head of the Hastings family, while sitting at the top of his own table, twice heard the sound of a carriage driving up to the main entrance when no carriage had arrived, then he knew that he would die before the year was out. Harry was too nervous and highly strung to ignore the legend completely.

Harry Hastings, 4th Marquis of Hasting, squandered a fortune equivalent to more than £30 million today in just five years. By 1868, at the age of 26, he was a pitiful sight, hunched over a walking stick, ruined in health, honour and estate. He died of kidney disease and was buried in a commoner's cemetery at Kensal Green in London, for there was no place for Harry in the family vault at Donington Park or Ashby de la Zouch. His widow, poor Florence Hastings, married George Chetwynd, 4th Baronet Chetwynd, of Brocton Hall in Staffordshire, in 1870.

With the death of the 4th Marquis of Hastings the title and other hereditary honours lapsed and the family estates had to be sold to meet his enormous gambling debts. The wines from the cellar, 500 paintings from the walls, 20,000 volumes from the library and vast quantities of furniture were offered at auction. *The Field,* a sporting magazine, spoke of the insanity by which he scattered his means and angrily criticized his lack of care for the hounds he kept for two seasons. *The Times* tried to emphasize his honourable heritage and beautiful wife, but had to confess to its readers that he was a wholesale and reckless gambler who owed no obligation to morality or respectability. *The New York Times* lamented the young man who had crowded into his brief existence an amount of romance and adventure seldom equalled by men thrice his age.

Edith Maud Rawdon-Hastings, 10th Countess of Loudoun (1833–1874)

With the 4th Marquis of Hastings dead and the possessions at Donington Hall sold, a decision had to be made about the property. Harry's eldest sister, Lady Edith Maud Rawdon-Hastings, Countess of Loudoun in her own right, was determined that the Donington Park Estate should not pass out of the family.

She was a woman of great common sense with an excellent capacity for business matters and fortunately she was wealthy. Her inheritance was from Sir Charles Abney-Hastings, the illegitimate grandson of Francis Hastings, 10th Earl of Huntingdon. Out of respect to her benefactor, she and her husband, Charles Frederick Clifton (1822–95), assumed the surname and arms of Abney-Hastings, dropping Clifton. The Countess of Loudoun had little problem in persuading her husband to purchase her late brother's estates and take up residence at Donington Hall, where she had lived as a child. The 10th Countess of Loudoun adored Donington Hall and spent the remainder of her short life restoring some semblance of gracious living at the mansion and raising her family. As mistress of Donington Park she regularly invited local children to tea on the lawn in front of the Hall. Her philanthropy did much to re-establish the Hastings family honour.

The Countess of Loudoun died of a stroke at the age of 39 in 1874. Like the 1st Marquis of Hastings she left a bizarre instruction in her will involving a severed hand. Hers was not to be saved and concealed in her husband's coffin, but to be buried in Donington Park overlooking the valley of the Trent with a cross to mark the spot. Her instructions were not carried out but a memorial to her memory was placed amidst the bracken and trees of Donington Park.

Charles Abney-Hastings, 1st Baron Donington (1822–1895)

Charles Abney-Hastings outlived his wife, Edith Maud, 10th Countess of Loudoun, by 21 years. Their eldest daughter, Lady Flora Abney-Hastings, married Henry Fitzalan-Howard, 15th Duke of Norfolk (1847–1917), the head of one of the oldest and noblest families in England, in 1877. The marriage was very happy but short, for sadly Flora, Duchess of Norfolk, died young, like her mother, as did two of her siblings, Henry and Sophia Abney-Hastings.

In 1880, Charles Abney-Hastings was honoured for his services to the Conservative party by being created 1st Baron Donington. During the late 19th century Lord Donington lived frugally at Donington Hall, maintaining only a skeleton staff and spending minimal sums on home comforts and clothes. He had no interest in continuing the patronage his late wife had extended to local shopkeepers and tradespeople. His land agent, John

The library at Donington Hall with floor-to-ceiling cedar bookcases, family portraits and comfortable furnishings, c.1890.

Gillies Shields, was more important to the local community in Castle Donington than he. Lord Donington's meanness was well known, stretching to conversing with friends in the dark rather than waste candles. He borrowed money from the bank at 5 per cent but only managed to generate income from his investments (collieries and ironworks) at less than 2 per cent. He would send a man 15 miles to Derby to purchase lemons at 5d because they cost 7d locally. Such economies verged on the ridiculous. Lord Donington did have one extravagance, however: he hungered to acquire land. Having purchased his late brother-in-law's estates and possession in the mid-1860s, he had little left to support his passion in his later years. He died of appendicitis in 1895, and is remembered not only for his thrifty nature and obsessions, but also as an unsociable and tight-lipped gentleman.

Two years before the death of Lord Donington, Donington Hall was featured in *The Illustrated London News* (1893):

THE ENTRANCE HALL

The pleasant entrance hall is all Gothic with a lofty groined ceiling. There is rich-coloured glass over the door and each compartment of the windows is gay with its shield whereon are the bearings of some ancient alliance of the family. In the two lower windows are the coats of arms of Edward I when he was Prince of Wales of Spain and England 'in pale' for Philip and Mary, crowned, and encircled by the Garter, and of Mary alone without the Garter. Here too is a great trophy of arms, with a complete suit of armour in the middle and on one wall are huge spreading antlers which were found buried in the sands in Ireland.

THE DINING-ROOM

On the right of the hall is the dining-room, a rather low room, yellow in its colouring with pink pillars at the end. It is an old-fashioned chamber full of noteworthy portraits. At the auction which followed the death of the last (4th) Marquis 550 paintings were sold, but the present owner bought back 150 of them and the house now has a collection of fine Holbeins, Jansons, Vandykes, Lelys, Reynolds, Romneys and Gainsboroughs including more than a dozen fine family portraits. The Holbein portrait of the Duke of Suffolk is as real as it can be.

THE DRAWING-ROOM

The Yelverton drawing-room, named after Barbara, 2nd Marchioness of Hastings, lies to the left of the hall and contains a most varied collection of very good portraits of her family, all of whom seem very satisfied with themselves. The most fascinating thing in the room is a splendid portrait of Robert Devereux, Earl of Essex, from whom George Hastings, 4th Earl of Huntingdon, purchased Donington Park in 1595. The room is a gay cream colour with gilt flowers running wild over its white ceiling. Above the doorway is a dark and purposeful portrait of Selina, Countess of Huntingdon. Hers is hardly what one would call a drawing-room face. Over the chimney piece hangs a grim portrait of the great Warren Hastings with his low forehead and large strong nose. Much more in keeping with the genius of the room is a handsome likeness of George IV, who was often here in the days when he was Prince of Wales.

THE LIBRARY

According to Lord Donington, Tom Moore the poet and author lived in this room for some years, enjoying the advantages of a fine collection of books and royal and noble letters. The room itself has a looking glass at the end to double its apparent length and a ceiling of cedar, not too lofty. The books were carefully classified by Mr. Edward Dawson during his stewardship at Donington Hall. Once again there are many handsome portraits in this room and like all those in this house nearly all of them have their names plainly painted for all the world to see – a plan which avoids a great deal of discussion, not always complimentary to the artist. Included in the library are portraits of Edward Stafford, the Duke of Buckingham, a pretty Jane Ford, Cardinal Pole, a King of Oude, and three portraits of the great Countess Selina, one with a very ugly baby, another a mezzotint which is nothing short of hideous.

Eight years after this article was written the precious collection of paintings, together with the great house and the beautiful park, had been sold.

The sale of the Donington Park Estate

On Thursday 24 October 1901, the stately mansion of Donington Hall with its deer park and woodlands amounting to nearly 2,000 acres fell under the auctioneer's hammer after more than three centuries of Hastings ownership. Another 3,000 acres of farms, inns, lime-works and land, valued at £8,000 a year, were sold in separate lots. The sale particulars of Lot One, 'the Stately Mansion', listed lengthy descriptions of the handsome well-proportioned rooms and domestic offices, the first-rate rabbit and partridge shooting, the excellent salmon and trout fishing, and the golf links, an unusual feature. It was pointed out that the sanitary arrangements had only recently been replaced with modern Doulton fittings and suggestions were made that electricity could and should be introduced for a small outlay. Very rarely did an English country estate only three hours from London come on to the market.

The Gothic entrance hall at Donington Hall displaying an extensive collection of swords and spears, c.1890.

LEICESTERSHIRE and DERBYSHIRE

3 hours' rail from London, and easy of access for Sheffield, Manchester and the North;

4½ miles from Kegworth Station on the main line of the Midland Railway; 9 miles from Ashby-de-la-Zouch. Tonge Station is on the Estate.

A Grand Sporting & Residential Domain of 1945 or 4914 Acres.

PARTICULARS, PLAN & CONDITIONS OF SALE

OF THE

FAMOUS FREEHOLD MANORIAL

Sporting and Residential Estate

DISTINGUISHED AS

"DONINGTON PARK,"

comprising within its borders some of the most beautiful scenery in the Midlands. It includes

THE STATELY MANSION,

well known as the Seat of the Marquess of Hastings, and formerly of the Earls of Huntingdon, which occupies a fine situation in a

MAGNIFICENT DEER PARK OF 400 ACRES

BOUNDED BY THE RIVER TRENT;

Following the death of Charles Abney-Hastings, 1st Lord Donington, in 1895, there began a systematic disposal of the Hastings family estates. The Donington Park Estate came under the hammer in October 1901.

John Gillies Shields (1857–1943) was the land agent at Donington Park for nearly fifty years. In 1930 Shields purchased the estate from John, 1st Baron Gretton, to save it from falling into the hands of speculative developers.

Donington Hall was purchased by Frederick Gretton, the younger brother of John Gretton of Stapleford Park, a Conservative politician. Frederick Gretton (1869–1928) was a millionaire from profits inherited from the family brewery business, but had no landed estates of his own. In the opening year of the new century he was actively looking for a suitable county seat, having just become engaged. Donington Hall would make the perfect family home and, what's more, it offered marvellous opportunities for shooting and hunting, Gretton's greatest pleasures. The purchase was completed but unfortunately nothing came of the courtship so Gretton never refurbished his country estate or lived at Donington Hall. He remained a bachelor and only visited the property when he fancied a day of sport with friends. Gillies Shields, previously Lord Donington's estate agent and now in Frederick Gretton's employment, continued to maintain Donington in the owner's absence. Shields, known as JG, lived nearby at Isley Walton.

The first decade of the 20th century was a peaceful time in the history of Donington Hall. Nothing much happened though Shields did offer hospitality on behalf of Gretton to local tenants, farm workers and tradespeople. To celebrate the coronation of George V in 1911 a magnificent party and tea was staged in front of the Hall attended by nearly the whole village of Castle Donington. By 1913, war in Europe was threatening. The conflict would have far-reaching consequences even in this sleepy corner of north-west Leicestershire.

Celebrating the coronation of George V at Donington Hall on 12 May 1911.

Barbed wire and sentry boxes

In the summer of 1914 Germany invaded Belgium, and Britain, though in many respects unprepared, was duty-bound to join the hostilities. The War Office lost no time in preparing camps for the reception of internees and prisoners-of-war. Donington Hall was one of the first places selected and requisitioned. Its transformation into a detention barracks was swift.

Barbed-wire entanglements were erected around the camp and sentry-boxes were constructed at strategic points. Electricity was installed at the Hall and stores and furniture arrived to meet the requirements of a camp destined to be home to hundreds of German soldiers and cavalry officers intercepted on the continent, and aviators forced down over England. The large and lofty bedrooms were furnished plainly with basic facilities for use as dormitories. In accordance with Ministry rules a number of the smaller bedrooms were set apart for prisoners holding the rank of Major and above. The Commandant of Donington Camp, Lieutenant Colonel Picot, was soon ready to receive the prisoners who would be in his charge for the duration of the war.

From the outset Donington Hall was the most talked-about internment camp in the land, a favourite topic of Parliamentary gossipmongers. Were the furnishings really as luxurious as rumour suggested? Did the American Bar really serve Fifth Avenue cocktails and Midland sherry cobblers? Did the inmates play polo in the park on ponies provided by the female cousins of Cabinet ministers? The reality of the situation was of course quite different. The prisoners were entitled to a reasonable amount of freedom inside the internment area, but all liberties were promptly curtailed following any contravention of camp rules. Some of the junior prisoners-of-war were compelled to serve their fellow officers, but otherwise the choice of study, work or amusement was up to the individual. Small carpentry workshops were set up in the basement rooms where the prisoners produced cabinets, window boxes and scenery for the drama group. Language classes were arranged and English newspapers were read in the common-room (drawing room), furnished now with simple wooden tables and chairs, but no carpets. A large home-made war map was hung on the wall and flagged to show the up-to-date position on western and eastern fronts. Artistic talents flourished with the production of wall paintings to decorate the bare dormitory walls. In the mess canteen basic rations were served, such as porridge, lentil soup, horse goulash and sauerkraut with potatoes. Privileges stretched to walks in the countryside, games of croquet and cricket on the front lawn, and attending orchestral concerts, theatre performances and chapel services. Lights had to be out by 10 pm.

Regardless of the conditions at Donington Camp during the First World War, it was the responsibility of every captured prisoner to try to escape. The Escapes Committee had an excellent espionage and intelligence system that ran with fastidious German efficiency. There were just four

During the First World War Donington Park and Hall was a prisoner-of-war camp to more than 1,300 men.

German prisoners relaxing at Donington Hall in 1915. Privileges included newspapers, hot baths and exercise in the park.

serious attempts to escape from Donington in the four years. Of these attempts, one was nipped in the bud, one was triumphant and two ended in recapture. The successful attempt to return to Germany was made by Ober-Lieutnant Gunther Pluschow, a pilot, who had escaped from China by aeroplane only to fall into the hands of the British at Gibraltar while on board an Italian ship. Pluschow's plan was simple but effective. He and his colleague, Trefftz, substituted two non-officer prisoners-of-war in their uniforms for evening roll-call. They then hid in damp shrubbery until nightfall, climbed over the barbed wire and escaped by bicycle to Derby. From there they made their way to London by train, after which they split up. Pluschow made his way back to Germany, but Trefftz was recaptured boarding a ship at Millwall Docks on the Isle of Dogs and returned to Donington Camp to face 48 days in solitary confinement. Another of the escapes involved three officers who placed dummies in their beds, then hid in a purpose-dug trench by the lawn tennis court, covered in fresh grass clippings, and finally escaped under the barbed-wire fence when all was clear. Unfortunately their command of English was poor and their liberty short-lived. The most industrious and plucky escape was staged by two German air officers, Thelen and Keilhack, who scooped out a tunnel more than 70 yards long with just an old tin shovel, a small zinc box for removing the debris and plenty of daring. They started in the reputedly haunted cellar under the drawing room, dug a shaft the height of a man, and then proceeded in a north-westerly direction until they were clear of the wire entanglements. They managed to reach a port and stow away in a lifeboat aboard a Dutch ship, but were recaptured on the high seas and returned to Castle Donington.

On 11 November 1918 the First World War ended with the signing of the Armistice, and another chapter in the history of the Donington Park Estate came to a close. The prisoners returned to their own countries, the barbed wire was taken down, the equipment and stores were removed, and finally, when the building had been renovated to an acceptable standard, it was handed back to the owner, Frederick Gretton. Life at Donington Hall reverted to minimum activity and occasional visits by Gretton and his friends.

COLONEL JOHN GRETTON.

Cigarette card of John Gretton (1867–1947), brewer and politician, drawn by John Cottrell. In 1929, Gretton inherited the Donington Estate from his brother, the late Frederick Gretton.

From manorial residence to country club and racing circuit

In 1928, Frederick Gretton died with no heir to inherit the property. The Donington Park Estate passed to his brother, John Gretton of Stapleford Park, who had recently been elevated to become 1st Baron Gretton. With no need of another country seat, particularly one in a dilapidated state of repair, the Baron immediately offered the property for sale. Donington Hall and park had great potential for a speculative developer to divide up and sell on.

A shooting party ready for a day's sport in Donington Park during the 1930s.

John Gilles Shields (JG) had other ideas. He had watched over the Donington Park Estate for 47 years and would not stand by and watch the Hall and park be destroyed by bulldozers. He had arrived at Donington in 1882 from the Loudoun Estates in Ayrshire to start a new life as estate agent to Lord Donington. Over the years he had matured from boy to man and accumulated large funds from wise investments, enough to purchase the estate for himself. To safeguard his new asset Shields had to be inventive. He had no intention of simply sitting back and enjoying the social and sporting life of a country squire.

Within months of JG's acquisition of Donington Hall and park they were opened to the public as a country club. Leisure activities were all the rage in the 1930s and people were looking for new and exciting ways to spend their spare time, preferably out of doors. The ancient deer park was cut back and restocked while the Hall was renovated with the introduction of central heating and mains water. The lake was redug and refilled in readiness for boating, a new hard-tennis court was laid and the existing golf links were restored. Advertisements in local guidebooks and newspapers attracted crowds in their hundreds. The all-inclusive price for a full day's entertainment was one shilling (5p) for adults and half price for children. For a little extra, visitors could inspect the historic mansion with its colourful wall paintings produced by the German prisoners-of-war, or make a tour of the walled garden, dairy and game-larder, where food had been grown, produced and stored for generations of earls and marquises. Another attraction was looking down the famous tunnel through which Thelen and Keilhack

A spectator event at Donington Hall Country Club during the 1930s.

had escaped. During the 1930s Donington Hall was available to rent for wedding receptions, birthday parties and private dances. For those who wanted a holiday, rather than just a day's outing, accommodation was available at competitive rates.

A further scheme for financing the upkeep of the Donington Park Estate was suggested by Lord Howe, Shields' neighbour, who reminded him that England badly needed a private road-racing circuit since road racing on public highways had been banned in the UK after the disastrous Paris–Madrid race of 1903. Shields

The Craner Curves on the Donington Park circuit seen here during a motorcycle event in the 1930s.

adored motor racing and was greatly enthused by the idea. He immediately contacted Fred Craner, a local garage owner and secretary of the Derby and District Motor Club. On visiting Donington Park Craner immediately recognized the potential of its long private roads. He envisaged laying out a tight motor-bike circuit that would climb and descend, sweep through the woods and under a stone bridge, and squeeze between the farmhouse and cowsheds beyond the Coppice Lodge entrance. Gillies Shields was encouraged by Craner's belief that such a scheme would draw thousands of visitors to the park and Hall. With the promise of the total gate money, a deal was signed.

The circuit, known simply as Donington Park, staged its first meeting in 1931. Within months the gravel surface had been tarred, the circuit had been extended and a modest grandstand and simple pit had been built. Within two years of opening, the track was widened to take cars as well as bikes, drawing in huge crowds on event days. The popularity and enthusiasm with which the

An early car race around the private roads of Donington Park, c.1933. This photograph shows the no-overtaking section in Coppice farmyard. After 1935, this bottleneck was altered when Grand Prix events were introduced.

motor racing was received ensured its continued success. Evelyn Waugh, whose novels depicted the English aristocracy, wrote about country house parties at which the guests spent their weekends at the Donington Park circuit.

The meetings at Donington Park were made up of short handicap races and trophy events. With the first Donington Grand Prix, in October 1935, racing in the park took a step forward. More powerful cars were introduced and lap records were continually being broken. Foreign drivers

Tazio Nuvolari in his trademark red helmet and yellow jersey leading the 1938 Donington Grand Prix.

became sufficiently interested to take part and used Donington Hall as their hotel for the duration of their stay. The injured were taken to the stable-block until the ambulance arrived. The bodies of those who tragically died going round the hairpin bend were taken to the old octagonal game-larder. In 1937, more than 50,000 people thronged around the circuit to witness a spectacle never before seen in this country. Mercedes-Benz and Auto-Union, the cream of the Grand Prix circus, were battling for first place on England's premier road circuit. Improvements had been made to the track and additional precautions were taken for the safety of the spectators. After a breathtaking battle Rosemeyer, the Auto-Union team captain, crossed the finish line to win at an average speed of 82.86 mph.

The 1938 Grand Prix drew an even larger crowd and had the added kudos of being flagged on its way by the Duke of Kent. After a masterly display of driving skill, involving daring manoeuvres to correct skidding, the Italian Nuvolari took the race in his V12 D-type Auto-Union. He returned to Mantua with two trophies for his collection – one for winning the Donington Grand Prix and another, a mounted stag's head, the one he had accidentally killed during practice the day before the race.

By 1939 political events in Europe had assumed ominous proportions, leading eventually to the closure of the country club and racing track. The facilities of Donington Park and Hall were abandoned and the premises invaded by people and motor vehicles of a very different kind.

Donington Park as an army base

Within five days of the declaration of war in September 1939, Donington Hall was cleared out and cleaned up from top to bottom and the estate evacuated.

The barbed wire went up again but this time no prisoners came. Instead trees were cut down, corrugated Nissen huts were erected and thousands of army vehicles were brought in across the golf course, race-track and undulating hills. Donington Hall was requisitioned as a billet for troops, and as an administrative headquarters and officers' mess. For the next 16 years Donington Park was used as an army transport base, one of the largest in the country.

The Craner Curves lined with military vehicles in the early 1950s when the reopening of the circuit was first considered.

When the military eventually left, in 1956, the Donington Park Estate was handed back to Major Gillies Shields, grandson of John Gillies Shields (JG), who had died in 1943. The Major had recently returned from East Africa to find his inheritance a mere shadow of its former self, and his fortune crippled by death duties. The army had carried out essential repairs to the fabric of the Hall, enough to ensure its well-being, but the park was littered with piles of rusty vehicle parts, the remains of air-raid shelters and neglected prefabricated structures. According to local magazine headlines more than half a million derelict vehicles had to be towed away for scrap.

With no time to spare, Major Shields began a ten-year salvage operation. The debris was cleared away, the fences were mended and those who worked the estate farms received the necessary help to become fully functional again. Thousands of pounds were spent on draining the land, replenishing the sheep and deer, planting hundreds of trees and preparing many acres of arable land for crops. In memory of his grandfather, from whom he inherited the Donington Hall Estate, Major Shields dug a ha-ha, a sunken fence, in front of Donington Hall, to allow animals to wander close by while offering unrestricted views across the park.

Major Shields never lived at Donington Hall, but that did not stop him from opening the door to others. It was a time of national upheaval, and through his generosity Donington Hall became a sanctuary and home to hundreds of European refugees and children, orphaned by the atrocities of war, under the care of the Ockenden Venture. The invitation to

The army finally leaving Donington Park in 1956 after 16 years of occupation.

enjoy the tranquillity of Donington Park and the facilities of the Hall was unconditional and open for as long as needed. The late 1950s and early 1960s were happy years, a time for working, playing and rebuilding both the estate and the lives of all those living there. The eventual departure of the Ockenden children and refugees, in the mid-1960s, coincided with the beginning of two great dreams that were to shape the future of the Donington Hall Estate.

Thoughts of a new racing circuit and family homes

The first scheme put forward to give the Donington Park Estate a new lease of life was the idea of Tom Wheatcroft, an entrepreneur who owned a magnificent collection of historic racing cars. Wheatcroft envisaged a stable for his fleet of valuable motors and had plans to reopen Donington's historic racing circuit. He remembered the heady days of the 1930s when, as a boy, he witnessed the magic of the race-track with its enthusiastic crowds, roaring cars and heroes. The second scheme belonged to Major Shields, who had thoughts of refurbishing Donington Hall as exclusive flats and even living in one himself. He remembered how as a boy he had marvelled at the Hall with its handsome rooms filled with admiring visitors and the sight of magnificent celebratory receptions. In 1971, two separate architects were commissioned to draw up plans for a purpose-built racing car museum by the Coppice Lodge entrance and to convert Donington Hall into apartments for leasing.

Tom Wheatcroft rejoicing in 1971 having just acquired part of the Donington Park Estate for his race-track and racing car museum.

For Tom Wheatcroft, his dream would become a reality. He had the financial backing needed to realize his plans. Before long he had purchased about 350 acres of Donington Park from the Major, paying the full six-figure asking price, and work had begun on creating a museum for his Grand Prix Collection. Rebuilding the derelict race track and reopening Donington Park as a major sporting venue took much longer, in fact six years of legal wrangling involving a catalogue of expensive planning appeals.

For Major Shields it was a different story. He had already spent most of his inherited fortune on maintenance and costly repairs. To generate income every conceivable money-raising scheme was considered. The stable-block and dairy were converted and rented out as residential accommodation and a suite of rooms in the Hall was leased to a computer company. A one-off opportunity was seized when the 4th Marquis' sunken plunge pool was wanted as a setting for a scene in a new film version of *Alice in Wonderland*. Major Shields' energy and determination were unquestionable, but there were never enough funds. In 1977, his dream finally ended. Donington Hall with its centuries of history and what remained of the beautiful park would have to be sold. For the rest of his life the Major lived with his memories and dreams at the family home at Isley Walton.

Desirable country residence for sale

In 1977, Donington Hall was offered for sale on the open market. With its beautiful setting and excellent location, within a stone's throw of East Midlands Airport and the M1 motorway, it was assumed that a suitable purchaser would easily be found. Many enthusiastic speculative developers and potential owners came to view the 25-acre estate with exciting plans and visionary schemes but no one put their money on the table. Many thought the Hall would become an up-market hotel to serve East Midlands Airport and Wheatcroft's race-track, but once again this opportunity was passed over. The restoration of Donington Hall would be an enormous challenge and financial commitment, and for more than three years nobody was prepared to take it on. The Hall began to look sad and neglected as the grass grew up beyond the ground floor windows and the long abandoned outbuildings became home to insects and wild animals.

In 1980, the fabric of Donington Hall was crumbling and the grass outside was waist deep. Within two years British Midland Airways had completely refurbished their new headquarters building, re-established their 25 acres of parkland, and moved in.

Eventually, in 1980, representatives of a company looking to relocate came to view the property. They were Stuart Balmforth and Colin Roberts of British Midland Airways, a small airline based mainly at East Midlands Airport, who to date had operated their business from pre-fabricated buildings scattered around the perimeter road of the airport. At the time, BMA flew a limited timetable of regional scheduled services and claimed a small slice of the transatlantic charter business. But the company were poised for serious expansion, having two years earlier been subject to a management buy-out. The new owners were Michael Bishop, Stuart Balmforth and John Wolfe (the BBW Partnership) and they were focused on winning for their airline the highly lucrative

The oval cantilevered staircase at Donington Hall, 1982.

trunk routes across the UK and into Europe. The fight would be hard, due to restrictive aviation legislation, but once won the business would grow rapidly and dedicated business premises would be crucial.

With encouragement from their American financial backer, Dr Robert Beauchamp, the three partners agreed that the acquisition of Donington Hall would be an excellent idea. A deal was struck at £185,000, a hefty drop from the asking price, and before long plans had been drawn up to restore and refurbish this historically important building as a computerized business headquarters. The project took 18 months and cost the company nearly £2 million, which included the purchase of the freehold. The end result was worthy of being voted the outright winner of the 1983 Business and Industry Premier Award, designed to identify environmentally conscious companies.

By the time British Midland Airways moved into their new premises, in 1982, the company had been granted the first of the licences they had been fighting for. Although it had been planned to rent out accommodation that was surplus to the company's needs, in the event the activities of the airline soon absorbed the whole premises. The library became the home of the reservations department while the bedroom floor was refurbished as offices for senior management. The billiard room and oval bedroom in the belvedere were converted into boardrooms for meetings and private

The entrance hall and reception area at Donington Hall in 2008.

luncheons, while the basement floor was set aside for storage, the post room and the company archive. Donington Chapel, a venue for religious worship for centuries, became the staff restaurant, retaining as many of its original features as possible. In 1987, plans were approved to utilize land behind Donington Hall for a new purpose-built 4,550 sq m office building to house more administrative staff. Hastings House, named after the family that had been associated with Donington Park for more than six centuries, was opened in the autumn of 1990.

Donington Hall and Hastings House, 2007.

Today, in 2008, Donington Hall, Hastings House and 25 acres of what remains of Repton's beautiful parkland are the pride of bmi.

Awards

1976 Contract Services Award in recognition of the 'Instant Airlines' worldwide operation. (*Air Transport World* magazine, US)

1979 Queen's Award for Export Achievement in recognition of the 'Instant Airlines' work

1983 Best UK Domestic Airline (*Executive Travel* magazine)

1984 Best UK Domestic Airline (*Executive Travel* magazine)

1986 Best UK Domestic Airline (*Executive Travel* magazine)
Anglo-Dutch Award for Enterprise, runner-up, for Heathrow –Amsterdam service

1987 Best UK Domestic Carrier (survey of 2,000 travel agents)

1988 Best UK Domestic Airline (*Executive Travel* magazine)

1989 Best UK Domestic Airline (*Executive Travel* magazine)

1990 Best Domestic Airline – Gold Award (Travel Agents' Awards sponsored by *Travel Trade Gazette* and *Express Newspapers*)
Best UK Domestic Airline (*Executive Travel* magazine)
Best Short-Haul Carrier – runner-up (*Executive Travel* magazine)
Best UK Domestic Airline (Silver Globe Awards sponsored by *Travel Weekly*)

1991 Best Scheduled Domestic Airline (*Travel Bulletin* magazine)
Best Airline – London to Ireland (Irish Air Transport Users' Committee)
Best UK Domestic Airline (Silver Globe Awards sponsored by *Travel Weekly*)
Best Domestic Airline – Gold Award (Travel Agents' Awards sponsored by *Travel Trade Gazette* and *Express Newspapers*)

1992 Best Domestic Airline – Gold Award (Travel Agents' Awards sponsored by *Travel Trade Gazette* and *Express Newspapers*)
Best UK Domestic Airline (*Executive Travel* magazine)
Best Short Haul Carrier (*Executive Travel* magazine)
Best UK Domestic Airline (Silver Globe Awards sponsored by *Travel Weekly*)
Anglo-Dutch Award for Enterprise (Netherlands – British Chamber of Commerce scheme for achievement in Anglo-Dutch trade)

1993 Best UK Domestic Airline (*Executive Travel* magazine)
Best Short-Haul Carrier (*Executive Travel* magazine)
Best Business Class, Dublin to London (Air Transport Users' Committee in Ireland)
Best Economy Class, Dublin to London (Air Transport Users' Committee in Ireland)
Best Domestic Airline – Gold Award (Travel Agents' Awards sponsored by *Travel Trade Gazette* and *Express Newspapers*)

1994 Best UK Domestic Airline (*Executive Travel* magazine)
Best UK Domestic Airline (Silver Globe Awards sponsored by *Travel Weekly*)

Best Short-Haul Airline (Institute of Travel Managers)
Best Domestic Airline – Gold Award (Travel Agents' Awards sponsored by *Travel Trade Gazette* and *Express Newspapers*)

1995 Best UK Domestic Airline (Silver Globe Awards sponsored by *Travel Weekly*)
Best Short-Haul Airline (Institute of Travel Managers)
Best UK Business Airline (Business Travel World awards)
Best Domestic Airline – Gold Award (Travel Agents' Awards sponsored by *Travel Trade Gazette* and *Express Newspapers*)

1996 Best UK Domestic Airline (Silver Globe Awards sponsored by *Travel Weekly*)
Best Domestic Airline – Gold Award (Travel Agents' Awards sponsored by *Travel Trade Gazette* and *Express Newspapers*)

1997 Best Domestic Airline – Gold Award (Travel Agents' Awards sponsored by *Travel Trade Gazette* and *Express Newspapers*)
Best UK Domestic Airline (*Executive Travel* magazine)
Best Short-Haul Carrier (*Executive Travel* magazine)

1998 Best UK Domestic Airline (*Executive Travel* magazine)
Best UK Domestic Airline (Silver Globe Awards sponsored by *Travel Weekly*)

1999 Best UK Domestic Airline (Silver Globe Awards sponsored by *Travel Weekly*)

2000 Best UK Domestic Airline (Silver Globe Awards sponsored by *Travel Weekly*)
Air Cargo Carrier of the Year
Best External/Community Communications award for 'Make the Air Fair' campaign (Communications in Business)
Best Short-Haul Airline (*Business Traveller* magazine)

2001 Best UK Domestic Airline (Silver Globe Awards sponsored by *Travel Weekly*)

2002 Best Domestic Leisure Airline (readers of *Conde Nast Traveller* magazine)
Five-star rating for Manchester–US service (*Business Traveller*)

2003 Best No Frills Airline – bmibaby (*Daily Telegraph* readers)
Best UK Domestic Airline (Silver Globe Awards sponsored by *Travel Weekly*)

2004 Best No Frills Airline – bmibaby (*Telegraph* Travel Awards)
Best UK Domestic Airline (Silver Globe Awards sponsored by *Travel Weekly*)
Best European Airline (Irish Travel Trade News)

2005 Best No Frills Airline – bmibaby (*Telegraph* Travel Awards)

2006 UK's most punctual airline – bmi regional (Flightontime website)

2007 UK's most punctual airline – bmi regional (Flightontime website)

Aircraft fleet – bmi group as at 30 September 2008

The details of the fleet are as recorded in the company archive.

TYPE	REG	NAME	CONSTRUCTION NO.	INTO SERVICE	ACQUIRED FROM
Miles M.38 Messenger IIA	G-AILL	—	6341	Aug-47	
Miles M.65 Gemini	G-AJZJ	—	6465	Mar-48	
De Havilland DH.89A Rapide	G-AIUK	—	6640	Jun-48	Kenning Aviation
De Havilland DH.89A Rapide	G-AKOV	—	6612	Aug-50	Inter-City Air Services
De Havilland DH.89A Rapide	G-AEAL	—	6325	Apr-53	Hunting Air Surveys
De Havilland DH.89A Rapide	G-AIUL	—	6837	Jun-54	Keale Street Pottery
Douglas C-47B Dakota 4	G-ANTD	*Dovedale*	14969	Apr-55	C E Harper Aircraft
Douglas C-47B Dakota 4	G-AOGZ	*Darley Dale*	16534	Jun-56	RAF ex-KN628
Douglas C-47B Dakota 4	G-APBC	*Derwent Dale*	15676	May-58	Transair
Douglas C-47B Dakota 4	G-AMSW	*Fern Dale*	16171	Apr-59	Cambrian
Douglas C-47B Dakota 4	G-AMSX	*Peak Dale*	16448	Apr-59	Cambrian
Douglas C-47 Dakota 3	G-AOFZ	*High Dale*	9131	Feb-60	Hunting Clan African
Douglas C-47A Dakota 3	G-AGJV	*Millers Dale*	12195	Mar-61	BEA
Douglas C-47A Dakota 3	G-AKJH	*Monsal Dale*	13164	May-61	BEA
Handley Page HPR.I Marathon	G-AMGW	*Millers Dale*	127	Mar-56	West African VR-NAN
Handley Page HPR.I Marathon	G-AMHR	*Monsal Dale*	129	Jul-56	West African VR-NAR
Handley Page Marathon T.I	G-AMEW	—	118	Jul-58	Ministry of Supply XA265
Canadair C-4 Argonaut	G-ALHS	—	164	Feb-62	Overseas Aviation (CI)
Canadair C-4 Argonaut	G-ALHY	—	170	Jun-62	Overseas Aviation (CI)
Canadair C-4 Argonaut	G-ALHG	—	153	Dec-62	Overseas Aviation (CI)
Canadair C-4 Argonaut	G-ALHN	—	160	–	Overseas Aviation (CI)
Canadair C-4 Argonaut	G-ALHP	—	162	–	Overseas Aviation (CI)
Canadair C-4 Argonaut	G-ALHV	—	167	–	Aden Airways VR-AAT
Handley Page Herald 211	G-ASKK	—	161	Feb-65	Handley Page (used)
Handley Page Herald 207	G-ATHE	—	165	Aug-65	Handley Page
Handley Page Herald 100	G-APWA	—	149	Apr-66	Handley Page
Handley Page Herald 214	G-ASVO	—	185	Mar-73	Sadia PP-SDG
Handley Page Herald 214	G-ATIG	—	177	Apr-73	Sadia PP-SDI
Handley Page Herald 214	G-BAVX	—	194	Apr-73	Sadia PP-SDN
Vickers Viscount 736	G-AODG	—	77	Jan-67	British United
Vickers Viscount 831	G-ASED	—	419	Feb-67	British United
Vickers Viscount 831	G-APNE	—	403	Apr-67	British United
Vickers Viscount 815	G-AVJA	—	336	Jun-67	HSA ex PIA AP-AJD
Vickers Viscount 815	G-AVJB	—	375	Jul-67	HSA ex PIA AP-AJF
Vickers Viscount 760	G-AWCV	—	186	Apr-68	Aden Airways VR-AAW
Vickers Viscount 785	G-AWGV	—	116	Apr-68	Alitalia I-LIRE
Vickers Viscount 831	G-APND	—	402	Jan-69	British United
Vickers Viscount 814	G-AWXI	—	339	Jan-69	Condor Flugdienst D-ANOL
Vickers Viscount 755	G-AOCB	—	92	Feb-69	Invicta Airways
Vickers Viscount 755	G-AOCC	—	93	Feb-69	Invicta Airways
Vickers Viscount 702	G-APPX	—	73	Apr-69	Field Aircraft Services
Vickers Viscount 833	G-APTD	—	426	Apr-69	British United
Vickers Viscount 813	G-AZLP	—	346	Jan-72	South African Airways ZS-CDT
Vickers Viscount 813	G-AZLR	—	347	Jan-72	South African Airways ZS-CDU
Vickers Viscount 813	G-AZLS	—	348	Feb-72	South African Airways ZS-CDV
Vickers Viscount 813	G-AZLT	—	349	Feb-72	South African Airways ZS-CDW
Vickers Viscount 813	G-AZNA	—	350	Mar-72	South African Airways ZS-CDX
Vickers Viscount 813	G-AZNB	—	351	Mar-72	South African Airways ZS-CDY
Vickers Viscount 813	G-AZNC	—	352	Mar-72	South African Airways ZS-CDZ
Vickers Viscount 814	G-BAPF	—	338	Feb-73	Nora Air Services D-ANUN
Vickers Viscount 814	G-BAPE	—	341	Feb-73	Nora Air Services D-ANIP
Vickers Viscount 814	G-BAPD	—	340	Feb-73	Nora Air Services D-ANAD
Vickers Viscount 814	G-BAPG	—	344	Feb-73	Nora Air Services D-ANIZ
Vickers Viscount 838	G-BCZR	—	446	May-76	Field Aircraft Services, ex Ghana 9G-AAU
Vickers Viscount 814	G-AYOX	—	370	Mar-78	Arkia 4X-AVA
Vickers Viscount 836	G-BFZL	—	435	Oct-78	Sultan of Oman's AF No. 501, then 3D-ACM

DISPOSAL	REMARKS	OPERATED BY
sold 1954, but flew until 1973		
sold 1956, scrapped 1967		
to Kenya as VP-KND 03/1955		
to Kenya as VP-KNC 03/1955		
to France as F-OAVE 03/1956		
to A S Hubbard 03/1957		
to Cameroon Air Transport as TJ-ACF 17/10/1968		
to Strathallan Air Services 01/04/1967		
to Southwest Aviation, Shoreham 30/04/1968	c/n of fuselage 27121, previous I-TRES	
crashed Pyrenees 07/10/1961		
to Guyana Airways as VP-GCF 22/12/1965		
to Gulf Aviation 22/03/1966		
to Air Envoy 13/03/1969		
to Gregory Air Services 10/1962		
withdrawn 25/07/1960, scrapped 04/1961		
withdrawn 18/07/1960, scrapped 07/1961		
withdrawn 27/09/1960, scrapped later		
withdrawn 16/10/1967, to Chartwell Aviation 19/10/1968		
withdrawn 06/11/1967, to Chartwell Aviation 19/10/1968		
crashed Stockport 04/06/1967		
broken up for spares		
broken up for spares		
broken up for spares		
to BUA (CI) 15/02/1967		
loaned until 15/09/1965		
loaned until 30/09/1966		
to British Air Ferries 07/01/1977		
to Brymon 01/01/1977		
to British Air Ferries 13/01/1977		
crashed East Midlands 20/02/1969		
to Alidair 19/05/1972		
to Arkia as 4X-AVE 21/09/1972		
crashed Manchester (training) 20/03/1969		
to Intra Airways Jersey 23/12/1976		
to A J Walter 08/1970		
withdrawn 1970 and scrapped		
to Arkia as 4X-AVF 21/12/1973		
engine fire Heathrow 12/1969, written off 22/01/1970		
withdrawn 01/1970 and scrapped		
to A J Walter 08/1970		
returned to Field 10/1969		
to Arkia as 4X-AVD 24/02/1970		
sold to BAe		
stored East Midlands for cabin crew training		
sold to BAe		
re-registered G-BMAT 1981, later sold to BAe		
sold to BAe		
sold to BAe		
sold to BAe		
to BAe 04/08/1987		
to Intra Airways Jersey 21/10/1977		
scrapped		
to Intra Airways Jersey 01/1978		
leased twice, returned 10/1977		
dismantled for spares 01/1984, fuselage		
Teesside fire practice		
return date unknown	operated by Manx from 16/11/1985	

TYPE	REG	NAME	CONSTRUCTION NO.	INTO SERVICE	ACQUIRED FROM
BAC One-Eleven 523FJ	G-AXLL	—	193	Jan-70	new
BAC One-Eleven 523FJ	G-AXLM	—	199	Feb-70	new
BAC One-Eleven 523FJ	G-AXLN	—	211	Mar-70	new
Boeing 707-321	G-AYBJ	—	17597	Apr-70	Pan American N719PA
Boeing 707-321	G-AYVE	—	18083	Apr-71	Pan American N757PA
Boeing 707-324C	G-AZJM	—	18886	Mar-73	British Caledonian
Boeing 707-373C	N370WA	—	19442	Mar-73	World Airways
Boeing 707-321	G-AYVG	—	17598	Feb-75	Pan American N720PA
Boeing 707-321F	G-AZWA	—	17605	Apr-75	Pan American N727PA
Boeing 707-321F	G-BAEL	—	17602	Aug-75	Pan American N724PA
Boeing 707-321F	G-AYXR	—	17608	Jan-76	Pan American N730PA
Boeing 707-338C	G-BFLD	—	19625	Mar-78	Qantas VH-EAE
Boeing 707-338C	G-BFLE	—	19293	May-78	Qantas VH-EBT
Boeing 707-321C	G-BMAZ	—	19270	Apr-79	Maverick (ex PanAm) N448M/TF-VLL
Douglas DC-9-15	G-BMAA	Dovedale The Shah Diamond	47048	Aug-76	Douglas N65358 ex Avensa YV-52C
Douglas DC-9-14	G-BMAH	Merseyside The Florentine Diamond	45712	Sept-77	Finnair OH-LYB leased
Douglas DC-9-15	N48075	Merseyside	45723	Feb-78	Southern, ex-Avensa, leased
Douglas DC-9-15	G-BMAB	The Great Mogul Diamond	45738	Nov-79	TWA N1057T
Douglas DC-9-15	G-BMAC	The Eugenie Diamond	45739	Feb-80	TWA N1058T
Douglas DC-9-15	G-BMAG	The Nassak Diamond	45719	Dec-82	KLM PH-DNB
Douglas DC-9-14	G-BMAI	The Star of Este Diamond	45713	Sept-83	Finnair OH-LYA
Douglas DC-9-32	G-BMAK	The Stewart Diamond	47430	Mar-84	Douglas N503MD, ex EAA
Douglas DC-9-32	G-BMAM	The Cullinan Diamond	47468	Apr-84	Douglas N504MD, ex EAA
Douglas DC-9-32	G-BMWD	The Orloff Diamond	47570	Oct-86	Adria YU-AJF
Douglas DC-9-32	G-PKBM	The Tiffany Diamond	47648	Jan-87	ALM PJ-SNA
Douglas DC-9-32	G-PKBD	—	47666	Aug-88	ALM PJ-SNB
Douglas DC-9-32	G-PKBE	—	47523	Oct-88	WJ Condren/ Swiss Air HB-IDE
Douglas DC-9-32	G-ELDG	—	47484	Apr-90	Electra Aviation OE-LDG
Douglas DC-9-32	G-ELDH	—	47555	May-90	Electra Aviation OE-LDH
Douglas DC-9-32	G-ELDI	—	47559	Apr-90	Electra Aviation OE-LDI
Douglas DC-9-32	G-BMWD	—	47570	Nov-88	Adria Airways 15/04/1990
Fokker F27-264	G-BMAE	—	10256	Oct-81	NLM
Fokker F27-241A	G-BMAS	—	10277	Nov-81	Danish Aero Lease, ex TAT F-BVTA
Fokker F27-242	G-BAUR	—	10225	Mar-82	Air UK, leased
Fokker F27-242	G-BLGW	—	10231	Apr-82	Air UK, leased
Fokker F27-286	G-BDDH	—	10289	Apr-82	Air UK, leased
Fokker F27-2100	G-BMAP	—	10302	Nov-82	Bangladesh Biman S2-ABF
Fokker F27-241	G-BHMW	—	10229	Dec-82	Air UK, leased
Fokker F27-237	G-BMAW	—	10212	Sept-83	Air Tanzania 5H-MRH, ex-5Y-AAC
Fokker F27-252	G-BMAU	—	10241	Oct-83	Air Tanzania 5H-MRO, ex 5Y-AAP
Fokker F27-101	G-IOMA	—	10106	Mar-85	Aviaco EC-BMJ
Shorts 330-200	G-BJFK	—	3077	Sept-81	new, leased from Shorts
Shorts 360	G-BKMX	—	3608	Mar-83	new, leased from Jetstream Aircraft Ltd
Shorts 360	G-BMAJ G-WACK	—	3611	May-83	new, leased from Nordic Leasing Services L
Shorts 360	G-LEGS	—	3637	Mar-84	new
Shorts 360	G-BMAR	—	3633	Mar-84	new, leased from Jetstream Aircraft Ltd
Shorts 360	G-ISLE	—	3638	Mar-84	new
Shorts 360	G-BLGB	—	3641	Mar-84	new, leased from Jetstream Aircraft Ltd
Shorts 360	G-RMSS	—	3604	Aug-85	Air Ecosse, leased
Shorts 360	G-SALU	—	3628	Jan-86	ex Maersk, leased from Shorts
Shorts 360 Advanced	G-BMLC	—	3688	Apr-86	new, leased from Lynrise Aircraft Financing
Shorts 360 Advanced	G-BMHX	—	3686	May-86	new, leased from Lynrise Aircraft Financing
Shorts 360 Advanced	G-BMHY	—	3687	May-86	new
De Havilland Canada DHC-7 Srs 102	G-BNDC	—	101	Mar-87	ex Newmans Air, leased from DHC
De Havilland Canada DHC-7 Srs 102	G-BNDC	—	101	Mar-87	ex Newmans Air, leased from DHC
De Havilland Canada DHC-7 Srs 102	G-BNGF	—	103	Apr-87	ex Newmans Air, leased from DHC

DISPOSAL	REMARKS	OPERATED BY
to TransBrasil as PP-SDT 05/05/1973		
to Court Line 26/09/1973		
to TransBrasil as PP-SDU 26/09/1973		
to Jet Power, Miami N43MA		
to Skyways International, Panama		
leased, returned 12/1975, IAL, Miami, N17323		
leased, returned 12/12/1978	later OO-SBU	
to Jet Power, Miami		
to International Air Leases, Miami		
to International Air Leases, Miami N2276X		
to International Air Leases, Miami N37681		
to Burlington Northern (Southern AT) N862BX		
to Burlington Northern (Southern AT) N861BX		
to Burlington Northern (Southern AT) N863BX		
returned to Ansett 08/02/1993	G-BFIH until 01/04/1980	bmi
returned to Ansett 08/02/1993	leased (Darley Dale), bought 23/06/1983, sale and leaseback with Nordstress 27/08/1987, lease assigned to Ansett and operated under lease from Ansett from 12/01/1988	bmi
returned 30/09/1978		bmi
returned to Ansett 12/08/1994	sale and leaseback with Nordstress 27/08/1987, lease assigned to Ansett and operated under lease from Ansett from 12/01/1988	bmi
returned to Ansett 08/1995	sale and leaseback with Nordstress 27/08/1987, lease assigned to Ansett and operated under lease from Ansett from 12/01/1988	bmi
returned to Ansett 24/03/1995	sale and leaseback with Nordstress 27/08/1987, lease assigned to Ansett and operated under lease from Ansett from 12/01/1988	bmi
returned to Ansett 06/04/1995	sale and leaseback with Nordstress 27/08/1987, lease assigned to Ansett and operated under lease from Ansett from 12/01/1988	bmi
returned to PLM 19/12/1994		bmi
returned to PLM 21/12/1994		bmi
returned to Adria 15/04/1990		bmi
returned to PLM date unknown		bmi
returned to PLM 31/01/1995		bmi
returned to Nordbanken Finans 14/12/1994	purchased by bmi, sale and leaseback with Nordbanken Finans	bmi
sold to Valujet 03/05/1996	leased and subsequently purchased by bmi, sold to Valujet	bmi
sold to Valujet 09/02/1996	leased and subsequently purchased by bmi, sold to Valujet	bmi
sold to Valujet 12/03/1996	leased and subsequently purchased by bmi, sold to Valujet	bmi
returned to Adria		bmi
sold to Northwest Aircraft Inc 11/1988	retained PH-KFH until 14/11/1982	bmi
returned OY-BST, later ZS-LMZ		
returned 09/1984		
returned 04/1984		
returned 02/1984		
sold to Northwest Aircraft Inc 11/1998	Loganair 05/1986, damaged and repaired	Loganair
returned 10/1983		
sold to Northwest Aircraft Inc 11/1988		bmi
crashed East Midlands crew training 18/01/1987		
traded in to Shorts 05/1986		
returned 01/01/1984		
	subleased by Loganair to British Regional Airlines Ltd at the time the companies left the group	BRAL
	re-registered for Manx 25/04/1986, retained by Manx when Manx left the group	Manx
sold by Manx to BAC Leasing Ltd 01/11/1996		Manx
	subleased by Loganair to British Regional Airlines Ltd at the time the companies left the group	BRAL
sold by Manx to BAC Leasing Ltd 01/11/1996		Manx
	subleased by Loganair to British Regional Airlines Ltd at the time the companies left the group	BRAL
returned to Jadepoint		
returned 09/03/1989	operated by Loganair, then (02/1988) Manx	Manx
returned 12/1994		Loganair
returned 12/10/1995	operated by BM until 02/04/1994, then leased direct to Loganair	Loganair
returned to Shorts 30/09/1988		
returned to DHC 04/1988		
returned to DHC 04/1988		
returned to DHC end 05/1988		

TYPE	REG	NAME	CONSTRUCTION NO.	INTO SERVICE	ACQUIRED FROM
De Havilland Canada DHC-7 Srs 110	G-BOAX	—	111	Apr-88	not previously delivered
De Havilland Canada DHC-7 Srs 110	G-BOAW	—	110	Apr-88	not previously delivered
De Havilland Canada DHC-7 Srs 110	G-BOAY	—	112	May-88	not previously delivered
De Havilland Canada DHC-7 Srs 110	G-BOAZ	—	77	May-89	Leasair Ltd and Aviation Enterprises 1988 In
BAe 146-100	G-OJET	—	E1004	Nov-87	ex SATA and others, leased
BAe 146-200	G-OLCA	—	E2099	Jul-88	new, leased from BAe plc
BAe 146-200	G-OLCB	—	E2103	Oct-88	new, leased from BAe plc
BAe 146-200	G-CLHA	—	E2024	Mar-00	leased from Bank of America Leasing and Capital LLC
BAe 146-200	G-CLHB	—	E2036	Apr-00	leased from British Regional Airlines Ltd
BAe 146-200	G-CLHC	—	E2088	May-00	leased from British Regional Airlines Ltd
BAe 146-200	G-CLHD	—	E2023	May-00	leased from Finova Capital plc
BAe 146-200	G-DEBE	—	E2022	Jun-00	leased from Flightline Ltd
BAe 146-200	G-CLHE	—	E2045	Sept-00	leased from P/F Atlantic Airways
BAe ATP	G-BMYK	—	2003	Jun-88	new, leased from Lombard Leasing Facilities
BAe ATP	G-BMYL	—	2004	Jun-88	new, leased from Lombard Leasing Facilities
BAe ATP	G-BMYM	—	2002	Jun-88	new, leased from Lombard Leasing Facilities
Saab 340	G-HOPP	—	8	Nov-86	Birmingham Executive, leased
Saab 340A	G-GNTA	—	340A-049	unknown	previously HB-AHK, operated by Business Air prior to acquistion of company
Saab 340A	G-GNTB	—	340A-082	unknown	previously HB-AHL, operated by Business Air prior to acquistion of company
Saab 340A	G-GNTC	—	340A-020	unknown	previously HB-ABE, operated by Business Air prior to acquistion of company
Saab 340A	G-GNTD	—	340A-100	unknown	previously SE-ISK, operated by Business Air prior to acquistion of company
Saab 340A	G-GNTE	—	340A-133	unknown	previously SE-ISM, operated by Business Air prior to acquistion of company
Saab 340A	G-GNTF	—	340A-113	unknown	previously SE-F13, operated by Business Air prior to acquistion of company
Saab 340A	G-GNTG	—	340A-126	unknown	previously HB-AHR, operated by Business Air prior to acquistion of company
Saab 340B	G-GNTH	—	340B-169	Jan-97	leased from Saab Aircraft Credit AB
Saab 340B	G-GNTI	—	340B-172	Jan-97	leased from Saab Aircraft Credit AB
Saab 340B	G-GNTJ	—	340B-192	Feb-97	leased from Saab Aircraft Credit AB
Fokker 100	G-BVJA	—	11489	Apr-94	new, leased from East Midlands Aircraft Finance (I) BV
Fokker 100	G-BVJB	—	11488	Jul-94	new, leased from East Midlands Aircraft Finance (I) BV
Fokker 100	G-BVJC	—	11497	Dec-94	new, leased from East Midlands Aircraft Finance (I) BV
Fokker 100	G-BVJD	—	11503	Dec-94	new, leased from East Midlands Aircraft Finance (I) BV
Fokker 100	G-BXWE	—	11327	May-96	ex EMAF PH-CFE
Fokker 100	G-BXWF	—	11328	Apr-96	ex EMAF PH-CFF
Fokker 70	G-BVTE	—	11538	Apr-96	new, leased from East Midlands Aircraft Finance (I) B.V.
Fokker 70	G-BVTF	—	11539	May-95	new, leased from East Midlands Aircraft Finance (I) BV
Fokker 70	G-BVTG	—	11551	Sept-95	new, leased from East Midlands Aircraft Finance (I) BV
Boeing 737-300	G-OBMA	—	23831	Nov-87	new, ex Ansett, leased
Boeing 737-300	G-OBMB	—	23832	Dec-87	new, ex Ansett, leased
Boeing 737-300	G-OBMC	—	24030	Jan-89	new, ex Ansett, leased
Boeing 737-300	G-OBMD	—	24090	Feb-89	new, ex Ansett, purchased
Boeing 737-300	G-OBMH	—	24460	Mar-90	new, ex Ansett, leased
Boeing 737-300	G-OBMJ	—	24092	Nov-93	new
Boeing 737-300	G-OBML	—	24300	Dec-91	ex ILFC, SE-DLA

DISPOSAL	REMARKS	OPERATED BY
sold to Air Associates Ltd 27/07/1990		London City
sold to Berjaya Air 19/06/1995		London City
sold to Berjaya Air 22/05/1992		London City
returned to Aviation Enterprises 1988 Inc on 22/11/1995		London City
thought to have been returned by Manx in 11/1992		Manx
returned 30/12/1991		Loganair
returned 30/12/1991		Loganair
returned 09/05/2002		bmi regional
returned 31/01/2002		bmi regional
returned 31/01/2002		bmi regional
returned 12/09/2003		bmi regional
returned 30/09/2000		bmi regional
returned 13/03/2002		bmi regional
	leased by bmi and then operated by British Regional Airlines Limited under a sublease from 07/12/1993	BRAL
	leased by bmi and then operated by British Regional Airlines Limited under a sublease from 27/03/1994	BRAL
	leased by bmi and then operated by British Regional Airlines Limited under a sublease from 07/12/1993	BRAL
returned to Saab 28/11/1987		Manx
returned to Swedish Aircraft Holdings AB 30/05/2000		bmi regional
returned to Swedish Aircraft Holdings AB 18/05/2000		bmi regional
returned to Saab Aircraft Credit AB 30/09/1999		bmi regional
returned to Swedish Aircraft Holdings AB 08/03/2001		bmi regional
returned to Swedish Aircraft Holdings AB 19/07/2001		bmi regional
returned to Swedish Aircraft Holdings AB 07/03/2001		bmi regional
returned to Swedish Aircraft Holdings AB 28/03/2001		bmi regional
returned 06/09/2001		bmi regional
returned 29/08/2001		bmi regional
returned 26/09/2001		bmi regional
returned to Aachen Aviation LLC 27/04/2004		bmi regional
returned to Aachen Aviation LLC 30/08/2004		bmi
returned to Castle Aircraft Finance (No.1) 24/01/2005		bmi
returned to Castle Aircraft Finance (No.1) 10/03/2005		bmi
sold to Phoenix Aircraft Leasing 28/06/2005	originally operated under lease from East Midlands Aircraft Finance, purchased by bmi in May 1998	bmi
sold to Ekspres Transportasi Antarbenua 12/04/2005	originally operated under lease from East Midlands Aircraft Finance, purchased by bmi in May 1998	bmi
returned to Castle Aircraft Finance (No. 1) 13/04/2005	lease transferred to Castle Aircraft Finance (No. 1), operated by bmi until 28/03/2002, then subleased to KLM Cityhopper. bmi's lease terminated 13/04/2005 and KLM entered into direct lease to CAF (No. 1)	bmi
returned to Castle Aircraft Finance (No. 1) 13/04/2005	lease transferred to Castle Aircraft Finance (No. 1), operated by bmi until 28/03/2002, then subleased to KLM Cityhopper. bmi's lease terminated 12/04/2002 and KLM entered into direct lease to CAF (No. 1)	bmi
returned to Castle Aircraft Finance (No. 1) 13/04/2005	lease transferred to Castle Aircraft Finance (No. 1), operated by bmi until 02/10/2002, then subleased to KLM Cityhopper. bmi's lease terminated 12/04/2002 and KLM entered into direct lease to CAF (No. 1)	bmi
returned to Ansett 15/11/1993		bmi
returned to Ansett 16/04/1993		bmi
returned to Ansett 14/01/1994		bmi
returned to Carlton Co. 30/12/1998	purchased from Ansett, sale and leaseback with Bishop Ltd, lease transferred to Carlton	bmi
return to Ansett 19/03/2001		bmi
returned to CIT Leasing Ltd 29/11/2000	purchased by bmi from Boeing, sale and leaseback with CIT Leasing Ltd	bmi
returned to IAI 11 Inc 12/05/1997		bmi

TYPE	REG	NAME	CONSTRUCTION NO.	INTO SERVICE	ACQUIRED FROM
Boeing 737-300	G-OBMP	*robin hood baby*	24963	Feb-91	new, leased from ILFC
Boeing 737-300	G-ECAS	—	28554	Dec-96	new, leased from Alnitak FSC One Corpn
Boeing 737-300	G-SMDB	—	28557	Mar-97	new, leased from Alnitak FSC Two Corpn
Boeing 737-300	G-OJTW	—	28558	Apr-97	new, leased from Alnitak FSC Three Corpn
Boeing 737-300	G-ODSK	*baby dragon fly*	28537	Jul-97	new, leased from Bowtie Leasing (Bermuda)
Boeing 737-300	G-BYZJ	*pudsey baby*	24962	Nov-99	ex GECAS, G-COLE
Boeing 737-300	G-OGBD	—	27833	Mar-04	ex ORIX, OY-MAR
Boeing 737-300	G-OGBE	*Derby's baby pride*	27834	Apr-04	ex Fleet Business Credit LLC, OY-MAS
Boeing 737-300	G-TOYA	*brummie baby*	26310	Jan-05	leased from ILFC
Boeing 737-300	G-TOYB	—	26311	Dec-04	leased from ILFC
Boeing 737-300	G-TOYC	—	26312	Jan-05	leased from ILFC
Boeing 737-300	G-TOYD	—	26307	Jun-05	leased from Castle 2003-2A LLC
Boeing 737-300	G-TOYE	—	27455	May-05	leased from AWMS 1
Boeing 737-300	G-TOYF	*rainbow baby*	28557	Nov-05	leased from AFT Trust Sub-1
Boeing 737-300	G-TOYG	*butterfly baby*	28872	Jan-06	leased from Celestial Aviation Trading 4 Ltd
Boeing 737-300	G-TOYH	*baby of the north*	28570	Dec-05	leased from LIFT Portugal LLC
Boeing 737-300	G-TOYI	—	28054	May-08	leased from ILFC
Boeing 737-300	G-TOYJ	—	28332	Apr-07	leased from Wells Fargo Bank Northwest, National Association
Boeing 737-300	G-TOYK	—	28870	May-07	leased from Wells Fargo Bank Northwest, National Association
Boeing 737-300	G-TOYM	—	29141	Aug-08	leased from Aviation Capital Group Corp
Boeing 737-400	G-OBME	—	23867	Oct-88	new, ex GPA
Boeing 737-400	G-OBMF	—	23868	Nov-88	new, ex GPA
Boeing 737-400	G-OBMG	—	23870	Mar-89	new, ex GPA
Boeing 737-400	G-OBMK	—	25596	Apr-92	
Boeing 737-400	G-OBMM	—	25177	Dec-91	new, ex GPA
Boeing 737-400	G-BOPJ G-OBMN	—	24123	May-90	ex Aeronautics H Inc
Boeing 737-400	G-OBMO	—	26280	Mar-92	new, ex ILFC
Boeing 737-400	G-SFBH	—	28723	May-97	new, ex GECAS
Boeing 737-500	G-OBMX	—	25065	Mar-93	ex SAS SE-DNE
Boeing 737-500	G-OBMY	—	26419	Apr-93	ex SAS SE-DNJ
Boeing 737-500	G-OBMZ	—	24754	Feb-93	ex SAS SE-DNK
Boeing 737-500	G-BVKA	—	24694	Feb-94	ex SAS SE-DNA
Boeing 737-500	G-BVKB	*foxy baby*	27268	Mar-94	new, ex SAS
Boeing 737-500	G-BVKC	—	26421	Apr-94	ex SAS SE-DNB
Boeing 737-500	G-BVKD	*ice ice baby*	26421	Nov-94	ex SAS SE-DNK
Boeing 737-500	G-BVZE	*little costa baby*	26422	Feb-95	ex SAS SE-DNL
Boeing 737-500	G-BVZF	—	25038	Mar-95	ex SAS SE-DND
Boeing 737-500	G-BVZG	—	25160	Apr-95	ex ILFC SE-DNF
Boeing 737-500	G-BVZH	*baby blue skies*	25166	Apr-95	ex ILFC SE-DNG
Boeing 737-500	G-BVZI	—	25167	May-95	ex ILFC SE-DNH
Boeing 737-500	G-OBMR	—	25185	May-96	ex Airplanes Finance Ltd XA-RJS
Airbus A330-200	G-WWBM	—	398	Apr-01	new, leased from ILFC
Airbus A330-200	G-WWBD	—	401	May-01	new
Airbus A330-200	G-WWBB	—	404	May-01	new, leased from Sierra Leasing Ltd
Airbus A321-200	G-MIDA	—	806	Mar-98	new, leased from ILFC
Airbus A321-200	G-MIDF	—	810	Apr-98	new, leased from ILFC
Airbus A321-200	G-MIDC	—	835	Jun-98	new
Airbus A321-200	G-MIDE	—	864	Aug-98	new
Airbus A321-200	G-MIDH	—	968	Mar-99	new
Airbus A321-200	G-MIDI	—	974	Mar-99	new
Airbus A321-200	G-MIDJ	—	1045	Jul-99	new
Airbus A321-200	G-MIDK	—	1153	Jan-00	new
Airbus A321-200	G-MIDL	—	1174	Feb-00	new
Airbus A321-200	G-MIDM	—	1207	Apr-00	new
Airbus A321-200	G-MEDF	—	1690	Feb-02	new

DISPOSAL	REMARKS	OPERATED BY
leased by bmi, lease transferred to NBB-24963 Lease Partnership	leased by bmi from Millerdell Limited	bmibaby
returned to AFT Trust-Sub 1 11/06/2005	leased by bmi, lease transferred to AFT Trust-Sub 1	bmibaby
returned to AFT Trust-Sub 1 14/03/2002	leased by bmi, lease transferred to AFT Trust-Sub 1	bmibaby
returned to AFT Trust-Sub 1 03/06/2005	leased by bmi, lease transferred to AFT Trust-Sub 1	bmibaby
	leased by bmi, lease transferred to NBB-BMA Lease Partnership Five	bmibaby
	leased by bmi, lease transferred to Celestial Aviation Trading 21 Ltd	bmibaby
	leased by bmi, lease transferred to Wells Fargo Bank Northwest, National Association	bmibaby
	leased by bmi, lease transferred to ORIX Aviation Systems Limited	bmibaby
	leased by bmi	bmibaby
	leased by bmi	bmibaby
	leased by bmi	bmibaby
	leased by bmi	bmibaby
	leased by bmi	bmibaby
	leased by bmi	bmibaby
	leased by bmi	bmibaby
	leased by bmi	bmibaby
	leased by bmi	bmibaby
	leased by bmi	bmibaby
	leased by bmi	bmibaby
crashed EMA 08/01/1989		bmi
returned to AerCo Ireland 03/11/2000		bmi
returned to ALPS 29/03/1999		bmi
returned to ILFC 05/04/1997		bmi
returned to AerFi Leasing USA 11 Inc 02/04/2003		bmi
returned to Castle Lease Co 19/12/1997	initially leased from Aeronautics, purchased bmi, sale and leaseback with Donington Lease Co, transferred to Castle Lease Co	bmi
returned to Tombo Aviation Inc. 16/05/2000		bmi
returned to FNBC Leasing Corporation 29/04/2002		bmi
returned to Snowfrog Co Ltd 23/03/2001	purchased from SAS, sale and leaseback with BBAM Aircraft Holdings 14, transferred to Snowfrog	bmi
returned to SAS 29/09/1998		bmi
returned to Oxford Co Ltd 22/12/2000	purchased from SAS, sale and leaseback with BBAM Aircraft Holdings 13 Ltd, transferred to Canterbury Co Ltd, novated to Oxford Co Ltd.	bmi
returned to NBB-BMA Lease Partnership One 28/02/2004	purchased from SAS, sale and leaseback with BBAM Aircraft Holdings 11 Ltd, transferred to NBB-BMA Lease Partnership One	bmi
	purchased from SAS, sale and leaseback with AWMS 1	bmibaby
returned to NBB-BMA Lease Partnership Two 30/06/2004	purchased from SAS, sale and leaseback with BBAM Aircraft Holdings 12 Ltd, transferred to NBB-BMA Lease Partnership Two	bmibaby
	purchased from SAS, sale and leaseback with AWMS 1	bmibaby
	purchased from SAS, sale and leaseback with AWMS 1	bmibaby
returned to BBAM Aircraft Holdings 39 Ltd 28/01/2000	leased by bmi from SAS, then BBAM Aircraft Holdings 39 Ltd	bmi
returned to NBB-BMA Lease Partnership Three 06/03/2008	purchased from ILFC, sale and leaseback with BBAM Aircraft Holdings 47 Ltd, transferred to NBB-BMA Lease Partnership Three	bmibaby
returned to Newport Co.Ltd 21/12/2007	purchased from ILFC, sale and leaseback with BBAM Aircraft Holdings 48 Ltd, transferred to Newport Co Ltd	bmibaby
returned to NBB-BMA Lease Partnership Four 16/05/08	purchased from ILFC, sale and leaseback with BBAM Aircraft Holdings 49 Ltd, transferred to NBB-BMA Lease Partnership Four	bmibaby
returned to Airplanes Finance Ltd 15/11/2000		hmi
	leased transferred to Wells Fargo Bank Northwest, National Association operated by bmi, leased from MALC Lease Four Ltd	bmi
	originally purchased by bmi, sale and leaseback with Singapore Aircraft Leasing Enterprise PTE Ltd, lease transferred to MALC Lease Four Ltd	bmi
		bmi
returned to Castle 2003-1A, LLC 30/03/2005	lease transferred to Castle 2003-1A LLC	bmi
returned 26/04/2005		bmi
	originally purchased by bmi, then sale and leaseback with ACG Trust 835	bmi
returned to AerCap Aircraft Leasing XIII BV 11/05/2006	originally purchased by bmi, then sale and leaseback with AerCap	bmi
returned to Sierra Leasing Ltd 27/03/2006		bmi
returned to Sierra Leasing Ltd 16/04/2006		bmi
returned to AerCap Aircraft Leasing XIV BV 23/11/2006	originally purchased by bmi, then sale and leaseback with AerCap	bmi
returned to ALS Irish Aircraft Leasing MSN 1153 Ltd 30/03/2007	originally purchased by bmi, then sale and leaseback with AerCap, transferred to ALS Irish Aircraft Leasing, MSN 1153 Ltd	bmi
	originally purchased by bmi, then sale and leaseback with ACG Trust 1174	bmi
returned to Gustav Leasing XII Ltd 11/05/2007	originally purchased by bmi, sale and leaseback with Indigo Aviation AB, lease transferred to Gustav Leasing XII Ltd	bmi
	acquired by bmi on acquisition of BMed in February 2007. BMed lease transferred to bmi in October 2007. Leased from ALS Irish Aircraft Leasing MSN 1690 Ltd	bmi

TYPE	REG	NAME	CONSTRUCTION NO.	INTO SERVICE	ACQUIRED FROM
Airbus A321-200	G-MEDG	—	1711	Apr-02	new
Airbus A321-200	G-MEDJ	—	2190	Apr-04	new
Airbus A321-200	G-MEDL	—	2653	Jan-06	new
Airbus A321-200	G-MEDM	—	2799	Jun-06	new
Airbus A321-200	G-MEDN	—	3512	May-08	new
Airbus A320-200	G-MIDZ	—	934	Jan-99	new
Airbus A320-200	G-MIDY	—	1014	Jun-99	new
Airbus A320-200	G-MIDX	—	1177	Mar-00	new, leased from Sierra Leasing Ltd
Airbus A320-200	G-MIDW	—	1183	Mar-00	new
Airbus A320-200	G-MIDV	—	1383	Jan-01	new
Airbus A320-200	G-MIDU	—	1407	Feb-01	new, leased from ILFC
Airbus A320-200	G-MIDT	—	1418	Mar-01	new
Airbus A320-200	G-MIDS	—	1424	Mar-01	new, leased from ILFC
Airbus A320-200	G-MIDR	—	1697	Apr-02	new, leased from Sierra Leasing Ltd
Airbus A320-200	G-MIDP	—	1732	May-02	new, leased from ILFC
Airbus A320-200	G-MIDO	—	1987	Apr-03	new
Airbus A320-200	G-MEDE	—	1194	Apr-00	new, leased from Singapore Aircraft Leasing Enterprise PTE Ltd
Airbus A320-200	G-MEDH	—	1922	Mar-03	new
Airbus A320-200	G-MEDK	—	2441	May-05	new
Airbus A319-100	G-DBCA	—	2098	Feb-04	new, leased from ILFC
Airbus A319-100	G-DBCB	—	2188	Apr-04	new, leased from ILFC
Airbus A319-100	G-DBCC	—	2194	May-04	new, leased from ILFC
Airbus A319-100	G-DBCD	—	2389	Feb-05	new, leased from ILFC
Airbus A319-100	G-DBCE	—	2429	Mar-05	new, leased from ILFC
Airbus A319-100	G-DBCF	—	2466	May-05	new, leased from Whitney Leasing Ltd
Airbus A319-100	G-DBCG	—	2694	Feb-06	new, leased from ILFC
Airbus A319-100	G-DBCH	—	2697	Feb-06	new, leased from ILFC
Airbus A319-100	G-DBCI	—	2720	May-06	new, leased from ILFC
Airbus A319-100	G-DBCJ	—	2981	Jan-07	new, leased from Eden Irish Aircraft Leasing 2981 Ltd
Airbus A319-100	G-DBCK	—	3049	Mar-07	new, leased from Eden Irish Aircraft Leasing 3049 Ltd
Embraer 145	G-RJXA	—	145136	Jun-99	new
Embraer 145	G-RJXB	—	145142	Jun-99	new
Embraer 145	G-RJXC	—	145153	Jul-99	new
Embraer 145	G-RJXD	—	145207	Feb-00	new
Embraer 145	G-RJXE	—	145245	Apr-00	new
Embraer 145	G-RJXF	—	145280	Jun-00	new
Embraer 145	G-RJXG	—	145390	Feb-01	new
Embraer 145	G-RJXH	—	145442	Jun-01	new
Embraer 145	G-RJXI	—	145454	Jun-01	new
Embraer 145	G-RJXM	—	145216	Apr-05	ex Regional Jet PJ-RXA
Embraer 145	G-RJXN	—	145336	Oct-06	ex ECC Leasing Company Ltd SP-LGI
Embraer 145	G-RJXO	—	145339	Oct-06	ex ECC Leasing Company Ltd SP-LGK
Embraer 145	G-CCYH G-RJXR	—	145070	Feb-05	ex Skyways Express
Embraer 145	CS-TPJ	—	145036	Mar-03	ex Portugalia
Embraer 135	G-RJXJ	—	145473	Jul-01	new
Embraer 135	G-RJXK	—	145494	Sept-01	new
Embraer 135	G-RJXL	—	145376	Dec-04	new
Embraer 135	SE-RAA	—	145210	Mar-03	ex City Airline AB
Embraer 135	G-CDFS	—	145431	Jan-08	LCY Flight Ltd
Boeing 757-200	G-STRX	—	25621	May-08	Astraeus Ltd
Boeing 757-200	G-STRY	—	28161	Mar-08	Astraeus Ltd

DISPOSAL	REMARKS	OPERATED BY
	acquired by bmi on acquisition of BMed in February 2007. BMed lease transferred to bmi in October 2007. Leased transferred to Cornelius Aircraft Leasing Ltd	bmi
	acquired by bmi on acquisition of BMed in February 2007. BMed lease transferred to bmi in October 2007. Leased from BOC Aviation Pte Ltd	bmi
	acquired by bmi on acquisition of BMed in February 2007. BMed lease transferred to bmi in October 2007. Leased from RBS Aerospace Ltd	bmi
	acquired by bmi on acquisition of BMed in February 2007. BMed lease transferred to bmi in October 2007. Lease transferred to Falak Lease Seven Ltd	bmi
	originally purchased by bmi, sale and leaseback with Aviation Leasing OpCo 7 S.a.r.l	bmi
	originally purchased by bmi, then sale and leaseback with Indigo Aviation, now leased from AerCo Ltd	bmi
	owned by bmi	bmi
		bmi
returned to Orix Aviation Systems Ltd 23/04/2007	originally purchased by bmi, then sale and leaseback with Orix Aviation Systems Ltd	bmi
returned to Orix Aviation Systems Ltd 21/02/2008	originally purchased by bmi, then sale and leaseback with Orix Aviation Systems Ltd	bmi
returned to ILFC 05/04/2008		bmi
	owned by bmi	bmi
		bmi
		bmi
		bmi
	owned by bmi	bmi
	acquired by bmi on acquisition of BMed in February 2007. BMed lease transferred to bmi in October 2007. Lease transferred to MALC Lease Three Ltd	bmi
	acquired by bmi on acquisition of BMed in February 2007. BMed lease transferred to bmi in October 2007. Leased from BOC Aviation Pte Ltd	bmi
	acquired by bmi on acquisition of BMed in February 2007. BMed lease transferred to bmi in October 2007. Leased from BOC Aviation Pte Ltd	bmi
		bmi
		bmi
		bmi
		bmi
		bmi
		bmi
		bmi
		bmi
		bmi
		bmi
		bmi
	purchased by bmi	bmi regional
	purchased by bmi	bmi regional
	purchased by bmi	bmi regional
	purchased by bmi	bmi regional
	purchased by bmi	bmi regional
	purchased by bmi	bmi regional
	purchased by bmi	bmi regional
	purchased by bmi	bmi regional
	purchased by bmi	bmi regional
	initially operated under lease from Regional Jet, purchased by bmi Dec 2005	bmi regional
	leased by bmi regional	bmi regional
	leased by bmi regional	bmi regional
	leased by bmi regional initially from Skyways Express AB and then Corporate Aircraft Leasing Ltd from 15/09/2006. Operated as G-CCYH until April 2008 when re-registered as G-RJXR. Lease transferred to Largus Aviation AB	bmi regional
returned to Portugalia 28/03/2004		bmi regional
	purchased by bmi	bmi regional
	purchased by bmi	bmi regional
	purchased by bmi	bmi regional
wet lease, returned to City Airline 26/03/2004		bmi regional
	purchased by bmi	bmi regional
	wet leased from Astraeus Ltd	bmi
	wet leased from Astraeus Ltd	bmi

Acknowledgements

At the outset I should like to thank the many individuals who have spoken to me so candidly about their recollections and experiences while working for bmi, British Midland and Derby Airways. Their engaging stories and thoughtful recollections were invaluable as I researched and wrote this narrative. The loan of precious memorabilia has been particularly illuminating and some of this has been reproduced as illustrations in the book.

Firstly I would like to express my gratitude to Sir Michael Bishop, Stuart Balmforth, John Wolfe, and Grahame Elliott for sharing with me their long-term memories and for their encouragement as the project took shape. I would then like to acknowledge the support of Stewart Adams, Chris Boylan, Tim Bye, Andy Cookson, Ray Eglington, Alex Grant, Ron Hardy, Debbie Haywood, David Hodge, James Hogan, Max Hunt, Peter Knapp, Aaron Lupton, Terry Liddiard, Geoff Linaker, Sam McKissock, Robert Nadin, Graham Norman, Austin Reid, Crawford Rix, Colin Roberts, Sue Roper, Jim Snee, Tim Sutton, Tony Topps, Nigel Turner, Tim Walden, Alison Wheatherley and Tony Whitby, who told me so much about the airline from their particular perspective and offered ongoing help and information as the months went by. Others who talked freely and offered me support were Peter Bell, Alison van Berkel, Ian Bloor, Pat Bohan, Vivian Bull, Stephanie Byre, Gareth Chappell, Adam Cook, Frank Cooper, John Corkill, Ellen Davies, Paul Drinkwater, David Edwards, Mike Esam, Linda Fergus, Simon Foster, Lorraine Hogan, Duncan Hope, Keith Jones, Linda Lazenby, Rosemary Mellors, Daren Monk, Charlotte Newall, Adrian Parkes, Adrian Piwowar, Peter Robotham, Paul Sanders, Susannah Saywood, Simon Scoggins, Richard Seymour, Liam Shaida, Alison Thompson, Ciara Thorn, and Grant Worsley. The penultimate thank you is to Tim Walden and Tim Bye who undertook the enormous task of reading and correcting the final drafts, and to whom I owe so much for their enormous input. Finally, I wish to mention Peter Dolton, whose creativity, tenacity and patience have brought the wealth of material I handed him to life.

The libraries I have worked in and the books and articles I have found helpful are: The RAF Museum, Hendon; Bill Gunston, *Diamond Flight*, 1988; B G Cramp, *British Midland Airways*, 1979; Robert M Stitt, 'Midland Memories', printed in *Air Enthusiast*, Issues 91 and 92, January and March 2001; Gordon Kniveton, *Wings of Mann*, 1997; Malcolm L. Giddings, *The Burnaston Story*, 1991; and Bob Walker, *The Airport serving the East Midlands for 40 years*, 2005, produced by Origination.

Photograph Credits

Air Enthusiast, pp.vii (centre), 7 (right), 8 (bottom), 10 (top), 11, 14 (bottom), 20–21, 27, 28 (top), 44 (bottom), 47–48, 50, 56–59, 60 (top), 64, 67, 76 (top left and right), 77 (bottom); Airbus, p.75 (bottom); BAA Aviation Photo Library, pp.28 (bottom), 53 (top); A J Best/*Airliner World*, 108 (top right); Freida Blickle/Lufthansa, p.77 (top); bmi, pp. vii (left), 1, 2 (top), 3 (top), 5, 7 (bottom), 8 (top left and right), 9, 13, 14 (top), 15, 16 (top), 17 (bottom), 19, 23 (centre and bottom), 25 (bottom), 26, 30 (centre), 32–33, 34 (top), 35, 36 (top), 37 (bottom left and centre), 39–40, 41 (top), 42, 43 (bottom), 45, 46, 51–52, 53 (bottom), 54–55, 61, 62, 63, 65 (top), 66, 69–71, 74, 75 (top left, centre and right), 76 (centre and bottom), p.79–85, 88–89, 90, 92 (top), 94 (top), 95, 96 (top), 97 (top), 98–99, 101–103, 104 (bottom), 105 (top), 107, 108 (top left and centre), 109; Chris Boylan, p.49; A J Bramson, p.4 (bottom); *The Daily Mail*: p.36 (bottom); Don Davidson/*Air Enthusiast*, p.3 (bottom); *Derby Evening Telegraph*, pp.2 (bottom), 4 (top), 10 (bottom), 18, 23 (top), 24, 29 (top), 30 (top), 34 (bottom), 37 (bottom right), 41 (bottom), 43 (top); Tony Dixon/*Airliner World*, p.96 (bottom); Frank C Duarte Jnr, p.65 (bottom); East Midlands Airport, p.22 (bottom); David Dyson; pp.vii (right), 86–87, 100 (bottom), 104 (top), 106 (bottom); Jim Halley, p.12 (top); Ron Hardy, p.68; Debbie Haywood, p.38 (top); George Jenks/*Air Enthusiast*, pp.6, 17 (top); Aaron Lupton, pp. v, 92 (bottom), 94 (bottom), 97 (bottom), 100 (top), 106 (top); Tony Marlow, p.93; Press Association, front cover; G Ricketts/*Air Enthusiast*, p.25 (top); Tony Topps, p.3 (centre); Roger Wise, p.37 (top); Tim Walden, p.12 (bottom); David Welch/*Air Enthusiast*, pp.7 (top left), 22 (top), 29 (bottom), 31, 32 (bottom), 38 (bottom), 44 (top), 60 (bottom), 72–73, 78 (top and bottom).

The history of Donington Hall

I should once again like to acknowledge the people, organizations and libraries that generously supplied research material and advice during my work on the first edition on this history back in 1990. I should particularly like to mention Major John Gillies Shields (now deceased) for his untiring enthusiasm and vivid memories. Others who offered their support and sound advice were Stuart Balmforth, Lady Gretton, the Countess of Loudon, John Shields, Robert Ward and Tom Wheatcroft.

The books and articles I read were: Henry Nugest Bell, *The Huntingdon Peerage*, 1820; Henry Blyth, *The Pocket Venice*, 1966; Brittin, *Leicestershire Delineated*, 1810; John Brushe, Wilkins senior's original design for Donington Park as proposed by Repton, *Burlington Magazine*, February 1979; Lt Colonel C E Cooke, *Donington Hall from Within*, 1919; Claire Cross, *The Puritan Earl*, 1966; Rev J Curtis, *Topographical History of the County of Leicestershire*, 1831; P Liddle, *A later medieval enclosure in Donington Park*, 1962; Marchioness of Londonderry, *A Memoir of Henry Chaplin*, 1926; Geoffrey Goddard, *Great Racing Cars of the Donington Collection*; Marilyn Palmer, *Francis Rawdon-Hastings, 1st Marquis of Hastings, 1780-1830*, 1992; Frederick Hingston, *Deer Parks of Great Britain*, 1988; Edward Rose, *Donington Park and Hall*, 1893; W. Scott, *The Story of Ashby-de-la-Zouch*, 1906; Gillies J Shields, A Refuge of two Centuries, *Country Life*, 22nd March 1979; Dorothy Stroud, Humphrey Repton, *Country Life*, 1962; John Throsby, *A History of Leicestershire*, 1791; Bruce Townsend, *Castle Donington in the Seventeenth Century*, 1971; and for this edition Tom Wheatcroft, *Thunder in the Park*, 2005.

Photograph credits
Photographs and drawings reproduced once again from the original history were supplied by Delia Astle, Gerald Dalby, the British Museum, Donington Park Museum, the Huntingdon Museum in California, the Leicestershire Museum, the National Portrait Gallery, Norris Pickford, the Royal Institute of British Architects and Bruce Townsend. New portraits and photographs for this edition have been supplied by the Cheshunt Foundation, Westminster College, Cambridge, pp.124, 125 (bottom); *Derby Evening Telegraph*, p.147 (bottom); John Higginson, pp.116–117; the National Portrait Gallery, pp.119, 123, 135,146 (bottom); the Royal Collection, p.132; and Tom Wheatcroft, pp. 148, 149, 150, 151.

Every effort has been made to obtain permission for the reproduction of the illustrations and photographs contained in this book; apologies are offered to anyone whom it has not been possible to trace or contact.

Published by Granta Editions, 25–27 High Street, Chesterton, Cambridge CB4 1ND, United Kingdom.
Granta Editions is a wholly owned subsidiary of Book Production Consultants Ltd.

ISBN 978-1-85757-095-3 Hardback
ISBN 978-1-85757-098-4 Paperback

A CIP catalogue record for this book is available from The British Library.

Designed by Peter Dolton.
Design, editorial and production in association with Book Production Consultants Ltd,
25–27 High Street, Chesterton, Cambridge CB4 1ND, United Kingdom.

Printed and bound in Italy by Studio Fasoli, Verona, Italy.

Printed on Hanno Art Silk paper, Sappi Europe SA
FSC Mixed Sources Certified Paper SGS-COC-003171

November 1972
Beginning of the era of
the Instant Airline

9 July 1977
Hijack of Boeing 707
(G-AZWA) flying in the livery
of Kuwait Airways

1982
Move to new company headquarters at Donington Hall

25 October 1982
Launch of the Heathrow to Glasgow scheduled service

1983
Manx Airlines begins operations

7 March 1983
Launch of the Heathrow to Edinburgh scheduled service

December 1983
BMA purchases Loganair

21 July 1978
Management buy-out
by Bishop, Balmforth
and Wolfe

29 October 1978
Swap day in Liverpool
with British Airways

26 March 1984
Launch of the Heathrow to Belfast scheduled servic

29 June 1986
Launch of the Heathrow to Amsterdam
route with Diamond Service

October 1987
London City Airways begins
operations

15 December 1988
SAS acquires a 40% st
in British Midland

8 January 1989
Boeing 737
(G-OBME) crash
on the M1 at
Kegworth

1970

Boeing 707

Douglas DC-9

1980

Shorts 360

Boeing 737

BAe 146

26 November 1983
Brinks Mat robbery at
Heathrow

7 February 1982
Laker Airways forced out
of business

1974
Clarksons and
Horizon Holidays
go into liquidation

Miner's Strike

4 May 1979
Margaret Thatcher
elected Prime Minister

Second oil crisis

1988
Personnel TV sets
introduced for airline
passengers

21 December 1988
Pan Am's Boeing 747
destroyed by a terrorist
bomb over Lockerbie

1973
First oil crisis

InterCity 125 train
introduced

1977
Bermuda II establishes
bi-lateral air service agreements

December 1987
British Caledonian taken
over by British Airways

February 1971
Rolls-Royce taken into state ownership